The International Society of Business, Economics, and Ethics Book Series

Volume 4

Series editors
Daryl Koehn
Ethics and Business Law, University of St. Thomas, Opus College of Business,
St. Paul, Minnesota, USA

Laura Spence
School of Management, Royal Holloway University of London, Egham, Surrey,
United Kingdom

The International Society for Business, Economics and Ethics is a global association for the study of social and moral aspects of business and the economy.

This book series draws from the worldwide membership of ISBEE and its associates to present truly international research and scholarship. The primary objective of the series is to promote business ethics globally by giving a voice to top scholars from around the world and reaching a similarly global audience.

This series encompasses manuscripts that focus on ethics in the international arena of business, particularly enabling comparative studies. There is a focus on research on the responsibilities, values and behaviour of business people and organizations as they interact with stakeholders including shareholders, employees, suppliers, customers, competitors communities and governments.

Incorporating a macro economic perspective, it is especially interested in considering new works dealing with globalization of business, *business in developing economies,* environmental questions, ethics and global communication, global economic growth, and sustainable development. The series embraces research and scholarship on all organisational forms relevant to business.

More information about this series at http://www.springer.com/series/8074

Sukhbir Sandhu • Stephen McKenzie
Howard Harris
Editors

Linking Local and Global Sustainability

 Springer

Editors
Sukhbir Sandhu
School of Management
University of South Australia
  Business School
Adelaide
South Australia
Australia

Howard Harris
School of Management
University of South Australia
  Business School
Adelaide
South Australia
Australia

Stephen McKenzie
School of Management
University of South Australia
  Business School
Adelaide
South Australia
Australia

ISSN 1877-3176
ISBN 978-94-017-9007-9
DOI 10.1007/978-94-017-9008-6
Springer Dordrecht Heidelberg New York London

ISSN 1877-3184 (electronic)
ISBN 978-94-017-9008-6 (eBook)

Library of Congress Control Number: 2014947971

Printed on acid-free paper

Springer is part of Springer Science+Business Media (www.springer.com)

Contents

Contributors

Pratima Bansal Ivey Business School, Western University, London, Canada

Don Clifton International Graduate School of Business, University of South Australia, Adelaide, South Australia, Australia

Ross Cullen Lincoln University, Lincoln, New Zealand

Andrew Fearne Centre for Value Chain Research, Kent Business School, University of Kent, Canterbury, Kent, England

Paolo Gaiardelli CELS—Research Group on Industrial Engineering, Logistics and Service Operations, University of Bergamo, Department of Engineering, Bergamo, Italy

Jijun Gao Asper School of Business, University of Manitoba, Winnipeg, Canada

Howard Harris School of Management, University of South Australia, Adelaide, Australia

Vandra Harris RMIT University Melbourne, Melbourne, Australia

Stephen McKenzie School of Management, University of South Australia Business School, Adelaide, Australia

Azmiri Mian Business School, University of South Australia, Adelaide, Australia

Lisa H. Newton Department of Philosophy, Fairfield University, Fairfield, USA

Wayne O'Connor Port Stephens Fisheries Institute, NSW Department of Primary Industries, Nelson Bay, Australia

Lucie K. Ozanne University of Canterbury, Christchurch, New Zealand

Janine Pierce Centre for Rural Health and Community Development, University of South Australia, Adelaide, Australia

Anna Pistoni Department of Economics, Insubria University, Varese, Italy

Department of Accounting, Bocconi University, Milan, Italy

Chris Provis Business School, University of South Australia, Adelaide, Australia

Barbara Resta CELS—Research Group on Industrial Engineering, Logistics and Service Operations, University of Bergamo, Department of Engineering

Sukhbir Sandhu School of Management, University of South Australia Business School, Adelaide, Australia

Clive Smallman Business School, University of Western Sydney, Sydney, Australia

Claudine Soosay School of Management, University of South Australia Business School, Adelaide, Australia

Mohsen Varsei School of Management, University of South Australia Business School, Adelaide, Australia

About the Authors

Pratima (Tima) Bansal is a Professor at the Ivey Business School, Western University in London, Canada. She also holds the Canada Research Chair in Business Sustainability and is the Executive Director and founder of the Network for Business Sustainability. Her research aims to understand sustainability, by bringing to bear a range of organizational theories and methodological approaches, especially concepts related time, space and scale. She has published in the *Academy of Management Journal, Strategic Management Journal, Journal of International Business Studies*, among others. She has also sat on seven journal editorial boards, and completed a term as an Associate Editor of the *Academy of Management Journal* in 2013.

Don Clifton holds an academic position at the University of South Australia International Graduate School of Business, and lectures in ethics, governance and sustainable business. In 2011, Don completed his PhD which focused on sustainability issues, taking a broad view of what it means for there to be a sustainable world and what might be needed to see this come about. Don's commercial background is in the financial services sector having spent over 30 years in that industry. During that time he held a number of senior positions with firms involved in investment funds management. In addition to his PhD, Don holds a Master of Advanced Business Practice, an Advanced Master of Business Administration, a Bachelor of Arts majoring in philosophy and psychology, and is a Graduate of the Australian Institute of Company Directors.

Ross Cullen was Professor of Resource Economics at Lincoln University, New Zealand until June 2012 when he departed to live in Oslo, Norway. His research examines a wide range of topics within agricultural, environmental and resource economics including measurement of change in levels of ecosystem services, willingness to pay for improved water quality, uptake of sustainable production practices, cost effectiveness of biodiversity conservation projects. Ross was co-editor of the Australian Journal of Agricultural and Resource Economics 2011–2013, and co-editor of a 2013 Special Issue of Wildlife Research on Prioritisation and Evaluation of Biodiversity Projects.

Andrew Fearne is Head of Kent Business School in the United Kingdom. He is also Professor of Food Marketing and Value Chain Management, and Director of the Centre for Value Chain Research. Drawing on more than twenty years of research into consumer behaviour, food marketing and the operation of supply and value chains, Professor Fearne's integrated approach has provided a way for many producers and suppliers in the UK, France, Ireland, Slovenia, Germany, North America, Australia and South East Asia to add value to their business and build consumer loyalty.

Paolo Gaiardelli is Assistant Professor and researcher at the University of Bergamo, Department of Engineering. His research activities mainly focus on servitization and product-service systems. In particular he is involved in studying how to support automotive and truck companies to develop new customer value propositions, operations and value chains in order to up hold the product-service business models. Paolo is also researcher of the ASAP Service Management Forum, an Italian joint industry-academic initiative that promotes the culture and the excellence of service management through research projects, practice, education and technological transfer.

Jijun Gao is an Assistant Professor at Asper School of Business, University of Manitoba. He received his PhD in Strategy from the Ivey School of Business, University of Western Ontario. His research has focused on corporate social responsibility and irresponsibility, business sustainability, and competitive advantage. He currently examines irresponsible innovations in the food industry, with particular interest in East Asia and North America. Applying both qualitative and quantitative methods in research, he has published in the *Organization Studies, Journal of International Business Studies* and *Journal of Business Ethics*, among others.

Vandra Harris is a Senior Lecturer in the graduate program in International Development at RMIT University. Vandra's publications are primarily focused on Australia's international policing in the Asia-Pacific region, and partnerships and cultural change in international development. She is particularly interested in the intersection of these two research interests, in the nexus between security and development. Her most recent book is *Conflict, security and nation-building in Timor-Leste: Cross-sectoral perspectives*, co-edited with Andrew Goldsmith (Routledge 2011), and she is currently conducting a major research project exploring the interaction between NGOs and militaries following conflict and disaster.

Azmiri Mian is a PhD candidate in the School of Management, University of South Australia Business School and a recipient of the Australia Postgraduate Award (APA) Scholarship. She also works as a Research Assistant and Tutor in Management. Her research interests are in social, organisational and ego networks and Indigenous business and workforce development. Azmiri has worked in both the Commonwealth and State governments and also non-government agencies in management and leadership roles. Through her experience, Azmiri has developed a commitment to Indigenous health, education and employment. She is also dedicated in educating others to learn and be involved in Indigenous life and economic outcomes.

Lisa Newton is Professor Emeritus in the Department of Philosophy at Fairfield University and founder of the Program on the Environment at Fairfield. In 2013 she was a recipient of the inaugural Leaders in Campus Sustainability Award for Lifetime Achievement for her efforts supporting campus sustainability and environmental education during her long and productive career at Fairfield. She is the author of *The American Experience in Environmental Protection* (Springer 2013).

Wayne O'Connor is a Principal Research Scientist at the NSW Department of Primary Industries' Port Stephens Fisheries Institute, and has played a leading role in the establishment of oyster farming in North Vietnam. He has over 25 years experience in aquaculture research, working on a variety programs including algal culture and the development of propagation techniques for a number of molluscs such as oysters (edible and pearl), scallops, mussels and clams. He is an Adjunct Associate Professor in the Faculty of Science Health and Education at the University of the Sunshine Coast, is a member of a number of molluscan societies and serves on the editorial boards for the journals Aquaculture and Aquaculture Research. He is the author of over 80 peer reviewed publications.

Lucie K. Ozanne is a Senior Lecturer in Marketing at the University of Canterbury in Christchurch, New Zealand. Lucie has a PhD and Masters from the Pennsylvania State University. Her research focuses on the natural environment, in particular how to encourage more environmentally responsible consumer and corporate behaviour. Recently, Lucie's research has begun to examine new forms of market exchange based on sharing, which include toy libraries, peer-to-peer renting and sharing skills through community time banks.

Janine Pierce is an adjunct research fellow in the Centre of Regional Engagement, University of South Australia and is involved in programs in the School of Management. Her PhD is from University of South Australia. Her current research particularly focuses on sustainability of people and place through the medium of Photovoice. Her recent projects have included working with ACIAR in Vietnam in exploring impact of aquaculture aid programs on communities, impact of energy prices on consumers, lives of parental carers of ASD children, and community visions and experiences for people in a South Australian urban area. Her current research focus is in further developing and assessing strategies for measuring community sustainability both within Australia and in developing countries, particularly in relation to climate change.

Anna Pistoni is Associate Professor of Management Control Systems in the Department of Economics at Insubria University (Varese—Italy). She is also teacher of Management Control Systems and Cost Accounting in the Department of Accounting at Bocconi University (Milan—Italy) and at the SDA Bocconi School of Management. Her main research interests are on the following topics: Corporate Social Responsibility and Performance Measurement Systems, Accounting and Sustainability, Servitization strategy and managerial control, Innovation and Managerial control. Anna is author of several national and international articles and books about these topics.

Chris Provis studied and taught philosophy, then worked for some years in industrial relations, and subsequently has taught and written in business ethics, publishing a number of articles and two books. He is now an Adjunct Associate Professor in the Business School at the University of South Australia. As well as his activities in teaching and research, he has undertaken consultancy work for a range of major public and private sector organisations. At present, he is editing a section on Confucianism for the forthcoming Springer Handbook of Virtue Ethics in Business and Management.

Barbara Resta got a master degree in Management Engineering (2008) and a Ph.D. in Logistics and Supply Chain Management (2012) at University of Bergamo with a dissertation on the *servitization* phenomenon and the impacts of introducing product-service offerings on the value network. Since 2012, she is a Research Assistant at CELS (Research Group on Industrial Engineering, Logistics and Service Operations) of the Engineering Department of the University of Bergamo. Currently, she is involved in the activities organized by ASAP Service Management Forum on the provision of product-service offerings in the automotive sector. Moreover, she is involved in research activities related to the application of sustainability principles to the textile sector.

Clive Smallman is Professor of Management and Dean, University of Western Sydney Business School, Australia. His research interests include process organisation studies, workplace risk management, decision-making, sustainability, organisational learning, organisational resilience, and positive psychology at work. His PhD is from Bradford University, UK.

Claudine Soosay is Associate Professor of Operations and Supply Chain Management at the University of South Australia Business School. Her current research areas include cold chain management, supply chain governance, sustainable operations and technology management. She has published in various journals and is actively involved in a number of industry associations in Australia.

Mohsen Varsei is a doctoral candidate in sustainable supply chain management at the University of South Australia Business School. He received his B. Sc. and M. Sc. with merit in industrial engineering and management science from Amirkabir University of Technology. His research interests include Integration of sustainability strategy into supply chain and operations management, at both strategic and operational level through framework and decision-making tool development, as to solve real business problems.

Sukhbir Sandhu is a Lecturer in the University of South Australia Business School, Adelaide, Australia. Her research interests include corporate social and environmental strategies, and base of the pyramid business strategies. Her PhD is from Lincoln University, New Zealand.

Stephen McKenzie was awarded a PhD in English from the University of South Australia in 2000. His doctoral research focused on conceptions of Asia in the medieval and early modern periods. He has undertaken research on the social aspects of sustainability. He is developing an interest in the intersection between religious ethics and social sustainability and has published in that area. He lived for a time in the Solomon Islands and later in Papua New Guinea.

Howard Harris teaches business and professional ethics at the University of South Australia. A member of the school of management in the UniSA Business School his main scholarly interest is in the relevance of traditional virtues including courage, justice and love in contemporary management. He is coeditor of *The Heart of the Good Institution* (Springer 2013). He came to academia after a career in industry where he saw at first hand the impact of personal decisions on organisational and social sustainability.

Chapter 1
Introduction

Stephen McKenzie, Sukhbir Sandhu and Howard Harris

Linking Local and Global Sustainability: A Model for Ethical Action

This book takes a holistic approach to sustainability, as a concern practical and philosophical, local and global. Through 12 chapters from a wide range of disciplinary backgrounds, we ask: how can individuals and institutions make judicious and well-managed contributions to the increasingly complex agenda of a sustainable world? We find ultimately, that the answer lies in processes of governance, management and decision-making.

One of the volume's central questions is: how do we know if what we are doing at a local level is actually sustainable at a global level? Despite being such a commonplace idea, a practical and workable definition for sustainability initiatives at the local level, which still contribute to the global agenda, remains elusive. The following discussion gives some insight into the problems of defining sustainability, and suggests a model for understanding it on six dimensions—simple, complex, local, global, ideal, and practical. Our definition of "local to global sustainability initiative" draws from all six of these dimensions.

A *simple* definition of sustainability is a short statement of basic premises—generally, that we must attempt to live in a way that not does draw from our various resources at a greater rate than they are replenished. Such brief definitions are usually also *ideal* rather than *practical*—that is, they describe an end-point at which we are attempting to arrive, rather than giving instruction on how we are to get there.

S. McKenzie (✉) · S. Sandhu · H. Harris
School of Management, University of South Australia
Business School, Adelaide, Australia
e-mail: Stephen.McKenzie@unisa.edu.au

S. Sandhu
e-mail: Sukhbir.Sandhu@unisa.edu.au

H. Harris
e-mail: Howard.Harris@unisa.edu.au

© Springer Science+Business Media Dordrecht 2014
S. Sandhu et al. (eds.), *Linking Local and Global Sustainability,* The International Society of Business, Economics, and Ethics Book Series 4, DOI 10.1007/978-94-017-9008-6_1

A *complex* definition of sustainability can be one that provides a detailed exposition of the precise nature of these resources—the Five Capitals framework derived originally from Pierre Bourdieu (and developed by the Forum for the Future), is an example (Bourdieu 1984). Alternately, a complex definition can provide more *practical* instruction into how we are to live without depleting these resources.

A *local* or "community" definition of sustainability is one that outlines the ideal conditions for a community or organization to live sustainably. Conversely, a *global* definition is one that outlines conditions for the whole world's resources to be used at a sustainable rate.

The oft-quoted Brundtland definition is an example of a simple, ideal, global definition. Sustainable Seattle's *Indicators of a Sustainable Community* is an example of a complex, ideal, local definition. As an example of a complex, practical, local definition, we cite the 12-page 'Model of Corporate Sustainability' in Marc Epstein's *Making Sustainability Work* (2008), and the original *Sustainability Reporting Guidelines* from the Global Reporting Initiative (2000).

Examples of complex, practical and *global* definitions are harder to come by. Where global sustainability is defined and discussed, it is inevitably very simple—such as the Brundtland definition—or, extremely complex, and requiring calculations about the impacts of all different aspects of modern life upon a wide range of resources, using data-sets from the United Nations and other global bodies (for example, the *Limits to Growth* reports, 1972, 2002 and 2012).

Neither of these two levels—simple or complex—are appropriate for the average business or organization. Simple definitions of global sustainability may be a source of inspiration, and a good place to begin a discussion, but they tend to beg the question, "so how do we achieve this ideal condition?". And in relation to complex definitions of global sustainability, most organizations simply do not have the capacity to make accurate calculations about every aspect of their operations against global resources, and if they did, it is questionable if this is even a valid activity. As Rob Gray warned in 2010, assessing the effect of the entire human population on the global environment is so complex that it is "difficult to really conceptualize at anything below planetary and species levels", and therefore, "any simple assessment of the relationship between a single organization and planetary sustainability is virtually impossible" (Gray 2010, p. 48).

Thus, this book centres on the concept of *local to global* sustainability, but without advocating for businesses or other organizations to account for their activities in relation to planetary resources. Our position is that organizations *can* make a valid contribution to the global agenda, without needing to make an overall assessment of their contribution to planetary sustainability.

To guide us as we develop this position, we construct a new definition of *a local to global sustainability initiative*, which blends the six dimensions we have discussed.

A *local to global sustainability initiative* is:

A collective, progressive and self-reflexive activity, undertaken within communities, designed to develop more sustainable relationships with the natural environment, including its own members and members of other communities.

We point to the following features within the definition:

- Sustainability is a collective activity. A sustainability initiative must engage different members of the community.
- Sustainability is a progressive activity. A sustainability initiative seeks to identify unsustainable practices and change them, or, to identify sustainable practices and develop or extend them.
- Sustainability is a self-reflexive activity. A sustainability initiative will improve in response to a self-relative critique of current practice.
- A sustainability initiative is undertaken and owned by a community or a number of co-operating communities. A community can include organizations of many different sizes and purposes.
- A sustainability initiative should develop a sustainable relationship with the natural environment. That is, it should ensure that the community's use of particular environmental resources is better than before it was implemented, and does not deplete resources at a greater rate than they can be replenished.
- Human communities are part of the natural environment. Thus, a sustainability initiative should improve and sustain relationships within its own community, and with other communities.

With this definition, we have departed from the standard practice of defining sustainability as an *ideal condition*, because as we have pointed out, such definitions are either too general or too complex to be workable for individual organizations. Instead, we are defining a model for human *activity* that begins at the local level and seeks ultimately to affect the wider world.

The move to define sustainability as a process of human activity which improves relationships draws us toward the field of business and organizational ethics, which is dealt with directly in the first section of the book. These chapters ask us to look beyond the view of sustainability as something that must be enforced through regulation and reported through accounting, and urge us to consider it as an ongoing and integral part of our responsibilities as human beings. As Chris Provis makes clear in the opening chapter, the situations that arise as modern businesses grapple with their social and environmental responsibilities are so nuanced and complex that rule-based systems of decision-making are inadequate. For instance, what does a manager do when an established product that has profound positive social and economic effects is suddenly shown to have an environmental down side? Ceasing production seems both the right and wrong choice. The triple bottom line formula of win-win-win is an aspirational goal that can only be achieved in some cases. In many others, we must decide what to do, and we must recognize that the issues we face are ethical ones, which cannot be delayed and avoided, and which require sound moral judgement and integrity.

Our definition of a local to global sustainability initiative is redolent of other models for virtuous organizational behavior. In particular, various writers in the volume have been influenced by the model of a "practice" developed by philosopher Alisdair MacIntyre in *After Virtue* (1985). Our suggestion is that sustainability initiatives are best defined as a continuous and self-reflexive process of seeking excellence in relation to the environment and human communities within it. A virtuous modern organization must strive for excellence in this endeavor, as well as seeking excellence in its particular field.

Stephen McKenzie's chapter discusses what sustainability would look like if it were a "practice" in the MacIntyrean sense—which currently, it is not. Sustainability is in a weak position, McKenzie argues, because it has no cohesive narrative of excellence, and is easily captured by different parties wishing it to be "about" different things. But if a global tradition of excellence in decision-making for sustainability were more formally recognized, then the contributions of individuals and their local organizations could be more easily fitted into this tradition. When managers attempt to make decisions about what was really sustainable, they would have this tradition to work within. This is not to say that rules for sustainability would be more formally developed, but that excellence in sustainable decision-making would be more understood, and managers would have more exemplar to follow.

Howard Harris' chapter, also based firmly in the tradition of virtue ethics, questions the notion that sustainability is primarily a matter of distributive justice, and a series of formulae for arriving at it. The problem, he argues, is that while human beings are encouraged to have the freedom to pursue the maximization of their own welfare, they will undoubtedly do so, and it is assumed that future generations will have at least the same or a greater level of welfare, otherwise their needs are compromised and the central tenet of the Brundtland definition has not been met. All this begs one of the central questions of sustainability: how much is actually enough? If sustainability is a simple matter of calculating maximum utility, we minimize its function as an ethical principle. Adopting it as a principle will be much harder than the utilitarian model, Harris writes, and will require the ongoing work of sustainability to be a self-reflexive critique of our actions as individuals.

Economic, Social and Environmental Relationships

For businesses, where profitability is often the central concern, the overlapping or "three pillar" model of sustainability can be appealing. Each sphere of activity is seen as essentially separate, and they can be portrayed as equal in size. The responsibilities of businesses to social and environmental stakeholders are found only in the places where those spheres overlap with their own, and true sustainability is found in the small area where all three intersect.

This model has been dubbed "weak sustainability" by Neumayer and others (see Neumayer 2003; Willard 2013) because it allows business to perceive that a large area of their profitability may exist independently of environmental and social concerns. It therefore positions sustainability as an "add-on" or adjunct to regular business behavior, something that must be addressed in particular situations to satisfy the needs of "external" stakeholders, but otherwise, should not interfere with the real business at hand, which is making money in the big red circle. In other words, it can serve to encourage business to "white-wash" or "green-wash" their behavior.

Fig. 1.1 The nested spheres
model

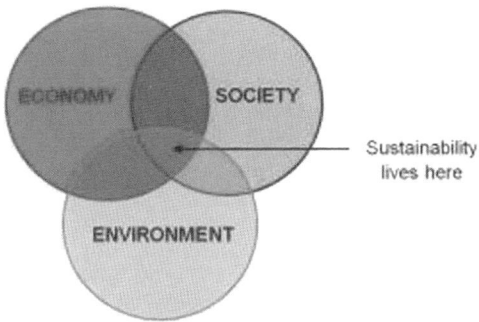

Our own criticism of the overlapping spheres model takes a different turn. In our view, the model is flawed because it suggests that true sustainability is a fragile and elusive condition, a miraculous balancing act between three competing forces, a compromise that is difficult to achieve and even harder to maintain. If we task modern organizations with such a near-impossible goal, is it any wonder that many of them continue to prioritize the economic sphere, and default to an economic definition of success in situations where the triple bottom line win turns out not to be achievable?

Our preferred conceptual model is the nested spheres (Fig. 1.1), in which the environment is all-encompassing, human communities are positioned within it, and the economy sits within those. In this model, there can be no economic activity that is somehow separate from its own environment or the communities in which the activity takes place.

This may seem an even more demanding model for profit-oriented businesses than the overlapping spheres model, because its appearance suggests that economic activity must *always* be subordinate to the needs of people and the environment. Profit is displayed as the smallest sphere, and therefore, it must come last. But in reality, the nested model is a more accurate description of how businesses really operate. They are housed within communities, which are in turn housed within the wider environment. Business organizations therefore have a "guest" relationship with communities and the environment which house them. Within such a model, we maintain that organizations can still be profit-oriented, but, they also have a natural interest in systematically improving their relationships with their hosts.

We know that there are many cases where the *current* relationships between organisations and their hosts are unhealthy, and unsustainable. This does not necessarily mean that such an organisation is to be condemned as a "bad guest"—corrupt, unethical or unsustainable. While we acknowledge that some organizations are corrupt, we also point to numerous examples of businesses that have seen weaknesses in their social and environmental relationships and voluntarily sought to improve them, without expecting economic or reputational reward for doing so. In other words, they have engaged in *local to global sustainability initiatives*.

In Section 2, "Economic, Social and Environmental Relationships", the chapter by Sukhbir Sandhu and colleagues (Sandhu, Smallman, Ozanne and Cullen) directly addresses this issue. It asks whether cost savings are really a main driver for companies to adopt environmentally sustainability measures, or if they are an incidental result of these measures. They conclude—after a literature review and extensive case study research in India and New Zealand—that in many cases, companies were going to adopt the environmental measures anyway, and that cost savings appeared as an unexpected bonus several years after adoption. They warn against the promotion of cost savings as a driver for environmental responsiveness, which will severely limit the amount and kind of initiatives that will be adopted.

The chapter by Claudine Soosay, Andrew Fearne and Moshen Varsei looks at sustainability measures in the supply chain management of a large Australian wine company (Yalumba). They highlight the supply chain as one of the key areas in which a large manufacturing company can address sustainability concerns in an effective way. Such research is a refreshing change from corporate sustainability activities based on philanthropy, which ultimately place sustainability outside the core business of the company. According to Soosay and her colleagues, sustainability concerns are imbedded in Yalumba's core business.

The section concludes with a chapter by Barbara Resta, Paolo Gaiardelli and Anna Pistoni, who also look at issues of supply and service delivery within a single car manufacturing company. Their proposal is that an analysis of sustainability concerns over the entire life of the company's vehicle is necessary if we are to arrive at an understanding of whether the production is really sustainable. As they point out, most of the emphasis on sustainability in the automotive industry thus far has been on the type of vehicle produced and in particular, its fuel consumption, and certain makes of vehicles can be labelled sustainable on this basis. But if things like maintenance and disposal of the car at the end of its life are taken into account, the view may change radically. This chapter presents a clear example of excellence in sustainable decision-making, and demonstrates how sustainability could be practiced locally, to make a global contribution—as a serious and concerted effort to examine all the implications of a course of action.

The section draws examples from developed countries (Australia, New Zealand and Italy) and one from a BRICs (Brazil Russia India China) country (India). The general conclusion to be drawn from all three chapters is that throughout the developed and emerging world, there are organizations that are voluntarily embarking on sustainability initiatives, and sustainability across the supply chain provides a key linking mechanism between local and global sustainability.

Responsibility for Sustainability

A recent internet search for "Responsibility of Society to Businesses" yielded no hits (all searches conducted on Google, October 16, 2013). A series of similar search phrases ("Social Responsibility to Businesses", etc.) also yielded nothing. Without the limiting quotes, hundreds of pages appeared in these searches in which the relationship is reversed, and the responsibility of corporations to society and the environment was discussed.

Fig. 1.2 The overlapping spheres model

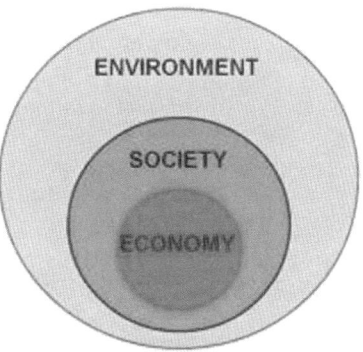

A Google Scholar search for "Responsibility of Society to Businesses" yielded only one result, a book by Satu Rintanen on corporate environmental management in the European meat sector. Rintanen points out that if all the responsibility for global sustainability is seen to rest with business organizations, there is a very real danger that they will be asked to solve very complex problems that they may not have caused, and that they are not capable of solving alone (Rintanen 2005, p. 40). Rintanen is guided here by the Italian ethicist Caselli, who wrote in 1998 that the environmental and social responsibility of companies must not be seen as a one-way relationship, and argued for a two-fold conception of social responsibility, which emphasized that companies should not be forced to take up objectives that do not ultimately belong to them, and should co-operate with communities in achieving sustainability objectives (cited in Rintanen 2005).

Such arguments are relatively uncommon, and the dominant discourse of sustainability at present is about the responsibilities of business to make sure they do not harm activity in the other two spheres. Collectively, what the discourse is saying is that businesses are responsible for our current *un*sustainability, and are therefore responsible for finding ways to address it.

Interestingly, another internet search for "Businesses are Vital to Sustainability" yielded no hits. "Businesses are Responsible for Sustainability" yielded nothing, either. Both search terms also yielded nothing on Google Scholar. Again, the removal of the limiting quotes drew up hundreds of pages in which the responsibility of businesses to society and the environment is discussed. While in many ways, the popular and academic discourses of sustainability locate responsibility for change within the economic sphere, they also do not like to admit that businesses are responsible for sustainability.

This paradoxical situation exists because many people still think in terms of the three areas of sustainability as separate and competing. Returning to the "overlapping spheres" model (Fig. 1.2), we note that it is not just the economic sphere that is pictured as having a partially separate existence from the others. All three are conceived in this manner. What might the three "unshared" areas actually contain? In the environmental sphere, the answer is clearly wilderness, areas of the environment removed from any human activity, economic or otherwise. In the economic sphere, we might find the quest for pure and unconstrained profit for shareholders, without heeding social and environmental constraints. And in the social sphere, we might imagine a civil and intellectual utopia in which the physical and emotional needs of all citizens was well cared for, irrespective of environmental or economic requirements.

While we do not think the overlapping model is a good description of what sustainability *should* be about, it is fair to say that much of the history of sustainability theory has been characterized by contestation between these three "different" areas of sustainability, with advocates for all three areas maintaining that their concerns should have primacy over the others, or at least that much of the activity within their particular sphere should remain separate from the other two. Such a model suggests that there can be large parts of human society which do *not* have any link to economic activity, and also, that human society can exist outside the natural environment. To us, both these propositions are just as implausible as the idea that there can be business activity that exists outside society.

All three chapters in the third section look at aspects of the history of this contestation, and make recommendations about how we might transfigure our understanding of sustainability towards a more co-operative model. The chapter by Pratima Bansal and Jijun Gao discusses the relatively new field of Organisations and Environment (O&E) research, and reviews its literature between 1995 and 2010. O&E research began its life with a dual nature. Researchers coming from the organizational side tended to view the environment as one variable among many that might explain organizational outcomes. On the other side, researchers with more of an environmental focus have viewed organizational structures as a means to the end of achieving a healthy environment. Only very recently has a more balanced discipline begun to emerge. This history of O&E in many ways mirrors the overall history of sustainability discourse. Many early forays were based strongly within one of the three spheres and looking to maximize the interests of that sphere. Only comparatively recently has a more balanced and cooperative understanding of sustainability begun to take shape.

The next chapter, by Don Clifton, looks at another field, Ecological Footprint Analysis (EFA), and concludes with a demonstration of the method in an Australian context. Here, the central issue is an argument between the "Reformist" and "Transformational" models of sustainability. The Reformist model posits continued economic growth and development, but in ways that are more "green and just" than they are at present. In this way, it is aligned with the dominant discourse of sustainability we have been describing. Within the Reformist model, the responsibility for sustainability still rests largely with businesses and regulators to change economic practices. The more radical Transformational model, however, sees continued economic growth as unsustainable and urges that we move away from an idea of human happiness and meaning based on consumption and affluence. In the Transformational model, much of the responsibility for sustainability rests with society in general, rather than with businesses. It is unreasonable to expect that we can continue to live the way we do as a society, thinking that businesses can be made solely responsible for making our current standard of living sustainable.

Lisa Newton's chapter, the last in the section, takes as its starting point a recent event in the U.S.: the proposition by two young thinkers that the tradition of environmentalism should simply be abandoned, as unwieldy, unworkable, and overly politicized. While Newton is not entirely in agreement with their initial argument, she is critical of environmentalism as a series of special interest groups, and she questions if conservation was ever really a progressive agenda, or, if liberalism was ever a true friend to the environment. Discarding "pure" environmentalism based on the desire for the preservation of wilderness, she calls instead for the unification of all the different rationales for the preservation of the environment, and a return to the classical conservatism and "concern for the commons". In Newton's analysis, the environment is neither separate from the economic realities of the world, nor intersecting with them only to a small degree. For this reason, environmentalism cannot be a special interest, in competition with other forces. Newton's paper predicts a future in which environmentalism must form part of the core practice of every business.

Sustainability Is Everywhere

In Section 2, "Economic, Social and Environmental Relationships", we examined case studies from developed and developing nations. The fourth and final section presents three case studies in which specific sustainability agendas in developing contexts are viewed through a global lens. The studies come from the Western Pacific, Indigenous Australian communities, and Vietnam. Our rationale for presenting case studies from some relatively unusual places is simple: for holistic, "local to global" sustainability to be truly effective, we must be able to identify and practice it everywhere.

Vandra Harris's chapter looks at Security Sector Reform (SSR) in the Solomon Islands. She argues that sustainability is about achieving positive medium- and long-term impacts that will expand people's choices and ensure an equitable distribution of resources. Law and justice sector reform are a critical aspect of sustainability, she argues, because a stable environment in which rule of law functions enables effective development in other areas. Harris' take on sustainable development is an interesting one. She argues that in many ways it is a tautology, because unless development is sustainable and equitable, it isn't actually development at all, but a maintenance of the status quo. This alerts us as to why case studies in developing countries are so useful. Much of what gets called sustainable development in developed countries is in fact the continuation of the economic status quo with slightly altered social and environmental practices. In a post-conflict environment like the Solomons, the need for development that *enables better community relationships* is strongly foregrounded. Self-reflexive activity is required to ensure that the development is genuinely having this effect.

Azmiri Mian's chapter on sustainable tourism also looks at development issues within indigenous societies, but her case study is less positive than the previous chapter. Her focus is on certification standards for Indigenous tourism operators in Australia through the program known as Respecting Our Cultures (ROC). Mian points out that while ROC has been established and run with good intentions, the outcome of the certification process has been that many Indigenous operators have lost control of their businesses and are now unable to deliver authentic cultural experiences. Vandra Harris' warning from the previous chapter is highly applicable here: if an intervention doesn't actually contribute to sustainability and equity, then it isn't development. The ROC hasn't worked well as a sustainability initiative because it has not effectively improved relationships between the organizations (the tourism operators) and the wider community. We are reminded again of how rule-based systems for sustainability can fail in practice, and how individual judgements based on moral integrity may provide a better path to sustainable outcomes in many cases.

The last chapter in the volume is Janine Pierce and Wayne O'Connor's examination of the impact of oyster farming on community sustainability in a Vietnamese village. Photo-voice devices were given to the farmers and they recorded information about what was important to them about the introduction of oyster farming to their region. Reading the chapter, the human and relational aspect of sustainability work becomes immediately clear. As well as an increased sense of personal pride and accomplishment, many of the farmers reported an increase in community spirit and co-operation. The chapter reminds us that sustainability initiatives in developing contexts need not be driven by a need for major profit, or implemented and analyzed in a top-down fashion according to predetermined criteria for sustainability. Locally-managed enterprises which are driven by small-scale economic need can increase a sense of stewardship and collective responsibility for social and environmental resources. The chapter thus provides a clear example of a local to global sustainability initiative and a fitting end to our volume.

For us, sustainability is not an ideal condition, but it is certainly more than a blanket term for anything that seems like a "good idea". It is about having the knowledge to weigh different claims of "good" with one other, the judgment to choose one course of action over another with competing claims, and the integrity to persist with courses of action into the medium- and long-term. We believe that the work of sustainability is about making these decisions in a concerted, informed and systematic way, with the intention of improving the relationships between organizations, society, and the global environment.

All 12 chapters here extend sustainability, conceptually, empirically and theoretically, and in doing so, provide insights into linking local and global sustainability. In the opening section, we are asked to view everyday decision-making as complex work, rather than as something that we can have done for us by formulae; in the second section, we see examples of various types of decision-making for sustainability, and how businesses in developed and developing economies are striving to undertake it in a cost effective manner; the third section looks at renewed theoretical approaches that will underpin the new work of sustainability as a co-operative rather than a contested space will look like; and the final section provides examples of the work in action, in a variety of development contexts.

References

Bourdieu, P. (1984). *Distinction: A social critique of the judgment of taste* (Trans. Nice, R.). Cambridge: Harvard University Press.

Epstein, M. (2008). *Making sustainability work: Best practices in managing and measuring corporate social, environmental and economic impacts*. San Francisco: Berrett-Koehler.

Global Reporting Initiative. (2000). *Sustainability reporting guidelines*. Amsterdam: Global Reporting Initiative.

Gray, R. (2010). Is accounting for sustainability actually accounting for sustainability … and how would we know? An exploration of narratives of organisations and the planet. *Accounting, Organizations and Society, 35,* 47–62.

MacIntyre, A. (1985). *After virtue*. London: Duckworth.

Neumayer, E. (2003). *Weak vs. strong sustainability: Exploring the limits of two opposing paradigms*. London: Edward Elgar.

Rintanen, S. (2005). *The establishment and development direction of corporate environmental management*. Tampere: Esa Print. (Publications of the Turku School of Economics and Business Administration, Series A-1).

Willard, B. (2013). Three sustainability models. http://sustainabilityadvantage.com/2010/07/20/3-sustainability-models/. Accessed 15 Oct 2013.

Part I
Philosophy and Ethics of Sustainability

These three chapters pose questions on the nature of sustainability, to be taken up in the sections that follow.

The first chapter asks—what sort of judgement and decision-making will we need if organisations are to become truly sustainable?

The second chapter explores decision-making for sustainable organisations.

The third chapter asks—how could sustainability function as an ethical principle?

1. Sustainability, Integrity and Judgement
2. A MacIntyrean Analysis of Sustainability Narratives in Modern Businesses
3. Sustainability is a Work of Justice: Virtue not Distribution

Chapter 2
Sustainability, Integrity and Judgment

Chris Provis

Sustainability is the focus of an enormous amount of discussion, and there is widespread agreement about its importance. There is no clear, precise definition of 'sustainability' that goes with the acceptance that sustainability is important (see e.g. Adams 2006, p. 2; Kates et al. 2005, p. 11) but many examples will be widely agreed. At present, prominent issues include climate change, sustainable agriculture, sustainable building practices, and many others. Examples from the past might include asbestos: for a long time long looked on as a wonder material for its fire-retardant properties, now reviled for its adverse health impact. Or we might think of the history of DDT, or the use of chlorofluorocarbons (CFCs) in refrigeration. Each of these has a claim to being a matter of sustainability: whether the production and use of these substances was a sustainable practice. One key thing about the cases is that each to some extent or other involves realization of bad effects based on study or understanding of a specific product or process. For us, they provide examples of sustainability issues that raise the specific question to be considered in this paper: To what extent do decisions about sustainable practices raise questions of individual moral integrity?

In particular, the paper focusses on decisions about sustainability made by individuals in large organisations. To that extent, it links the discussion to issues of corporate social responsibility. There has been extensive discussion and debate about DuPont's role in CFC production, and the company's response to emerging evidence about CFC effects on the Earth's ozone layer (see e.g., Maxwell and Briscoe 1997; Mullin 2002). Corporate producers and users of DDT were prominent in hearings about its continued use in the United States (U.S. EPA 1975). There has been widespread discussion of the role played by asbestos producers in asbestos-related disease (Edley and Weiler 1993; Dawson 2004). In each of these cases there has been some debate about what appropriate courses of action were, and whether corporations did in fact behave responsibly, but what is clear is that the issues cannot be divorced from matters of corporate social responsibility. Often, in discussions

C. Provis (✉)
Business School, University of South Australia, Adelaide, Australia
e-mail: Christopher.Provis@unisa.edu.au

© Springer Science+Business Media Dordrecht 2014
S. Sandhu et al. (eds.), *Linking Local and Global Sustainability,* The International Society of Business, Economics, and Ethics Book Series 4, DOI 10.1007/978-94-017-9008-6_2

about sustainability, focus on individuals relates to their roles as consumers, or as citizens (see e.g., Dower 2011; Kent 2011). Kent contends that "there is an inherent emphasis in developed societies on locating responsibility for climate change, both in terms of its causes and effects, with individual actors" (2011, p. 67). In fact, corporations and other organizations are key players in sustainability. Corporations directly produce a great deal of the world's pollution, and derivatively produce a great deal more, in the goods and services that they offer to consumers. Investments by corporations determine how jobs and production are distributed, and what form they take. In agriculture, in manufacturing, in provision of power, water and transport, and through innumerable other activities, the behavior of corporations is a key to sustainable future. Here, then, we focus especially on decisions made by individuals in those many organisations that have some responsibilities for sustainable practices.

It may be question to what extent focus on individual judgment and decision can improve organizational judgment and decision, in ways that allow corporations to discharge their social responsibilities. In this context, I want to make two suggestions. One is that the idea of integrity may be a useful one in considering how individuals' decisions contribute to sustainable activity by corporations, and the other is that individuals' choices will have to emerge from well-developed reflective judgment. If we want corporations to act in ways that are morally, socially and ecologically sustainable, we need them to contain individuals who act with integrity on the basis of well-developed reflective judgment. The next section reminds us of the moral complexities and conflicts that are faced by individuals in large organizations that have corporate social responsibilities. Later sections suggest that such problems are exacerbated by sustainability requirements. We may attempt to reconcile the conflicting moral demands on us through decisions that fit into a coherent personal story, but to do so is especially difficult in matters of sustainability that require us to deal with new, complex and possibly unwelcome information. Then, it is a requirement of integrity for us to revise our beliefs when necessary, and behave accordingly.

Sustainability, Corporations and Individuals

In matters of sustainability, there is often contestation about factual issues. The facts about the effects of CFCs on the ozone layer or the effects of DDT on the environment required sophisticated scientific investigation. There is still debate about the extent to which corporations like DuPont were honest in the way they responded to claims that were made about their products. Mullin has carefully set out the history, and has pointed out ways in which decisions by DuPont executives were reasonable, and suggests that, despite some shortcomings, "DuPont's reaction to the CFC crisis appears overall to be an example of doing things right" (2002, pp. 216–217). Here, we do not need to determine where responsibility lies in that or any particular example, but Mullin's account certainly identifies points about the pressures on corporations like DuPont. The key point for us is that the corporation had a moral responsibility to take seriously the claims that were being made and to assess the evidence in an objective way. The fact that assessment of such claims is complex and demanding has to be set against the magnitude of the harm that may occur if they are dismissed. During the period when the effects of atmospheric CFCs were being considered, one of the problems was the possibility that conclusive evidence might become available only after they had done irreversible damage (Mullin 2002, p. 210).

In such cases, individuals have to make decisions about advice and recommendations in situations where they are subject to multiple competing demands and pressures. Solomon sets out the general difficulty of saying what implications there are for individuals from the responsibilities of the corporations they work in:

> Consider a disastrous decision or mishap of moderate proportions. A middle manager insists that he was 'just doing what he was told,' and his supervisor claims that she was 'just following orders.' Her boss in turn was only doing what he thought the top executives wanted done and the executives themselves, even the chief executive of the company, insist that they had no such intention and place the blame squarely on those to whom they had delegated such responsibilities. The board of directors, who are supposedly the overseers of the entire operation, claim to have had no knowledge of what was going on. And the stockholders, who in theory 'own' the company, find themselves out of the loop where such decisions are made. Where is the responsibility to be laid? (1997, p. 219)

Solomon uses this to extend the argument put forward earlier by others, most notably by French 1979, that responsibility must eventually be assigned to the corporation itself. He gives the Exxon *Valdez* case as a vivid example where responsibility seems to be diffused unclearly amongst a variety of individuals.

However, even if we accept Solomon's argument that the diffusion of responsibility confirms the need to attribute responsibility to organizations, that does not mean that we can push aside the question how to attribute responsibility to individuals. If it is unclear how to attribute responsibility to individuals when things go wrong, it can be equally unclear how individuals' obligations and duties figure in ensuring that things go right. Nevertheless, individuals in large organizations need to determine their duties and responsibilities. How may they do so? The problem emerges partly from individuals' responses to the expectations they perceive others to have of them: the supervisor claims that she was 'just following orders', her boss was only doing what he thought the top executives wanted done, and so on. A finite set of instructions can only very seldom define fully what an individual in a corporation is to do (and jobs where this is most possible are gradually being replaced by computer technology). In determining their duties and responsibilities, it is quite right for individuals to take account of others' legitimate expectations, but inevitably their understanding of others' expectations is a matter of inference and interpretation. Those inferences and interpretations will be based on many factors, including the individuals' own personal characteristics, feedback they have received in the past, present cues from others, and stated organizational policies and values.

Organizations are complex networks of roles and social relationships. Individual managers within business organizations have multiple calls on them, all of them quite legitimate. Typically, a manager's organizational duties go beyond responsibility for a single issue like product safety. They may include other policy matters like occupational safety and health, but also supervising other employees. Usually, they involve providing reports on past actions, as well as deciding on future actions. Sometimes, they involve direct contact with clients, suppliers, government officials or members of the public, as well as with other members of the organization. The fact that the corporation has certain social responsibilities does create obligations for individuals in the corporation, but they have other obligations as well. These also include other obligations to people outside the corporation, who have nothing especially to do with the corporation: most obviously, for example, obligations to their families, or other close associates, but also general obligations of honesty, fairness and benevolence to others. Individuals have ethical obligations to help their organizations meet responsibilities for sustainable products and processes, but their obligations to one another, to friends and family, the obligations they have in other social roles, all these and others also place moral demands on them, no different in their fundamental moral character than the demands on them to help the corporation fulfil its social responsibilities. All of these obligations are associated with a need for understanding of the relevant issues. This is true in general, and in particular it is true in cases where decisions have to be made about harmful products or processes.

Of course, it is not only as members of corporations that we face conflicts amongst different moral demands. We may do so in many other situations, whether as small businesspeople, family members, churchgoers or in any of our many other activities. Demands of honesty, to report things truly, may conflict with demands of fairness, to give someone the benefit of the doubt, or a promise I made to one person may conflict with the need to help another. And so on. Often, we can hope that our moral development allows us to deal simply and easily with situations where different factors pull us in contrary directions, but sometimes we face real dilemmas. That we have to make choices in such situations is an important aspect of human life generally. Nevertheless, it is especially salient within large organizations, because their complexity tends to proliferate demands on us, and increase the possibility of conflict.

As a result, large organizations often aim to assist their members with codes that set out the moral demands they recognize that may loom largest. However, such codes cannot be expected to serve as rules or checklists that can resolve dilemmas in a routinized way. In general, checklists and codes identify types of obligations, and suggest ways to approach them. As guidelines, they are useful. It is not a corporate code, but the Rotary Four-Way Test (Rotary International 2012) provides a clear, simple example:

Of the things we think, say or do

1. Is it the TRUTH?
2. Is it FAIR to all concerned?
3. Will it build GOODWILL and BETTER FRIENDSHIPS?
4. Will it be BENEFICIAL to all concerned?

In the sort of case we are envisaging, like DuPont's production of CFCs, questions like "Is it the truth?" and "Will it be beneficial to all concerned?" are very much to the point. The trouble is, such questions are not at all easy to answer in the sorts of cases we are envisaging. So far as beneficial effects are concerned, products like CFCs, asbestos and DDT certainly do have some benefits. CFCs were introduced to replace ammonia as a refrigerant, just because of ammonia's potentially harmful effects (Mullin 2002, p. 208). Asbestos was widely used because of its benefits in fireproofing, and DDT was used to combat the mosquitos that spread malaria. The question in each case is not whether the product is beneficial but whether its benefits outweigh its harmful effects. More than that, though, the issue is about potential benefit versus risks of harm, and then the question "Is it the truth?" becomes prominent. In the sorts of cases we are considering, that is not clear-cut.

Heuristics like the Four-Way Test are useful, but that is what they are: heuristics, which often but not always point out the right path to follow. Many codes of conduct for organizations and professions have a similar structure, outlining several principles or values to which the organization or profession is committed: respect for others, perhaps, or honesty, justice, kindness, accountability and others. But they will not replace situation-specific judgment. This may well be recognized in the code itself. BHP Billiton's *Code of Business Conduct* says, quite reasonably, "The Code does not remove the need for all of us to exercise good judgment—it just makes it easier for every one of us to do so" (BHP Billiton 2012, p. 8). The contents of a code, like the Rotary Four-Way Test, can assist, but not provide some unreflective step-by-step routine. Whatever principles and values may be identified, there is room for an individual to face conflict amongst them in certain situations, and only individuals' judgment can resolve it.

This is especially so in matters of sustainability, where factual issues are sometimes very difficult (see e.g., Holling 2001). As a result, individuals have new calls on their judgment. Immediately after the statement quoted above from the BHP Billiton code, it goes on "We all have a responsibility to work with integrity and good judgement". In what follows I shall make some suggestions about the way that this is especially important in connection with sustainability. Corporations' social responsibilities include sustainable choices, but corporations' choices will only be sustainable if the individuals within them show integrity in their judgments as well as their decisions.

Decisions, Integrity and Belief

Concern about sustainability has grown enormously over the past few years, at least in part because of our increasing awareness that common practices that have been taken for granted for years may have effects that are both unanticipated and unwelcome. These range from global issues like effects of CFCs on the ozone layer to local issues like the effect of discharging pollutants into a creek. Because sustainability so often involves emergence of new and unwelcome information, it raises special issues of individual judgment and integrity.

We might aim to classify sustainability problems using Jennifer Jackson's distinction: she says that "There are two kinds of difficulties in ethics: difficulties in identification—of what is your duty in a particular situation, for example; and difficulties of compliance—of doing your duty once you know what it is" (1996, p. 8). She notes that "perhaps the public's perception of business ethics reflects its awareness of the latter (compliance) problem—how to prevent skulduggery, mischief and negligence" (1996, p. 8). Compliance problems, cases where individuals fail to heed a fairly clear obligation, where they act in ways that are clearly wrong, have been and continue to be the focus of a good deal of writing in business ethics (see e.g., Bazerman and Tenbrunsel 2011; Messick and Tenbrunsel 1996). However, even if members of the general public believe that ethical failures in business are largely failures to do what is clearly right, it is unsurprising that people in business are nevertheless aware of 'identification problems': not problems of doing what ought to be done, when that is known, but problems of working out what ought to be done in the first place (Jackson 1996, p. 8).

Certainly, in some cases, issues of sustainability seem to raise straightforward compliance problems. Consider the case of asbestos production. Concerns about asbestos did not emerge all at once. Alleman and Mossman note that although such concerns came to a head in the 1970s, "problems stemming from the inhalation of exceedingly high levels of asbestos in milling and manufacturing plants had actually been observed since the turn of the century" (1997, p. 74). There is some evidence that executives of manufacturing plants understood but suppressed such concerns: "From the point of view of the plaintiffs' bar, the true disgrace of the asbestos story is their belief that senior executives of some of the country's leading producers—particularly Johns-Manville—were not only aware of these risks, but took active steps to suppress knowledge of the danger in order to protect the sales of their product" (Edley and Weiler 1993, p. 388). To the extent that they did so, the ethical issue is not a problem of identification, in Jackson's terms, but a problem of compliance.

However, there are many other cases where things are less straightforward. Modern research is greatly increasing our understanding of human judgment and decision processes (see e.g., Kahneman 2011; Lehrer 2009), and advances in our understanding of judgment and decision are making us aware that 'compliance problems' start to overlap with 'identification problems', as individuals fail to see ethical implications of their own actions, even though these seem to be clear to observers (e.g., Bazerman and Tenbrunsel 2011, pp. 4–9). Further, individuals may be confronted not just with failure to see implications, but difficulties working out how to deal with contrary moral demands. They may see the different demands more or less clearly, but not be clear how to resolve the tension. Recently, Reynolds and colleagues have noted such situations, in their discussion of 'moral stress': "a psychological state (both cognitive and emotional) marked by anxiety and unrest due to an individual's uncertainty about his or her ability to fulfil relevant moral obligations" (2012, p. 492). They note in particular that the conflict is not well characterized as an individual having to choose between right and wrong. They cite Waters and Bird's acknowledgment that "moral stress may also result from the conflict of equally morally legitimate obligations"(Reynolds et al. 2012, p. 493, referring to Waters and Bird 1987). Reynolds and colleagues place the idea of moral stress in the context of psychological research on stress more generally. For example, they note that unlike 'challenge stressors' such as deadlines and workloads, which may be dealt with through increased effort, conflicts of obligations seem to be debilitating 'hindrance stressors', which cannot.

We noted some such problems in the previous section, where corporate managers may be caught in the midst of conflicting obligations. Sometimes, they have to choose between two or more alternatives that would fulfil different and conflicting obligations, and the individuals have to 'identify' which course is appropriate. On other occasions, however, they have to work out what to do without being quite clear what obligations they have: their problem is not so much one of conflict amongst clearly perceived obligations, but of perceiving only dimly what obligations they have. These kinds of problems are all too likely to arise when sustainability is an issue, and they make a special sort of call on individuals' integrity.

Recent work on the notion of integrity has focused on integrity as consistency between an individual's words and actions, sometimes referred to as 'behavioral integrity' (e.g., Kannan-Narasimhan and Lawrence 2012; Palanski and Yammarino 2007; Simons 2002), but the cases that arise in the sort of context we are considering call for integrity that goes beyond words and actions: it revolves around consistency of words and actions with an individual's beliefs. We are all familiar with situations where we harbor misgivings about a course of action, but we persist with it in the face of our misgivings, for one reason or another. We are uncertain about the competence of a prospective student, but bow to pressure to fill a quota, regretting it later as we have to use extra resources to support him. Or a bicycle manufacturer wonders if the junction of parts made with two new alloys may be weakened by reaction between them, only for the issue to be pushed aside by other demands, until eventually a rider is injured when the joint fails. And so on. In corporations, managers are confronted with various kinds of influences that push aside their doubts. Sometimes, they may be dimly aware of concerns, but subject to great pressures to proceed. For individuals, the pressures are often social pressures to conform to group norms (Provis 2011, Chap. 5), sometimes conceived as requirements of 'team play' (Jackall 1988, pp. 54–56). Often, this may lead to inconsistency between individuals' private beliefs, on the one hand, and their words and actions, on the other.

So far as consistency amongst words and actions is concerned, there need be no problem. The shortcoming of emphasis on 'behavioral integrity' is that words and actions may be consistent with one another, but not accurately reflect underlying doubts or beliefs. Consistency of words and actions can become second nature, as individuals manage their self-presentation so that it becomes a matter of course for their behavior to conform to others' expectations. Jackall comments that:

> Managers at Alchemy Inc., for instance, simply shrug at many of the widely trumpeted hazards of toxic waste; here, one person's hysteria and cause for moral outrage is another's familiar and somewhat dull routine. (Jackall 1988, p. 194)

He discusses concerns over the exposure of workers to cotton dust, for example, and the health risks it posed, and in another company rather similar concerns about the effects of noise on workers' hearing. 'White', a manager who raised concerns about the noise, found those concerns pushed aside by his peers and superiors (Jackall 1988, pp. 101–105). If those individuals lacked integrity, it was not necessarily because of inconsistency between their words and actions: it was because they did not face up to the doubts raised by White, and accept the facts he put before them.

As Jackall describes the case, failure by senior managers to heed White's concerns was caused largely by the potential costs of remediation and of compensation payments to affected workers. To that extent, the issue was essentially a compliance problem, where ethical concerns were set aside in favor of self-interested fears about company profits and personal position. The case may resemble early concerns about asbestos, noted above. In such cases, managers can be strongly tempted, since in many cases definite conclusions about costs and benefits will only be available after many years. Going back to the case of asbestos, for example, Edley and Weiler note that "asbestos-produced disease has a lengthy latency period—anywhere from ten to forty years" (1993, pp. 387–388), and as Jackall says, "managers think in the short run because they are evaluated by both their superiors and peers on their short-term results" (1988, p. 84). However, the pressures on them are exacerbated by the changes and developments in scientific understanding about the effects of products and processes. Jackall quotes vividly from the account given by one middle-level manager he interviewed:

> Well, from 1957 through 1962, I was intimately involved with the manufacture of DDT. During that time, we doubled production and sold almost all of it to Africa and India. And I knew and went home *knowing* that I was saving more lives than any major hospital was capable of doing. I *knew* that I was saving thousands of lives by doing this.
>
> Then Rachel Carson's *Silent Spring* came out and not only did I become a murderer of falcons and robins, but also one of the mass murderers of the world. I was now doing evil things to the world. (Jackall 1988, p. 155, italics in Jackall)

The manager goes on to recount similar occurrences with regard to the production of CFCs and soda ash. Such experiences are likely to be regular occurrences in matters of sustainability, as information accumulates about the effects of products and processes. One of the pre-eminent aspects of sustainability-related research findings is how they identify previously unrealized connections (see e.g., Kates et al. 2001). This may be a matter of scientific study, or of other research. For example, we may suddenly face suggestions that our organization is part of a supply chain that relies on exploited labour in other countries or uses materials with a large carbon footprint.

Then, the temptations to suppress information deliberately will be compounded by the difficulties of changing one's views about the merits of what one is doing. The manager interviewed by Jackall had been heartened by the good he was doing; suddenly, he had to deal with claims that it was not good but harm. The difficulty is not just a temptation to conceal evidence for the sake of company profits and personal position: it is a matter of weighing factual evidence about effects, adding evaluative issues about the relative magnitude of harms versus benefits, and resolving the question without being unduly influenced by regard for one's self-image as someone whose work is good and worthwhile. Then, we have to assess evidence knowing that we have obligations on either hand: obligations to shareholders and customers, on the one hand, and obligations to exploited workers or future generations, on the other. What do we do?

Integrity and Judgment

Situations like this can be referred to as 'right-versus-right' conflicts. Kidder (1995) and Badaracco (1997) both identify the problem of 'right versus right', and each makes suggestions about how such conflicts may be dealt with. Kidder identifies a need for integrity, and associates it with organizational culture. He says:

> The creation of a stronger sense of individual integrity, the development of a finer sense of character in our top leaders—while these are laudable, they won't do the trick… [W]hat's needed is not a moral makeover at the top but an ethical climate change throughout the organization. What's needed, in other words, is a wholesale effort to create cultures of integrity. (1995, p. 227)

However, that takes us no closer to how integrity bears on specific cases where individuals are confronted with new and disconcerting information, which forces them to re-evaluate their actions and strategies. To promote an organizational culture that supports integrity in the relevant way, we need an idea of how integrity sustains good decisions in those sorts of cases. What is at issue is integrity of judgment, as well as integrity of speech and action. 'Integrity' was mentioned in the BHP Billiton statement that "we all have a responsibility to work with integrity and good judgement". But how is integrity related to judgment? In particular, how is it related to matters of judgment about sustainable corporate processes and practices?

Suggestions that integrity can be reduced to consistency of words and actions is plausible, related to integrity's undoubted sense of wholeness and unity, but in the context of sustainability it is often crucial that we show integrity also in our beliefs and judgments. The outstanding feature of issues like climate change and environmental degradation is the extent to which they present new, uncomfortable information that requires effortful revision of our past, well-established beliefs, and of the ingrained, habitual ways of life that are based on those beliefs. Integrity cannot only involve people's words and actions, however much that might appeal to students of observable behavior. Integrity also involves consistency of one's words and actions with one's beliefs. If we are to act with moral integrity then we must be consistent between what we do and what we believe we ought to do. To act with integrity is at least in part to resist temptation, setting aside my own interests and inclinations in favor of my obligations. I must do so if I am to retain the wholeness and unity that integrity connotes. Failure to do so injects some fragmentation between my ideal self and my actual self.

What that can mean is shown in Badaracco's account, which revolves around the idea that such choices often constitute 'defining moments': moments that reveal and develop one's character and commitments. On his view, moments where managers have to deal with conflicts of right-versus-right are moments where individuals' choices play a crucial part in the development of their lives. The choices made by individuals reflect their past and shape their future. Similarly, the choices made by senior managers in organizations reflect the organizations' commitments and values, and shape the organizations' futures.

Badaracco's account is consistent with an emerging view that our decisions may be based on considering how different possible choices might fit into the story of my life. MacIntyre earlier made the point that this bears on one's obligations and responsibilities:

> To be the subject of a narrative that runs from one's birth to one's death is … to be accountable for the actions and experiences which compose a narratable life. It is, that is, to be open to being asked to give a certain kind of account of what one did or what happened to one or what one witnessed at any earlier point in one's life than the time at which the question is posed. (1985, pp. 217–218)

On this account, dealing with conflicts of obligations, or decisions about right-versus-right, is a matter of narrative coherence: discerning which choice best fits into the story of my life. Rather than considering whether a decision might conform to one or another rule or principle, and rather than considering whether it might have better or worse consequences than other options, I have to reflect on how things will seem subsequently, if I fulfil one obligation rather than the other, and compare my vision of how they will seem if I keep the other, rather than the first. Which obligation I fulfil, and which I renounce, adds to the story of my life, and as Kahneman has said recently, "we all care intensely for the narrative of our own life and very much want it to be a good story, with a decent hero" (2011, p. 387).

Kahneman's phrasing is suggestive, conjuring up an idea of us mentally looking at different possible movie scripts, with ourselves as the leading character in each, choosing the scenario that makes for the best story, choosing the action that allows us to figure in the movie in the way we would wish to see ourselves as observers. This is a metaphorical account, but perhaps a suggestive and useful one. In particular, this account of ethical decision-making implies an account of integrity: to choose and act with integrity is to make choices and perform actions that fit into a coherent, integrated narrative. Reflecting on such a possible narrative may be construed as the exercise of 'moral imagination', but moral imagination in which evaluation of the possible narrative relies on its intelligibility and coherence (Johnson 1993, Chap. 8).

However, the coherence of a narrative is not only a matter of our words and actions, but also of our beliefs and desires. Stanovich notes that it is unique to humans that we have "metarepresentational abilities to enable a cognitive critique of our beliefs and our desires" (2011, p. 82). In their uniqueness, these abilities create a unique problem: how to be honest with ourselves. Nowadays, we can start to articulate this idea in a way that makes it clearer than it may have been in the past. Stanovich argues convincingly for a model of human mental functioning that gives a prominent role to a reflective component: an aspect that monitors other functioning. The case he makes includes reference to modern work on brain structures and processing, as well as close reference to work in experimental psychology. A key element of his model is that the reflective component of mental processing can be distinguished both from autonomous cognitive functioning—the sort of functioning that enables us to drive a car safely to our destination without paying close attention to what we do, and without much memory of it—and from the sort of algorithmic cognitive functioning that is measured by intelligence tests. A good deal of work has been done on the notion of 'reflection' (see e.g., Harris 2008 and references therein), and much of it is consistent with Stanovich's account, but his account is both precise and considers exhaustive empirical evidence. Individual differences in the reflective mind account for such things as differences in tendencies toward 'myside thinking' and 'one-sided thinking' (2011, p. 34). Most importantly for our present purposes, "thinking dispositions (sometimes termed cognitive styles) are measures of the functioning of the reflective mind. Many thinking dispositions concern beliefs, belief structure, and, importantly, attitudes toward forming and changing beliefs" (2011, p. 35). Then, as we form our beliefs, we have to exercise judgment that takes account of factual evidence, of risks and possible consequences, of what we see as important, and of the stories we want our lives to be.

This is especially relevant to individuals in corporations whose actions help or hinder sustainable life. Michaelis and Lorek note the importance of people's internal discourse and narrative in guiding their decisions toward sustainable consumption (Michaelis and Lorek 2004, pp. 66–67). The same point can be made about the choices people make in guiding the policies and practices of their organizations: our internal narratives are our basis for choice as members of organizations when we are confronted by conflicting obligations. In Kahneman's words, we seek choices that allow us to portray our stories as good stories, with decent heroes. The extent to which our choices fit into a coherent story shapes the extent to which we act with integrity. However, that is not in itself enough. We create these internal narratives for ourselves on the basis of information we accept, and it is difficult to accept new and disturbing information. Integrity not only requires our words and actions to be consistent with our beliefs: it is also a matter of how we reach our beliefs. We must be willing to accept unpleasant truths, resisting the temptation to turn a blind eye or look the other way.

Conclusion

Corporations can only fulfil their responsibilities for sustainable policies and practices if individuals in them show moral integrity in dealing with concerns about products and processes. Our focus has been on individuals in large organisations, individuals whose decisions are tied to the organisations' own corporate responsibilities. The cases we have looked at illustrate the problems that arise. Integrity does not only require consistency of word and action: it also requires consistency of our words and actions with our beliefs. It is possible that the point may be generalised beyond the policies and practices for which specific corporations can be held responsible. Issues of sustainability highlight the need for our judgments and beliefs to be arrived at and held with integrity. Psychologists' models of cognitive functioning emphasize that it is always tempting to push aside anything on the periphery of our attention that looks as though it may require hard mental work to deal with. The part of our mental system that involves careful thinking is demanding and effortful, and that often we sidestep its demands in favour of simpler issues (Kahneman 2011, p. 31; Stanovich 2011, p. 29). Moral integrity involves acceptance of that effort. When we have only some peripheral awareness that an issue may have some ethical dimension, it is all too easy to turn a blind eye: moral integrity involves looking more closely, accepting the demands the issue can make on us. In matters of sustainability, there are all too many pieces of unpalatable information that make such demands, but the effort is something morally required of us.

References

Adams, W. M. (2006). The future of sustainability: Re-thinking environment and development in the twenty-first century, report of the IUCN renowned thinkers meeting, 29–31 January 2006. http://cmsdata.iucn.org/downloads/iucn_future_of_sustanability.pdf. Accessed 16 July 2012.

Alleman, J. E., & Mossman, B. T. (1997). Asbestos revisited. *Scientific American, 277*(1), 70–75.

Badaracco, J. L., Jr. (1997). *Defining moments: When managers must choose between right and right.* Boston: Harvard Business School Press.

Bazerman, M. H., & Tenbrunsel, A. E. (2011). *Blind spots.* Princeton: Princeton University Press.

BHP Billiton. (2012). Working with integrity: Code of business conduct. http://www.bhpbilliton.com/home/aboutus/ourcompany/Pages/codeofbusconduct.aspx. Accessed 7 July 2012.

Dawson, D. F. (2004). Report of the special commission of inquiry into the medical research and compensation foundation, NSW Government. http://www.dpc.nsw.gov.au/_data/assets/pdf_file/0020/11387/01PartA.pdf. Accessed 7 Dec 2012.

Dower, N. (2011). Climate change and the cosmopolitan responsibility of individuals: Policy vanguards. In P. G. Harris (Ed.), *Ethics and global environmental policy* (pp. 42–65). Cheltenham: Edward Elgar.

Edley, C. F., Jr., & Weiler, P. C. (1993). Asbestos: A multi-billion-dollar crisis. *Harvard Journal on Legislation, 30,* 383–408.

French, P. A. (1979). The corporation as a moral person. *American Philosophical Quarterly, 16*(3), 207–215.

Harris, H. (2008). Promoting ethical reflection in the teaching of business ethics. *Business Ethics: A European Review, 17*(4), 379–390.

Holling, C. S. (2001). Understanding the complexity of economic, ecological, and social systems. *Ecosystems, 4*(5), 390–405.

Jackall, R. (1988). *Moral mazes.* New York: Oxford University Press.

Jackson, J. (1996). *An introduction to business ethics.* Oxford: Blackwell.

Johnson, M. (1993). *Moral imagination.* Chicago: University of Chicago Press.

Kahneman, D. (2011). *Thinking, fast and slow.* New York: Farrar, Straus and Giroux.

Kannan-Narasimhan, R., & Lawrence, B. S. (2012). Behavioural integrity: How leader referents and trust matter to workplace outcomes. *Journal of Business Ethics, 111*(2), 165–178.

Kates, R. W., Clark, W. C., Corell, R., Hall, J. M., Jaeger, C. C., Lowe, I., McCarthy, J. J., Schellnhuber, H. J., Bolin, B., Dickson, N. M., Faucheux, S., Gallopin, G. C., Grübler, A., Huntley,

B., Jäger, J., Jodha, N. S., Kasperson, R. E., Mabogunje, A., Matson, P., Mooney, H., Moore, B. III., O'Riordan, T., et al. (2001). Sustainability science. *Science, 292*(27 April), 641–642.

Kates, R. W., Parris, T. M., & Leiserowitz, A. A. (2005). What is sustainable development? Goals, indicators, values, and practice. *Environment, 47*(3), 8–21.

Kent, J. (2011). Individual responsibility and voluntary action on climate change: Activating agency. In P. G. Harris (Ed.), *Ethics and global environmental policy* (pp. 66–88). Cheltenham: Edward Elgar.

Kidder, R. M. (1995). *How good people make tough choices*. New York: William Morrow.

Lehrer, J. (2009). *How we decide*. Boston: Houghton Mifflin Harcourt.

MacIntyre, A. (1985). *After virtue* (2nd ed.). London: Duckworth.

Maxwell, J., & Briscoe, F. (1997). There's money in the air: The CFC ban and DuPont's regulatory strategy. *Business Strategy and the Environment, 6*(5), 276–286.

Messick, D. M., & Tenbrunsel, A. E. (Eds.). (1996). *Codes of conduct: Behavioral research into business ethics*. New York: Russell Sage.

Michaelis, L., & Lorek, S. (2004). Consumption and the environment in Europe: Trends and futures. Danish Environmental Protection Agency, Environmental Project No. 904. http://www.mst.dk/Publikationer/Publications/2004/03/87-7614-193-4.htm. Accessed 16 July 2012

Mullin, R. P. (2002). What can be learned from DuPont and the Freon ban: A case study. *Journal of Business Ethics, 40*(3), 207–218.

Palanski, M. E., & Yammarino, F. J. (2007). Integrity and leadership: Clearing the conceptual confusion. *European Management Journal, 25*(3), 171–184.

Provis, C. (2011). *Individuals, groups and business ethics*. New York: Routledge.

Reynolds, S. J., Owens, B. P., & Rubenstein, A. L. (2012). Moral stress: Considering the nature and effects of managerial moral uncertainty. *Journal of Business Ethics, 106,* 491–502.

Rotary International. (2012). Guiding principles. http://www.rotary.org/en/aboutus/rotaryinternational/guidingprinciples/pages/ridefault.aspx. Accessed 6 July 2012.

Simons, T. (2002). 'Behavioral integrity: The perceived alignment between managers' words and deeds as a research focus. *Organization Science, 13*(1), 18–35.

Solomon, R. C. (1997). *It's good business: Ethics and free enterprise for the new millennium*. Lanham: Rowman & Littlefield.

Stanovich, K. E. (2011). *Rationality and the reflective mind*. New York: Oxford University Press.

U.S. EPA. (1975). 'DDT regulatory history: A brief survey (to 1975). http://www.epa.gov/aboutepa/history/topics/ddt/. Accessed 7 Dec 2012.

Waters, J. A., & Bird, F. (1987). The moral dimension of organizational culture. *Journal of Business Ethics, 6*(1), 15–22.

Chapter 3
A MacIntyrean Analysis of Sustainability Narratives in Modern Businesses

Stephen McKenzie

Introduction: Accounts of Sustainability

In a recent landmark paper, Rob Gray (2010) has noted that a great deal of business reporting on sustainability has little, if anything, to do with sustainability as it is actually defined in the academic literature. In fact, such reports more often contain a view of how businesses *want* sustainability to be perceived, rather than how it is actually being outlined in that literature.

> In doing so, business is in the process of constructing the dominant discourse around sustainability, but in a way which—at best—ignores discourse in both the development literature and the development community, as well as the growing body of scientific consensus. (Gray 2010, p. 48)

This is an alarming observation, all the more so for being backed up by a range of recent literature reviews (Gray 2006; Gray and Milne 2002; Milne et al. 2006, 2003). To begin with, it renders redundant, at least potentially, a huge amount of academic activity with the purpose of assisting businesses who genuinely *want* to become more responsible and sustainable. It also leaves the door open for 'greenwashing' and other behaviours in which unscrupulous businesses may give the illusion of sustainability to increase their social credibility, without making any genuine change. But on a more profound level, it calls into question what organizations *are* actually doing when they attempt to give an 'account' of sustainability, and, whether such a process even has any value.

Gray's paper hinges on the concept of 'accounts', which he also calls narratives (a word to make any student of Alisdair MacIntyre take note). He defines accounts as articulations and justifications for behavior, against claims made by other parties. When we ask businesses to report to the community on their environmental and social responsibility, we are asking them to give an account of themselves in relation to the needs of a range of stakeholders.

S. McKenzie (✉)
School of Management, University of South Australia Business School, Adelaide, Australia
e-mail: Stephen.McKenzie@unisa.edu.au

© Springer Science+Business Media Dordrecht 2014
S. Sandhu et al. (eds.), *Linking Local and Global Sustainability,* The International Society of Business, Economics, and Ethics Book Series 4, DOI 10.1007/978-94-017-9008-6_3

When the process of public accounting began, the main stakeholders were the shareholders, through the financial bottom line, and the wider community through adherence to corporate law. But as the previous century progressed, a company's range of stakeholders grew to include wider social and environmental concerns, and by the 1990s, when sustainability began to be seen as a corporate responsibility, the stakeholders of a large corporation had become global in scope.

> No longer were accounts potentially parochial things, loosely articulated through ill-specified notions of accountability and responsibility—they had become the contested terrain of global planetary desecration, of human and other species suffering and of social justice addressed through the language of sustainability, sustainable development and commerce. (Gray 2010, p. 48)

Gray's subsequent argument, to which I shall be returning throughout this chapter, is that through this process we have devalued sustainability and created a system of reporting that has little or no meaning. He states that the *modern understanding of global sustainability is so complex that it has no real operational meaning at the level of an individual organization*, and therefore any valid assessment of the relationship between an individual organization and global sustainability is impossible. Whatever we have been asking organizations to report on for the last few decades, it *isn't* actually sustainability. It is something else, and at this stage, we do not know what it is, or if it has any value.

In this chapter I want to take a MacIntyrean perspective on Corporate Social Responsibility (CSR) reporting. I want to look at Alisdair MacIntyre's conceptions of *practice and narrative*, and explore the implications of these concepts for what corporate sustainability reporting could *actually* be about. In particular, I want to examine the theoretical implications of viewing sustainability as a *practice*, as MacIntyre suggests it could be.

> In the ancient and medieval worlds, the creation and sustaining of human communities— households, cities, nations—is generally taken to be a practice in the sense that I have defined it. (MacIntyre 1985, pp. 187–188)

In a previous paper (McKenzie 2012) I have examined the implications of viewing sustainability as a practice, using Toyota Australia's annual sustainability reports as a case study, and looking for ways in which companies like Toyota could begin to focus on their own internal goods of excellence as evidence of a socially sustainable approach to manufacturing. Here, I want to take another angle, and suggest that if sustainability is a practice, then, it is being dominated by its various institutions. I conclude by looking at ways for it to become a stronger practice.[1]

---

[1] I make it clear from the outset that I do not consider myself to be a sustainability practitioner, or even an applied theorist in strong sustainability. My interest here is in exploring the ethical bases on which strong sustainability could be developed as a practice. For me to self-identify as a sustainability practitioner, I would need a qualification in sustainability accounting.

Sustainability as a Universalized Concept

The notion of a 'sustainable society' has become such a central and over-arching concept in the last 20 years that it can now be found *as a stated goal* in a wide range of discourses. A Google Scholar search for this year's papers featuring the term 'sustainable society' (July 2012) yields results on research methodologies, urban planning, vegetarian diets, computer circuit design, telecommunications policy, waste management, and local governance in the Amazon; and that is just the first few pages of results. All these papers argue that the adoption of their particular idea or program will contribute to 'a sustainable society'.

It is hard to think of another formal term that would lead to such a wide array of uses, and I suggest that this is because 'sustainable' is not really a formal term at present. Just as a writer may use terms like 'peaceful', 'democratic' and 'tolerant', or even 'modern' and 'post-modern' without being formally trained in their meaning, so too does the mention of a 'sustainable' society pass in many cases without the need for further explanation. If it is called sustainable, it is good, and that has become self-evident. The sustainable society has become a universalized concept.

On one hand, this acceptance of sustainability as a common good may be seen as an indicator of success for the project. When writers like John Elkington (1994) began to call for a unified approach to sustainability in which economic, social and environmental factors were all considered, they may have been happy to know that in future decades, this goal would shared by so many thinkers and researchers in so many different fields. But in another sense, the growth of sustainability into a universalized concept has had some profound negative effects, and I will outline these here.

Gray and many others have argued that the uncritical acceptance of the 'sustainable = good' formula means that the term is entering common discourse emasculated and largely trivialized, and it no longer really means anything other than what groups and individuals want it to mean on the day. Sustainability, in this light, has become one of the chief fictions by which big organizations justify their continuation of business as usual.

In terms of a MacIntyrean analysis, I would put it differently. I suggest that sustainability is a *practice* that has lost track of its own narrative, and has become dominated by its various institutions. I will explain this further in the next section. For now, I will give a background on how this situation came to be.

Sustainability theory and research is now so diffuse that it would be almost impossible to undertake a systematic and informed review. Even if such a review only considered papers on general sustainability theory, it would still be an undertaking of several years, but when we add in all the many disciplinary and interdisciplinary papers that feature the 'sustainable society' as a key agenda, we see that the pan-academic complex that has been created is far too great for any such overview to be obtained. (And whether such a document would even be useful is highly questionable.)

The lack of agreed boundaries for sustainability research, or any systems of disciplinary governance, means that there is currently no accepted way for an individual piece of research to be assessed outside of its own discipline. What is 'good' sustainability research? And who would know? While there have been numerous attempts to make frameworks for what quality sustainability research would *ideally* look like (such as Kobayashi et al. 2012), these often spring from individual disciplines, and are not necessarily adopted, or even noticed, by other actors in the field. In addition, such frameworks are aspirational and forward-looking rather than attempting to be at all retroactive. It is clear that no one could ever effectively review the last 40 years of sustainability discourse and determine what worked, what didn't, what should be kept, and what should be discarded.

In such a diverse and confusing environment, it is easy for an individual to get lost in a maze of literature in which many disciplines and political agendas are at play, and in which foundational words are used to mean entirely different things. And as it becomes increasingly difficult to build on sustainability's 'past', more commentators elect to look forward, developing their own positions without necessarily referencing prior work.

A related issue is the way in which the evolving sustainability mega-discourse has subsumed previous bodies of knowledge, or at least set up a parallel discourse in the same subject, without anyone necessarily acknowledging that it is doing so. In several previous papers I have pointed out that social policy organizations which set out to define social sustainability through a process of community consultation are actually engaging in a process that bears very strong resemblance to normative ethics and value mapping (McKenzie 2004, 2006). But such organizations may not realize the similarities of their approaches to earlier ones, and do not look back for ideas on how to proceed. In this way, the wheels of sustainability are reinvented regularly, and the long history of related discourses gets overlooked.

In terms of sustainability reporting, I will make a similar point: the concept of business responsibility towards the environment and society is not very recent *at all*, but many recent writers do not fully recognise this, and consequently, they do not build on a strong tradition with a cohesive narrative of how such things may best be pursued. I expand this point in the following section.

CSER, CSR, Social Auditing, BSC and the TBL

Corporate social and environmental reporting (CSER) is defined by Gray et al. (1996, p. 3) as the "process of communicating the social and environmental effects of organisations' economic actions to particular interest groups within society and to society at large". As Branco and Rodrigues point out in their recent review of the field, the basic concept of CSER is not new. The first attempts, while not actually bearing the name CSER, date to the beginnings of the twentieth century (see the review in Maltby 2004). The practice gained importance in the 1960s, particularly in regards to environmental protection, but declined in the face of neo-liberalism in the 1980s. It has lately seen a resurgence, which has been largely driven by the related field of sustainability reporting (outlined in KPMG's survey of CSER reporting in 2005).

In 1999, Archie Carroll published a historical survey of the development of Corporate Social Responsibility (CSR). Early definitions for this field state that it is about *business decisions and actions taken for reasons at least partially beyond the firm's direct economic or technical interest*. Carroll traces the origins of the movement to works such as Theodore Kreps' *Measurement of the social performance of business* (1940) and in particular, Howard R. Bowen's *Social responsibilities of the businessman* (1953). Works on the subject continue all the way through to a special issue of the *International Journal of Management Reviews* in 2010 (see especially Lindgreen and Swaen's overview of the field 2010.

At least superficially, we might expect these two fields to have considerable overlap and shared academic history—after all, CSR is essentially about making socially and environmentally responsible business decisions, and CSER is about ways of reporting to the public on the outcome of these decisions. Yet a comparison of the bibliographies of these two papers—Branco and Rodrigues (2007) and Carroll (1999)—show almost no convergence. Both used Abbott and Monsen's 'On the measurement of corporate social responsibility' from 1979, and they cited different papers by R. E. Freeman on strategic management from the 1980s (not cited here). But that is all. The Branco and Rodrigues paper has 45 references (which date from before Carroll's paper), while Carroll's itself has 54. That means 99 pieces of contemporaneous literature have been used in the two reviews of CSR and CSER, and only *one* of these pieces of literature is deemed to cross over both discourses.

To be fair, the two reviews are not intended to be complete, and, the two practices are sufficiently different that the authors may have excluded works that did not fit precisely. But I think it is revealing that, while an array of academic material has been produced on how to make socially responsible decisions in a business, the literature on how to *report* on socially responsible actions is almost entirely different, at least in this example.

Should this be the case? CSER is likely to include a more full disclosure where strong CSR exists within the company—that is to say, companies with responsible decision-making practices will naturally have *more to say* in their reports. Thus, the lack of overlap between the two discourses creates an image of a business world in which the internal goods of socially responsible decision-making *do* exist, but, as reporting is an external activity, we do not necessarily get to hear about these goods in CSER reporting, in or triple bottom line (TBL) reporting, either.

Elkington's development of the TBL concept in his book *Cannibals with Forks* (1998) is often cited as a major idea in the discourse of sustainability. Something about the simplicity of the phrase appears to have stuck, but this is not to say that what Elkington said was ultimately that revolutionary. As we have seen, the origin of CSER dates from the 1960s at latest, and has its genesis in ideas that were around at the turn of the century.

In addition to CSER, academics like Freer Spreckley began talking about the need to develop business tools for economic, social and environmental *auditing* in

the 1970s, and in 1981 she provided a detailed questionnaire proforma for organizations to map their 'social responsibility', including elements of demographic
equity, job satisfaction, and worker input into decision-making (Spreckley 1981). It
is one of the earliest such attempts to create a proforma for employees to give input
on these issues, and it is still quite applicable to firms today. Yet Spreckley's work
is not cited in Elkington's *Cannibals with Forks*, and nor is it cited in Branco and
Rodrigues, Lindgreen and Swaen, or Carroll's reviews of CSER and CSR. I think it
is fair to ask, why not?

A third point along these lines regards research literature on the Business Case
for Sustainability (BCS). The BCS literature review by Salzmann et al. in 2005
defined BCS as being a *discourse about attempts to prove or disprove the sound
economic rationale for corporate sustainability management*, which they define
as a strategic and profit-driven corporate response to environmental and social issues caused through the organization's primary and secondary activities. In other
words, BCS is about determining the precise economic cost to a business of decisions based on concerns over social and environmental sustainability.

In terms of a shared disciplinary background, one might expect a tighter fit between BCS and CSR. But Carroll's paper (1999) has 54 references, and Salzmann's
team cite 49 works (that were published before Caroll's paper). Out of a total of 103
references they might have shared, only 6 actually are. (Salzmann does also cite
Carroll's review, and, there are two other circumstances in which the two papers cite
different works by the same author.) Incidentally, there is no overlap *at all* between
Salzmann's review of BCS and the CSER review by Branco and Rodrigues. It is as
though CSER and BCS are entirely different fields of endeavour. But, would not
literature that is about making a *financial case* for sustainability benefit from input
from the long-standing tradition of *reporting* on sustainability?

Salzmann's team also makes comments about the state of BCS research that are
instructive about the sustainability field overall. There are far too many case studies,
they say, which showcase excellence in a chosen area but have little transferrable
value, and there are also a plethora of 'coaching' tools (methodologies and other
forms of instruction) which do not actually get used by managers in real businesses
because they don't have time, or because the tools don't work in practice. In terms
of the quantitative studies, the data gathered is often of little value, primarily because BCS is hard to quantify and the methodologies employed are inadequate to
capture its complexity (Salzmann et al. 2005, pp. 31–33). Such observations could
also be levelled at CSR, or CSER, without having to change a word.

My final point here concerns transdisciplinary, and macro or meso-level
approaches to sustainability research. There have been repeated calls that sustainability is a complex solution requiring transdisciplinary, or at least *comprehensive*
solutions, and writers like Kobayashi et al. (2012) have stated that most sustainability research suffers from being too domain specific. It is, unfortunately, very easy
to be cynical about such claims. His own review, and proposed model, does not cite
the 2006 review of transdisciplinary sustainability research by Hirsch Hadorn et al.
(2006), which makes the same basic claim. In fact, out of 70 pieces of literature
from both papers, only *one* is shared. Kobayashi's paper has a focus on engineering

and design, and Hirsch Hadorn's paper stems from environmental science and accounting. Naturally, most of the references are from those respective areas. So, although the two both make claims about the importance of transdisciplinary work in sustainability and accuse other work of being too domain specific, both still exist very much in their own academic spheres.

I believe such parochialism is unavoidable. How many disciplines are meant to be included in a macro-level or even a meso-level approach to sustainability research? And who could possibly master the basics of even a fraction of them, well enough to make true or worthy statements within each discipline? If there is such a noticeable disjunct between two related fields like CSR and CSER, the prospect of having a *truly* interdisciplinary framework linking fields like botany, engineering and accounting is almost impossible. As things stand, attempts along these lines will simply result in yet more literature that is disjointed from what already exists.

To make my point explicit: the meta-/mega-discourse of sustainability has become so large and diffuse that different aspects of it are not properly communicating with each other, and never really have done so. In consequence, the practice and accompanying narrative of sustainability are both weak. This situation is leading to a great deal of research and reporting that is unnecessary, irrelevant, or, not reaching its intended audience. When businesses claim that 'better models for CSR/BSC/ social auditing are required', it is tempting to dismiss this as a delaying tactic, a parallel move to the persistent claim that not enough climate change research has been done. But I believe that this is not the case. What businesses are really saying is that sustainability has a weak narrative, and they cannot follow it. The problem is *not* a lack of information, but the lack of a unifying structure in which the information could be situated.

Thus, the reason why sustainability has been captured by business interests in the way that Gray describes is because its narrative is weak, and the needs of the institutions that house it—primarily businesses and government agencies—have been allowed to dominate over the practice of creating and maintaining a sustainable society.

Practices as Historical Objects

Here I turn to the description of practices and their narratives in Alisdair MacIntyre's *After Virtue* (1985 edition), using Christopher Lutz's (2004) monograph on MacIntyre's concept of tradition as a secondary guide.

A *practice*, to paraphrase MacIntyre's definition in *After Virtue*, is a formal set of human activities characterized by standards of excellence, and developed within a tradition, within which new practitioners can learn. An institution is the physical and financial infrastructure that houses a practice; for example, law is the practice and a law firm is the institution. Central to MacIntyre's schema is that virtuous behavior will tend to result when institutions remain focused on the practice, rather than allowing the needs of the institution to dominate. In this situation, the internal goods of excellence in the practice will be the main reward for pursuing it, and financial and other external concerns will be secondary, although not unimportant. This is MacIntyre's model of a virtuous organization.

Practices, and their standards, do not come fully-formed from nothing. As Lutz points out, the current standard of professional football would have been unthinkable when the first professional games were played in the US less than a century ago (2004, p. 41). Practices are the sources of standards, and develop through a striving for betterment. Consequently, they are not static, because they do not have fixed goals, and excellence is not perfection, simply the furthest point we have yet reached on a continuum.

The way in which members of a practice describe their progress along this continuum may be called a 'narrative' for the purposes of this chapter.[2] According to Lutz, "[n]arratives are the myths, histories and theories that specify the methods, principles, purposes and standards of practices" (Lutz 2004, p. 43). In other words they are the way in which a practice communicates within itself about what it is, where it has come from, where it is going, and how it will get there. For a practice to have strong standards of excellence, it must have a strong and cohesive narrative, so that this communication will be clear.

It is perhaps facile to look at the history of a developing set of human activities and ask, at what point did it become a fully-fledged practice in the MacIntyrean sense, whereas before it might have something less than that. However, we can derive from MacIntyre (and Lutz) several major guidelines for the development of a practice over time.

1. The practice must have *practical goals*, as well as *ideal goals*.
2. The practitioners must be *aware that they are members of a practice*.
3. The practice must be able to explain itself and *transmit its knowledge* to new members.
4. The practice must have sufficient intellectual capacity to *deny or disprove rival claims* to knowledge.

In the final sections of this paper I work through these four observations in order, looking at the implications for sustainability accounting as a practice, in its current state. I will also be imagining an ideal state in which sustainability accounting might become strong enough to stand up to the institutions that house it.

---

[2] This leaves the term 'tradition' to refer more specifically to the macro-level social and historical knowledge structures in which smaller practices are located; i.e. Western scientific thought, Enlightenment morality, Christian religious belief, and so on. In fact, MacIntyre and others do sometimes use the term 'tradition' to refer to the traditions of excellence within practices, but for the sake of clarity I will refrain from doing likewise.

Sustainability as a Practice

Practical and Ideal Goals

On this point about goals, Lutz notes that a definition of a practice that only ever considers its practical goals is incomplete, because current practitioners can never see what the goals of the future may be (Lutz 2004, p. 44). For example, if the aim of automotive engineering were merely to make a functional car, progress would have ceased a long time ago. Clearly, the actual goal is to make the *best possible* car on the day. The ideal is more important than whatever initial goal is posed, and so a practice must be about more than achieving a set and finite goal.

It is clear that sustainability has an ideal goal of balanced human living, upon which standards of excellence could be based. At this point the ideal goal has been well articulated, through the Brundtland definition and others. But the practical goals are myriad, and, it is often unclear as to how the individual practical goals of a sustainability project will contribute to the ideal goal of balanced living. Thus, it becomes hard to link the contribution of the individual to the long-term of ideal, in such a way that human powers to achieve excellence in sustainability are systematically extended.

Membership

To contextualize my point about the members of practices being *aware* of their membership, we may try to imagine a field of endeavour in which individual operators did not recognize that they were part of a practice, and pursued their own agendas without communicating their successes and failures to others who were pursuing the same goal. Religious cults and high school cliques spring to mind—there is obviously an art to establishing and maintaining such groups, but there is certainly no systematic attempt to extend human ability to do so, because each individual group would not recognize that it was part of a larger 'practice'.

I suggest that the situation with sustainability bears some unfortunate similarities to this situation. At this time, *anyone* can write about sustainability, and begin to build up a reputation in the field, without considering themselves as members of a practice, and consequently, while the systematic extension of human ability to achieve sustainability *is* ongoing, it is entirely piecemeal and no cohesive narrative can be formed. It is difficult to imagine at this time what the narrative of sustainability would actually be, if one were trying to explain it to new members.

Transmission of Knowledge

Members of well-established practices such as law and medicine receive specialist training in those fields and are granted licence to practice by governing bodies, after it has been established by other members of the profession that they can operate to a sufficient standard. In some cases the professional standards are reinforced by legislation. (A simple example is the UK Medical Act of 1858, designed to create a registry of recognized medical professionals, so that the public would know who was actually a doctor.)

At this time, there is no formal learning requirement to practice or teach sustainability. For example, in Australia, you can teach sustainability theory at tertiary level with a background in education studies, engineering, financial accounting, or botany, without the need to do any further specific training. The transmission of knowledge to new members is not only piecemeal, but entirely dependent on what the individual teacher decides is relevant.

We may try to imagine what sustainability would look like if practitioner membership and systems of instruction *were* clearly defined. In Australia, there might be a technical course (equivalent to Australian TAFE Certificate IV standard) for all those who wished to instruct tertiary level students in sustainability. Staff who had this award would be given preference by employers for teaching positions. Other technical awards, such as the various certificates available in Australia in home sustainability, business sustainability and operational sustainability, would all be taught by people who had this instructional qualification, as well as the relevant experience to teach the particular qualification. From this, a National Board of Sustainability Educators could be formed. (Currently, many such organizations exist at a private or quasi-autonomous level, but no such organization exists in Australia that can fully certify trained sustainability educators.)

Denying Rival Claims

On my final point, we must look again to the history of well-established practices and note that at some point, many of them had to establish their primacy against rival claims to truth; scientific medicine against quackery, chemistry against alchemy, formal Westminster common law against *ad hoc* regal or judicial proclamations, and so on. In short, an important feature in the historical development of a practice is the ability to say what the practice is *not*. Any practice that fails to do so may be overrun by many things that claim to be genuine and effective, but which aren't.

This ability to define the boundaries of the practice is part of what MacIntyre, in a well-known passage, calls the 'argument' that takes place within the practice.

> So when an institution—a university, say, or a farm, or a hospital—is the bearer of a tradition of practice or practices, its common life will be partly, but in a centrally important way, constituted by a continuous argument as to what a university is and ought to be or what good farming is or what good medicine is. Traditions, when vital, embody continuities of conflict. (1985, p. 194)

In terms of its internal argument, sustainability is in a very weak position at present. While it is often said that sustainability is a contested concept, only some of this contestation is happening within the sort of narrative framework that MacIntyre lays out as the true pathway to develop a good practice. Ideally, most of the contestation over sustainability accounting should be *a continuous argument about what good sustainability accounting is*. It should be an argument in which contestants are formally engaged with each other in trying to establish the truth of this matter, for the good of the practice.

But as we know, contestation over sustainability is far more likely to take a passive form—that is, participants will not acknowledge that what they are saying and doing is in disagreement with rival claims. They simply make whatever claims they wish to make, and label their outcome as progress towards sustainability. Sustainability theory *as a body* currently has no systematic way to deal with these claims. It cannot accurately define what it is not.

A Broader Theory of Weak and Strong Sustainability

In modern sustainability discourse, the 'strong' model of sustainably promotes the biosphere as the most important, over-arching element, and situates the society and economy within it. This is contrasted with the TBL and other sustainability models that have been labeled 'weak' because while they give the illusion of equality among the three elements, in reality, the economy always predominates (Neumayer 2003).

I promote a use of the words 'weak' and 'strong' that expands on this sense. For me, 'strong' sustainability should relate to the entire practice in an ethical sense. The development of a model which is easy to explain, and also, which is capable of defining weakness, is certainly a step in the right direction. It is, potentially, the beginning of the process by which sustainability could define what it is not. But far more than that will be required, if sustainability is truly to become a strong practice.

As both MacIntyre (1985) and Moore (2012) note, institutions are powerful and *will* tend to dominate their practices over time unless they are kept in check, creating greedy companies which damage the economy, the society and the environment. The problem is that sustainability reporting was meant to be *the means by which these companies could be kept in check*. But as Gray points out, sustainability has been captured, and is now a toothless beast with little power to make real change in company behavior. Companies are creating narratives of their behavior that bear little or no relation to real sustainability. These narratives are not their internal narratives of progress toward excellence, either. What they are is a systematic attempt to define sustainability in a way that suits their own interests. Businesses are in a position to do this because the narrative of sustainability is so weak that there are very few people in the world who can definitively tell them that what they are doing *isn't* sustainability.

Strong sustainability will need to address this. It will need to refine its goals so the link between local projects and global outcomes is far more clearly articulated. It will need to inculcate a sense of self-identification of its members, who must be more than good citizens seeking to do the right thing, and must become aware that they are members of a specific practice in which certain things are done and not done. It will need to strengthen the transmission of appropriate forms of knowledge (for example, through the formation of a nationally-based training curriculum). And above all, sustainability practitioners must sharpen their ability to weed out ideas and behaviours that have the appearance of sustainability, but which are in fact rival claims to knowledge.

References

Abbott, W. F., & Monsen, R. J. (1979). On the measurement of corporate social responsibility: Self-reported disclosures as a method of measuring corporate social involvement. *Academy of Management Journal, 22,* 501–515.

Bowen, H. R. (1953). *Social responsibilities of the businessman.* New York: Harper and Row.

Branco, M., & Rodrigues, L. (2007). Issues in corporate social and environmental reporting research: An overview. *Issues in Social and Environmental Accounting, 1*(1), 72–90.

Carroll, A. (1999). Corporate social responsibility: Evolution of a definitional construct. *Business Society, 38,* 268–295.

Elkington, J. (1994). Towards the sustainable corporation: Win-win-win business strategies for sustainable development. *California Management Review, 36*(June), 90–101.

Elkington, J. (1998). *Cannibals with forks: The triple bottom line of 21st century business.* Oxford: Capstone.

Gray, R. (2006). Does sustainability reporting improve corporate behaviour? Wrong question? Right time? *Accounting and Business Research (International Policy Forum), 36*(Suppl. 1), 65–88.

Gray, R. (2010). Is accounting for sustainability actually accounting for sustainability … and how would we know? An exploration of narratives of organisations and the planet. *Accounting, Organizations and Society, 35,* 47–62.

Gray, R. H., & Milne, M. (2002). Sustainability reporting: Who's kidding whom? *Chartered Accountants Journal of New Zealand, 81*(6), 66–70.

Gray, R., Owen, D., & Adams, C. (1996). *Accounting and accountability: Changes and challenges in corporate social and environmental reporting.* Hemel Hempstead: Prentice Hall.

Hirsch Hadorn, G., Bradley, D., Pohl, C., Rist, S., & Wiesmann, U. (2006). Implications of transdisciplinarity for sustainability research. *Ecological Economics, 60,* 119–128.

Kobayashi, H., Uwasi, M., Hara, K., & Umeda, Y. A. (2012). Framework for comprehensive sustainability research focusing on the meso-level. In M. Matsumoto, Y. Umeda, K. Masui, & S. Fukushige (Eds.), *Design for innovative value towards a sustainable society* (pp. 571–756). Dordrecht: Springer.

KPMG. (2005). *KPMG international survey of corporate responsibility reporting 2005.* De Meern: KPMG.

Kreps, T. J. (1940). *Measurement of the social performance of business. An investigation of concentration of economic power for the temporary national economic committee* (Monograph No. 7). Washington: U.S. Government Printing Office.

Lindgreen, A., & Swaen, V. (2010). Corporate social responsibility. *International Journal of Management Reviews, 12*(1), 1–7.

Lutz, C. S. (2004). *Tradition in the ethics of Alasdair MacIntyre: Relativism, thomism, and philosophy.* Lanham: Rowman and Littlefield.

MacIntyre, A. (1985). *After virtue.* London: Duckworth.

Maltby, J. (2004). Hadfields Ltd: Its annual general meetings 1903–1939 and their relevance for contemporary corporate social reporting. *The British Accounting Review, 36*(4), 415–439.

McKenzie, S. (2004). *Social sustainability: Towards some definitions*. Hawke Research Institute Working Paper Series No. 27. Magill: Hawke Research Institute, University of South Australia.

McKenzie, S. (2006). *Social sustainability and religious ethics*. The International Journal of Cultural, Economic and Social Sustainability: Proceedings of the Second International Conferee on Environmental, Cultural, Economic and Social Sustainability. Champaign: Common Ground Publishers.

McKenzie, S. (2012). Thoughts on a MacIntyrean approach to social sustainability reporting. In H. Harris, G. Wiejesinghe, & S. McKenzie (Eds.), *The heart of the good institution: Virtue ethics as a framework for responsible management* (pp. 161–168). Dordrecht: Springer.

Milne, M. J., Tregigda, H. M., & Walton, S. (2003). The triple bottom line: Benchmarking New Zealand's early reporters. *University of Auckland Business Review, 5*(2), 36–50.

Milne, M. J., Kearins, K. N., & Walton, S. (2006). Creating adventures in wonderland? The journey metaphor and environmental sustainability. *Organization, 13*(6), 801–839.

Moore, G. (2012). Re-imagining the morality of management: A modern virtue ethics approach. In H. Harris, G. Wiejesinghe, & S. McKenzie (Eds.), *The heart of the good institution: Virtue ethics as a framework for responsible management* (pp. 7–34). Dordrecht: Springer.

Neumayer, E. (2003). *Weak vs. strong sustainability: Exploring the limits of two opposing paradigms*. London: Edward Elgar Publishing.

Salzmann, O., Ionescu-Somers, A., & Steger, U. (2005). The business case for corporate sustainability: Literature review and research options. *European Management Journal, 23*(1), 27–36.

Spreckley, F. (1981). *Social audit. A management tool for co-operative working*. Leeds: Beechwood College.

Chapter 4
Sustainability Is a Work of Justice: Virtue Not Distribution

Howard Harris

The argument most frequently used to justify the call for sustainability in business and in life or society more generally is based on notions of distributive justice (see for instance Dobson 1998; Jacobs 1999; Tencati and Perrini 2011). This chapter sees a strong link between sustainability and justice, but in a different way, concerned more with the development and exercise of the virtue of justice by individuals. Sustainability is thus more personal, and is something involving personal effort. It is a work of justice.

The first section provides a short restatement of the conventional view that sustainability is principally about intergenerational justice, and introduces some alternative positions. This is followed by a section in which the three main approaches to justice—utilitarian, rights and virtue—are outlined (after Cotton 2001). The third section is concerned with the argument that justice is a virtue, that it is a quality of character as well as a measure of distribution, and that this personal virtue can be developed in community. The fourth section considers the interrelationship between sustainability and the virtue of justice, and shows that both sustainability and justice require personal effort. The conclusion reinforces the argument that runs through the chapter that sustainability is something to be worked at now, that a commitment to sustainability is not a wish for the future but an action in the present.

Introduction

The Club of Rome report in 1972 drew attention to the possibility that the earth faces 'limits to growth', and that these limits might be reached within the lifetime of many of its current inhabitants unless the then equations or paths of growth were attenuated (Meadows et al. 1972). The term sustainability gained recognition and authority by its use in two United Nations sponsored activities—the 1987 report of

H. Harris (✉)
School of Management, University of South Australia, Adelaide, Australia
e-mail: Howard.Harris@unisa.edu.au

© Springer Science+Business Media Dordrecht 2014
S. Sandhu et al. (eds.), *Linking Local and Global Sustainability,* The International Society of Business, Economics, and Ethics Book Series 4, DOI 10.1007/978-94-017-9008-6_4

the World Commission on Environment and Development (WCED), the *Brundt-land Report* (1990), and the 1992 Earth Summit held in Rio de Janeiro. The theme of both is development, especially development for what was then called the Third World. The intergenerational element is clear in both the report's title *Our common future* and in Brundtland's definition: "Sustainable development seeks to meet the needs and aspirations of the present without compromising the ability to meet those of the future" (Brundtland 1990, p. 84, 1.49). A slightly different form of this definition, found a little later in the WCED report, has found much wider usage, often as a definition of sustainability in general. Under this formulation, the focus on future generations is explicit and the reference to aspirations dropped, as has the concept of seeking, resulting in the phrase "meets the needs of the present without compromising the ability of future generations to meet their own needs" (Brundtland 1990, p. 87, 2.1). This underpins much of the writing and practice about sustainability. It can be found in numerous books, curriculum materials, and websites, and in the sustainability reporting guidelines of the Global Reporting Initiative (GRI 2006). On this approach, "Futurity: An explicit concern about the impact of current activity on future generations" and equity are core ideas in the discussion of sustainability (Jacobs 1999, p. 26).

This approach to the definition of sustainability is contested. This did not go un-noticed by the WCED team as they included in their report a comment by a speaker at public hearings conducted by them in Sao Paulo as they prepared their report. The unidentified person told the Commission, "You talk very little about life, you talk too much about survival" (Brundtland 1990, p. 84). In a similar vein Amartya Sen has expressed concern that the emphasis is on needs and not on capabilities. He writes (Sen 2004, p. 11):

> The world has good reason to be grateful for the new prominence of this idea, yet it must be asked whether the conception of human beings implicit in it is sufficiently capacious. Certainly, people have 'needs', but they also have values, and, in particular, they cherish their ability to reason, appraise, act and participate. Seeing people in terms only of their needs may give us a rather meagre view of humanity.

Another concern (of which more later) is that the WCED definition does not provide any guidance on what is to be distributed justly across generations. Some activists in the environmental justice movement argue that "the environment is a particular form of goods and bads that society must divide among its members" (Dobson 1998, p. 20) while other environmentalists have wider concerns such as the preservation of wilderness (Carter 2009, p. 449), and supporters of the triple bottom line (Elkington 1999) will be concerned about an even broader canvas including social and economic sustainability as well as the environment. That we do not know what the needs, let alone the aspirations, of future generations will be makes it difficult to decide what we should constrain, or distribute. This may be one reason why there are so many definitions of sustainability—the number exceeded 300 and was still rising when Dobson (1998) did a count over a decade ago.

A major tenet of the WCED report, the Brundtland definition, the Rio conference and the protocols that have followed it is the view that sustainability is attainable—'If only a new binding treaty were adopted all will be well'. But this sustainability may be unattainable. Sustainability that meets the needs of today and those of tomorrow may not be achieved in practical or political terms as an effective agreement between the many nations and other players may not be reached and it may be unachievable because it is a mistake to consider sustainability as an object or state that can be definitively achieved as "perfect justice or an ideal state (or society) is conceptually impossible" (Berlin in Slote 2011, p. 6). Isaiah Berlin's claim is developed by Michael Slote in his book *The Impossibility of perfection* where he argues that the choices between virtue and happiness, or between adventure and security, say, can never be perfectly resolved for an individual (Slote 2011, p. 7), let alone for a society or across the entire planet. Can conscientious adherence to a perceived duty to protect a particular endangered species or a specific stretch of wilderness be just when it leads to illegal activity or disrespectful behavior toward human beings? It would seem that a choice must be made, "that things can/could never be as good for us as we might wish them to be" (Slote 2011, p. 34). This is perhaps even more starkly so when it is realized that the sustainability being sought in the conventional definition is sustainability at a global level and "the idea of global justice without a world government is a chimera" (Nagel 2005, p. 115).

Approaches to Justice

In this chapter I accept, after Jacobs (1999), that the future and equity are important elements in the concept of sustainability and that sustainability and justice are linked, but not that the relevant linkage mechanism is to be found in the concept of (intergenerational) distributive justice. I will argue that by considering justice as a virtue a broader notion of sustainability will be fostered, one in which individuals today will be engaged, and perhaps working hard. Before embarking on that argument it is necessary to outline the three main approaches to justice—utilitarian, rights and virtue. The description that follows is based on the introduction provided by Michael Sandel who describes the ideas behind these three ways of thinking about justice as "maximising welfare, respecting freedom, and promoting virtue" (2009, p. 6). Whilst what follows is principally in the Western philosophical tradition, links to Confucianism will be made as the argument develops to show how the concepts are also relevant in that important Eastern ethical and political tradition, one which is "the most influential source of non-Western values" in many of the economically advancing societies in East Asia (MacIntyre 2004, p. 204).

Under the popular definition sustainability means that the needs of both current and future generations will be met. In a utilitarian approach to ethical decision-making the goal will be to maximise welfare. If this approach is adopted to assist in the understanding and practice of sustainability questions will arise as to what is to be included in the calculation of welfare, as to the time period over which the maximization of welfare is to be sought, and as to the extent that the distribution of welfare is to be taken into account both within any one generation and across generations (Sinnott-Armstrong 2012). If future generations have an uncompromised ability to meet their needs that would seem to suggest that they will be able to achieve a level of welfare at least equal to that of the present generation or that they will have a modified set of needs, perhaps having cut their coat to match their cloth. But is that just? The concern is for a just allocation.

Another approach is to focus attention on freedom and to say that the most important element to be sustained is human freedom, without which there can be no justice. Some might consider the key freedom to be the opportunity to participate in a free market and to make free choices in it, including choices about what to value. Others, after Kant, might consider the central freedom to be the capacity to choose under which rule they should live. Thus for sustainability this approach to ethical decision-making will tend more to focus on the maintenance of certain fundamental rights. As Sandel notes, "making sense of Kant is not only a philosophical exercise; is also a way of examining some of the key assumptions implicit in our public life" (2009, p. 104).

The third approach is concerned not with the justice that is demonstrated in an appropriate level or measure of welfare, or the justice demonstrated in the existence of certain freedoms or rights, but with that quality of character known as justice, one of the virtues "on which the good society depends" (Sandel 2009, p. 8).

At this stage I will note some of the difficulties which come from using either the utilitarian or the rights approaches when considering the link between sustainability and justice. The conventional definition holds that sustainability is about just allocation. Basing sustainability in utility makes it a matter of calculation rather than principle. If that is so then it lessens the grounds on which sustainability can make a moral claim on individuals (and society). If sustainability is not a principle to be fought for or defended, but the result of a calculation, then its attraction will be lessened. In the context of sustainability utilitarianism is not only subject to the criticism that there is no single measure available with which to calculate the various individual utility functions, but to the added difficulty that any calculation involving intergenerational justice will have to span long periods of time.

If, as Nozick (1993) for instance argues, each individual has a right to make a free choice about what they value, then the concept of intergenerational justice is perhaps thwarted, deprived of any power to move society toward a goal of sustainability. Each can make his or her own decision as to what needs (and aspirations, even capabilities) to seek in the present, but the needs which the future generation will be meeting cannot be foretold. That makes it difficult to justify or to mount any coordinated effort to protect or develop a particular element of society or the environment. That applies as much to action by government or some other authority to enforce actions in support of sustainability as it does to any autonomously evolving campaign. Rawls establishes a right to just distribution in the deliberations of the 'original position' where no one knows their ultimate status in society (Rawls 1971), but this still leaves open how things are to be valued.

It is to this difficulty in determining what is to be valued that the virtue approach can make a contribution. While virtue, like utilitarianism and rights, does not have a universally accepted position on what should be valued, it does have a process for investigation. The virtue approach involves cultivating the attitudes and dispositions on which society depends and "reasoning about the common good" (Agosto et al. 2008, p. 8). This is both an individual and a communal activity, personally cultivating virtue and collectively debating the right way to value things. As I will argue below, both these are important elements of sustainability.

A disadvantage or difficulty of the virtue approach is that it is personally demanding in a way that the other two approaches are not. No longer is sustainability something I can commit to and perhaps follow some rules or possibly burdensome strictures in support of it. It is work, for the discussion and cultivation requires work by both individuals and communities. Having the discussion about what to value is work as much as personally cultivating a disposition toward justice.

Justice as a Virtue

The linking of justice with issues of sustainability and distribution brings to the fore the social role and organisational nature of justice. It is here that Rawls begins *A theory of justice*, calling justice "the first virtue of social institutions" and making "the basic structure of society" its primary subject (Rawls 1971, p. 3). However, it is the idea of justice as an individual virtue that is the focus of this chapter. That particular virtue or moral excellence is principally concerned with "moral issues having to do with goods or property" (Slote 2010) and the concept can be traced back at least as far as Plato.

This "conception of individual justice…ties justice (acting justly) to an internal state of a person rather than to (adherence to) social norms or good consequences" (Slote 2010), thereby rejecting the utilitarian and rights/freedom approaches and making it an example of the virtue approach. Put in perhaps simpler terms, "only the just can know what justice is" (Hamilton 1961) or "we become just by acting justly" (Aristotle Nicomachean Ethics, 2:1). Both these statements point to the dynamic nature of the moral virtues, that they can be developed through practice and from example. This will be important when considering sustainability as a work of justice.

The purpose of the *polis*, the engagement of individuals in the life of the society or state, is "to form good citizens and cultivate good character" (Sandel 2009, p. 193). To determine which virtues are to be honoured and rewarded in society involves reason and argument, to determine the "goods internal to practices" (MacIntyre 1985, p. 198) which contribute to the growth and enjoyment of the individual undertaking some practice and seeking to do it well. Aristotle's examples range from the practical in the playing of flutes through the building of houses to the development of courage and the capacity to act justly. The purpose of every art, job, or practice, he argues (Politics, 3.8), is some good. To determine its value we need to understand its purpose or essential nature, in the sense that the purpose of flutes is to be played well. I would argue then that the purpose of sustainability is to allow, encourage and enhance the good society and its physical, intellectual and moral virtues. Sustainability is a debate about purpose.

A similar notion, that virtue is a human quality and that the highest expression is found in harmonious relationships between humans and nature is found in the teachings of Confucius (Analects 12.24), and that a person of virtue "should sustain others if he wishes to sustain himself", which leads to a requirement to "understand others' situations and care for them" (Li 2008, p. 181 after Analects 6.30).

The Journey Aspect—Working Toward Sustainability

This section considers the interrelationship between the virtue of justice and sustainability, and shows that both sustainability and justice require personal effort.

The first Brundtland definition (1990, p. 84, 1.49) included an aspect of incompleteness and mission—"sustainable development seeks to meet…"—which is lost in the second and much more widely used statement that sustainability "meets the needs…" (1990, p. 87, 2.1). The active verb 'seeks' with its connotation of expeditions and discovery has been replaced by the passive 'meets' with the implication that the task has already been achieved. The idea that we should be "working toward" justice and sustainability not only acknowledges that this is unfinished business requiring an ongoing effort but also recognizes that there is no sufficiently well-defined set of universal values with which to assess the relative merit of trees, jobs and health.

This plurality of values in the contemporary world could be used as a reason to do little if anything to seek out more than the broadest definition of sustainability, sustainability light, as it were. Support could be found in at least two arguments—that failure is certain and so any effort would be wasted, or that it would be a repudiation of individual freedom to seek to change another person's view of the relative worth of those various things which are held to be valuable. Virtue provides grounds for rejecting this do-little approach. Aristotle, the Confucians and MacIntyre point to the personal benefit which can come as one seeks to develop moral virtue and understand purpose. For Aristotle, to be a better person, to have a virtue or any number of them more deeply than before, or to understand more clearly how particular virtues that one has relate to each other and to the whole, are sufficient reason to engage in the development of one's moral capabilities even if of no immediate use. Similarly in Confucian thought it is through the practice of self-cultivation that one becomes a "perfected person" (Nosco 2008, p. 26).

Where there are goods internal to the practices then there will be a benefit for the practitioner even when the intended external goal is not met. MacIntyre acknowledges the importance of flow and time when he writes, "I can only answer the question, 'What am I to do?' if I can answer the prior question, 'Of what story or stories do I find myself a part?' " (1985, p. 201). That there are multiple stories, that each of us might be part of more than one is a challenge and an opportunity to exercise reason, rather than an invitation to inaction. The plural society need not inhibit debate, indeed it heightens the need for the development of virtue and the capacity for reflection (Harris 2008). Furthermore, Gardner (2011) argues that, even where there is widespread acceptance of a multiplicity of views about what constitutes truth, beauty and goodness, engagement in a 'movement toward' truth is essential if truth and society are to be sustained. The questions raised by any examination of what is meant by sustainability and how it is to be achieved cannot be answered without consideration of ethics, and "our debates about justice unavoidably embroil us in substantive moral questions" (Sandel 2009, p. 243). Thus an attempt or desire to introduce a form or process of sustainable allocation on the basis of equivalence will lead to consideration of whether the future generations will (or should) attribute the same value to the item being allocated as we do in this generation. Those in Gen Y, we are told, have different values, honor and reward different virtues to those from the Babyboomer generation. Is it sustainable that what is sustained changes from generation to generation? Sandel acknowledges the link between allocation, value and justice when he writes: "Justice is not only about the right way to distribute things, it is about the right way to value things" (2009, p. 261).

In concluding this section on the characterization of sustainability as a journey I return to the idea that sustainability may be an impossible or unattainable goal, a notion linked in that earlier part of the chapter to the work of Berlin and Slote. Amartya Sen writes at length in *The idea of justice* (2011) about the impossibility of the transcendental concept of justice—that there is a definable ideal state and that the knowledge of this is necessary to guide just action. This is not a cause for hopelessness in Sen's view as action to relieve manifest injustice is clearly possible without the need for a completed picture of perfect justice (or, I suggest, sustainability). As he puts it "the demands of justice have to give priority to the removal of manifest injustice…rather than concentrating on the long-distance search for a perfectly just society" (Sen 2011, p. 259). The requirement is to work at the diagnosis of injustice, "including the exercise of individual duties and responsibilities" a process which for Sen would include the application of Social Choice Theory (2011, p. 22). Himself extending the argument so that the parallel with sustainability is apparent, Sen writes,

> And yet, through lack of reasoned engagement and action, we do still fail to take adequate care of the environment around us and the sustainability of the requirements of good life. To prevent catastrophes caused by human negligence or callous obduracy, we need critical scrutiny, not just goodwill toward others. (2011, p. 48)

The first Brundtland definition with its 'seeking', Aristotle Confucius and MacIntyre who see the value of personal virtue, Gardner with the 'movement toward' truth in plural societies, and Sen with the idea that we progress toward justice with each injustice that is removed, all support the concept of sustainability as a journey.

…A Work of Justice

If sustainability is a journey and not an end, what is the nature and value of the work involved in making that journey, a journey which I believe should be considered to be a work of justice. The discussion which follows draws on MacIntyre (1985,

1988) and the notion of goods internal to practices to show how such work can contribute to personal fulfilment, result in tangible benefits to society and enhance engagement in a community, all at the same time. Both MacIntyre and Aristotle tell us, from their positions over 2,000 years apart, that the cultivation of virtue is not easy; it requires practice. This is part of the work of justice. Any moral virtue in its desired state lies in a mean between the extremes of excess and deficiency, courage for instance between rashness and cowardice, justice between the extremes of giving too much and too little. As this mean is not one calculated arithmetically by summing and dividing, to find the mean requires the application of reason, and engagement in a process of moral decision-making. One aspect of the work is participation with others in the process. Earlier I referred to unavoidable debates. Participating in those debates—enunciating a position, listening intently to different views, seeking common ground—requires effort. "We have reason to listen and pay some attention to the views and suggestions of others" even though the result will not always be satisfactory (Sen 2011, p. 88). It may be that the debate is conducted through stories, as different tales capture the reality of variations in the value and honor attached to specific items at different times and in different places. The work is not only in the telling of the story for sometimes the story will become real and its implementation unavoidable. Telling the story, looking after it and nurturing it is a responsibility, for "you can't really take pride in your country [or profession, or wilderness] and its past if you're unwilling to acknowledge any responsibility for carrying its story into the present, and discharging the moral burdens that may come with it" (Sandel 2009, p. 235).

This has implications for ethics education and sustainability education throughout the education system, organizations and society. Where case studies are used the cases should be chosen to encourage debate rather than unalloyed condemnation or praise for one participant at the expense of another. Cases where the same item—a stream, the companionship of domestic animals, the classics of art and literature, for instance—is valued differently by a number of different participants in the case, and where there is a matrix of stakeholders and valued goods, will provide a greater opportunity to discuss what is necessary to maintain the society and the environment for generations to come than two-party, A against B, cases. Case studies can be put to a number of purposes; open-ended cases can invite the search for a solution, others may be chosen to demonstrate the application of a particular theory or principle, some may be examples of good practice or the consequences of despicable behavior. In the teaching of ethics, especially to adults, cases which allow and encourage those studying them to examine how the participants responded to the conflicts of values and the interplay of internal and external goods have been found particularly effective (O'Donovan 2002).

A specific example of sustainability as a work of justice, a case study using the example of sustainable agriculture, is given by Lisa Stoen Hazelwood (2000). Agriculture, Hazelwood argues, provides a "concrete starting point from which to discuss the implications of unsustainable relations…and evaluate more mutual, ecological, economic and communal arrangements" (2000, p. 2). As she examines the nature of sustainable agriculture, "explicating an ethic of whole justice for a whole biosphere…justice itself is reconceptualised as sustainability" and a sense of justice becomes the guide for addressing the complex problems of sustainability in "agricultural practices and structures, from household to global levels" (Hazelwood 2000, p. 1). For her,

> Justice located in the matrix of sustainable mutual relations—ecological, economic, and social—is a justice that fits the challenge. An expanded moral domain, while messy and full of ambiguities, lays the groundwork for messy, ambiguous, but more inclusive ways of dealing with issues that affect people, land, and economies—in overlapping, untidy, ever-shifting communities. (Hazelwood 2000, p. 66)

Even from these short extracts the untidiness and imperfection which has been enunciated by Slote, the need for work in dealing with people seeking solutions as explained by Sen, and the links between justice and sustainability described by Jacobs are apparent. Hazelwood's holistic model of sustainability is one with 'transformative potential', it is not an end-state but a process, not a "particular collection of organic, integrated cropping and animal husbandry techniques" but a shared passion for justice (2000, p. 5).

Conclusion

Although the most common framing of sustainability is in terms of intergenerational (distributive) justice, that view is open to criticism both practical and conceptual. It will be more helpful, I argue, to consider justice as an individual virtue than as a social virtue. On this basis sustainability is something to be worked at now; a commitment to sustainability is not a wish for the future but an action in the present.

Sustainability is a debate about purpose, a debate about what to value in a world where there are wide differences about how some goods are to be valued. That debate occurs both within communities and between communities. Understanding the traditions which have led to the practices of the community in which one is placed, and of the other communities with which one engages in a search for sustainability will be enhanced by a disposition to openness and to justice.

References

Agosto, D. E., Gasson, S., & Atwood, M. (2008). Changing mental models of the IT professions: A theoretical framework. *Journal of Information Technology Education, 7,* 205–221.

Aristotle. (1953). *Nicomachean ethics.* Harmondsworth: Penguin Books.

Aristotle. (nd). *Politics* (Trans. Warrington, J.). Publication details not stated: Heron Books Series, published in assoc with JM Dent.

Brundtland, G. H. (1990). *Our common future* (Australian ed.). Canberra: World Commission on Environment and Development.

Carter, A. (2009). Distributive justice and environmental sustainability. *Heythrop Journal, XLI,* 449–460.

Confucius. (1997). *The analects* (Trans. Leys, S.). New York: Norton.

Cotton, A. H. (2001). Private thoughts in public spheres: Issues in reflection and reflective practices in nursing. *Journal of Advanced Nursing, 36*(4), 512–519.

Dobson, A. (1998). *Justice and the environment: Conceptions of environmental sustainability and theories of distributive justice*. Oxford: Oxford University Press.

Elkington, J. (1999). *Cannibals with forks: The triple bottom line of 21st century business*. Oxford: Capstone.

Gardner, H. (2011). *Truth, beauty, and goodness reframed: Educating for the virtues in the twenty-first century*. New York: Basic Books.

GRI. (2006). *Sustainability reporting guidelines G3*. Amsterdam: Global Reporting Initiative.

Hamilton, E. (1961). Introduction to The Republic. In E. Hamilton & H. Cairns (Eds.), *The collected dialogues of Plato* (1st ed., pp. 575–576). New York: Pantheon Books.

Harris, H. (2008). Promoting ethical reflection in the teaching of business ethics. *Business Ethics: A European Review, 17*(4), 379–390.

Hazelwood, L. S. (2000). *Sustainability as justice: Toward a Christian, ecofeminist ethic of sustainability using the example of sustainable agriculture* (PhD). Union Theological Seminary, New York.

Jacobs, M. (1999). Sustainable development as a contested concept. In A. Dobson (Ed.), *Fairness and futurity: Essays on environmental sustainability and social justice* (pp. 21–45). Oxford: Oxford University Press.

Li, C. (2008). The Confucian concept of ren and the feminist ethics of care: A comparative study. In D. A. Bell (Ed.), *Confucian political ethics* (pp. 175–197). Princeton: Princeton University Press.

MacIntyre, A. (1985). *After virtue* (2nd ed.). London: Gerald Duckworth.

MacIntyre, A. (1988). *Whose justice? Which rationality?* Notre Dame: University of Notre Dame Press.

MacIntyre, A. (2004). Questions for Confucians. In K.-l. Shun & D. B. Wong (Eds.), *Confucian ethics: A comparative study of self, autonomy, and community* (pp. 203–218). Cambridge: Cambridge University Press.

Meadows, D. H., Meadows, D. L., Randers, J., & Berhens, W. W. III (1972). *The limits to growth: A report to the club of Rome's project on the predicament of mankind*. London: Earth Island.

Nagel, T. (2005). The problem of global justice. *Philosophy and Public Affairs, 33*(2), 113–147.

Nosco, P. (2008). Confucian perspectives on civil society and government. In D. A. Bell (Ed.), *Confucian political ethics* (pp. 20–45). Princeton: Princeton University Press.

Nozick, R. (1993). *The nature of rationality*. Princeton: Princeton University Press.

O'Donovan, O. (2002). *Common objects of love*. Grand Rapids: Eerdmans.

Rawls, J. (1971). *A theory of justice* (1st ed.). Cambridge: Harvard University Press.

Sandel, M. J. (2009). *Justice: What's the right thing to do?* London: Penguin.

Sen, A. (2004). Why we should preserve the Spotted Owl. *London Review of Books, 26*(3), 10–11.

Sen, A. (2011). *The idea of justice*. Cambridge: Belknap-Harvard

Sinnott-Armstrong, W. (2012). Consequentialism. In E. N. Zalta (Ed.), *The Stanford encyclopedia of philosophy* (Winter 2012 ed.). http://plato.stanford.edu/archives/win2012/entries/consequentialism/.

Slote, M. (2010). Justice as a virtue. In E. N. Zalta (Ed.), *Stanford encyclopedia of philosophy* (Fall 2010 ed., pp. 429–448). http://plato.stanford.edu/archives/fall2010/entries/justice-virtue/.

Slote, M. (2011). *The impossibility of perfection: Aristotle, feminism, and the complexities of ethics*. Oxford: Oxford University Press.

Tencati, A., & Perrini, A. (Eds.). (2011). *Business Ethics and Corporate Sustainability*. Cheltenham: Edward Elgar.

Part II
Case Studies in Sustainable Decision-Making

The three papers in this section take up the questions posed in the previous section, and look at sustainable decision making in small and medium-sized organisations.

Chapter four challenges the popular assertion that cost savings are a driver for environmental responsiveness and instead proposes resource dependence dynamics of organizations on powerful stakeholder as motivations to engage in environmental responsiveness.

Chapter five looks at the supply chain as a means for organisations to extend their sustainable practices beyond the limits of their own organisation and into the wider business community and provides an example of this process in action.

Chapter six looks at life-cycle analysis as a mechanism for understanding the environmental impacts of products and employs these insights to propose how organizations can improve their relationship with environment.

Chapter 5
Environmental Responsiveness and Cost Savings: Effect or Driver?

Sukhbir Sandhu, Clive Smallman, Lucie K. Ozanne and Ross Cullen

Introduction

Corporate environmental responsiveness is an established if contentious domain of professional practice and research (Banerjee 2011; Hart 2007). It refers to the *recognition of the importance of the natural environment by business organizations and its integration into strategic decision-making* (Banerjee 2002; Sandhu et al. 2012). It includes both compliance-based environmental responsiveness as well as voluntary initiatives (e.g., investing in environment management systems, product stewardship and a commitment to sustainable development).

Accordingly, organizations that are environmentally responsive will comply with the environmental regulations and will also exhibit some or all of the following criteria such as: having a written environmental plan, communicating this plan to stakeholders, rewarding environmental performance, conducting regular environmental audits, having top management support for environmental issues and encouraging employee environmental training (Menguc and Ozanne 2005; Sandhu et al. 2012). These organizations may also try to integrate environmental issues into strategic planning process. Among the strategic actions influenced by environmental concerns are decisions such as investing in technology development in pollution prevention and waste management (Hart 2007; Sandhu et al. 2012).

Although perhaps counterintuitive, there is a body of literature that argues that being environmentally responsive leads to cost savings for business organizations

S. Sandhu
School of Management, University of South Australia
Business School, Adelaide, Australia
e-mail: Sukhbir.Sandhu@unisa.edu.au

C. Smallman
Business School, University of Western Sydney, Sydney, Australia

L. K. Ozanne
University of Canterbury, Christchurch, New Zealand

R. Cullen
Lincoln University, Lincoln, New Zealand

© Springer Science+Business Media Dordrecht 2014   55
S. Sandhu et al. (eds.), *Linking Local and Global Sustainability,* The International Society of Business, Economics, and Ethics Book Series 4, DOI 10.1007/978-94-017-9008-6_5

(Clemens 2006; Hart 1995, 1997, 2007; Hart and Ahuja 1996; Porter 1991; Porter and Linde 1995a, b; Porter and Reinhardt 2007). Such savings have been reported both as a consequence of compliance with regulations (Porter 1991; Porter and Linde 1995a, b), and also as a consequence of environmental investments that extend beyond compliance (Hart 2007; Hart and Ahuja 1996; Russo and Fouts 1997). For example, Dow Chemicals redesigned its production process in the US in response to revised waste water storage regulations. Caustic soda usage was reduced considerably as was the production of hydrochloric acid waste. The investment of US$ 250,000 gave a return of US$ 2.4 million (Porter and Linde 1995a). Beyond compliance, 3M's voluntary program PPP (Pollution Prevention Pays) has, since 1975, resulted in cost savings of more than US$ 1.2 billion for 3 M (Hart 2007).

However, both proponents (Hart 2007) and critics (Cairncross 1994; Walley and Whitehead 1994) of the relationship between environmental responsiveness and cost savings are clear that "only under the right circumstances... [can] ... firms... lower costs by internalizing externalities through pollution prevention" (Hart 2007, p. 13). Similarly Schendler (2002), although an advocate of corporate environmental responsiveness, argues that selling environmentalism on the basis of a favourable economic argument is fundamentally flawed.

Yet, despite these cautionary notes, a recent trend in the broader environmental literature has begun to advocate the idea that businesses should choose to be environmentally responsive as this *leads* to cost savings (Crawford and Scaletta 2006; DeSimone and Popoff 1997; Holliday et al. 2002; Schmidheiny 1992). This hypothesis suggests that significant reductions in costs can be achieved through focusing on efficient manufacturing processes driven by environmental responsiveness.

Therefore, following both arguments environmental responsiveness can (sometimes) *lead* to cost reduction and the promise of cost reductions can be portrayed as a *driver* for corporate environmental responsiveness. This raises the question of causality. Does the promise of cost savings motivate organizations to be environmentally responsive or do organizations enjoy cost savings vicariously? Rather than a question of semantics, this causal concern influences the nature and type of environmentally responsive projects that organizations may adopt. If cost savings are deemed as a significant driver, (rather than a consequence), then only the environmental projects that result in tangible savings will be favoured by organizations. However, if cost savings are merely a consequence, the projected cost savings will not influence the selection of environmental initiatives by organizations. This contradictory body of knowledge leads us to question whether cost savings are an effect or a driver of corporate environmental responsiveness?

Research Design

As discussed in the introductory section, both sides of this question have been extensively discussed in the literature, but they have not thus far, been assessed as a whole. Hence, we observe that the work thus far, whilst of value, is inadequate and does not address the question of whether cost savings are an effect or a driver of corporate environmental responsiveness. The existing literature also indicates that corporate environmental responsiveness covers a wide range of concepts from a great many sources. Hence, the choice of a multiple case study approach seemed appropriate (Eisenhardt and Graebner 2007; Yin 2003). While single cases can provide rich descriptions (e.g., Dutton and Dukerich 1991; Siggelkow 2007; Weick 1993), multiple cases facilitate replication logic (Eisenhardt and Graebner 2007; Yin 2003). This allows the cases to be treated as a series of experiments wherein each case serves to confirm or disconfirm the inferences drawn from others (Eisenhardt and Graebner 2007; Graebner and Eisenhardt 2004; Yin 2003). This ensures that the insights gained are not idiosyncratic, but instead are consistently replicated (literally or theoretically) across multiple cases. This leads to more robust theory development (Eisenhardt and Graebner 2007).

We theoretically sampled cases from amongst larger organizations (in terms of employee numbers and revenue) both in India and New Zealand. The rationale for focusing on larger organizations is explained by previous research which suggests that only larger organizations tend to exhibit proactive environmental responsiveness that extends beyond compliance (Arora and Cason 1995; Sharma and Henriques 2005; Sharma and Vredenburg 1998). Furthermore, previous research in the Indian context has specifically indicated that corporate environmentalism in India is limited to larger organizations (D'Souza and Peretiatko 2002; Sandhu et al. 2010). The criterion for more specific selection of the organizations from amongst the top organizations was an established reputation for environmental responsiveness (based on our earlier definition), which we assessed through content analysis (Malhotra et al. 2006) of the websites and environmental reports of the top 100 organizations in India and New Zealand, the analysis of environmental awards and media reports, and conversations with corporate communication directors.

Tables 5.1 and 5.2 describe the fit between the definition of corporate environmental responsiveness as employed in this research and its manifestation in the case studies. To ensure confidentiality, names of both the participating organizations and the managers who were interviewed in each organization, have been changed.

We included organizations from both India and New Zealand in this study because we sought to examine whether this relationship differed between organizations in developing countries and developed countries.

Data Sources

Interviews with senior managers—responsible for environmental issues—in 23 environmentally responsive organizations were the primary data source. To ensure reliability, we triangulated the interview data through extensive examinations of the company websites and documents such as annual reports, environmental or sustainability reports, business publications, brochures and other material (including copies of public presentations made by the respondents). Where possible, we interviewed multiple respondents (Eisenhardt and Graebner 2007). Fifty-one interviews of between 60 and

Table 5.1 Summary of environmental measures in the case study organizations in India

Organization	ISO 14000	Environment policy	Environment report	Distinct environment division	Employee environment training	Environment awards	Environmental benchmarking against other organizations	Pollution prevention and waste reduction
Cosmos	√	√	√	√	√	√	√	√
ICLL	√	√	√	√	√	√	√	√
Endeavour	√	√	√	√	√	√	√	√
Valiance	√	√	√	√	√	√	√	√
Cottex	√	√	√	√	√	√	√	√
Tripax	√	√	√	√	√	√	√	√
Organochem	√	√	√	√	√	√	√	√
Mayer	√	√	√	√	√	√	√	√
Pharmachem	√	√	√	√	√	√	√	√
Sun	√	√	√	√	√	√	√	√
Raj	√	√	√	√	√	√	√	√

90 min duration were conducted over a period of 21 months from 2005 to 2007, and the majority were recorded and transcribed verbatim. When further clarifications were needed, follow-up questions were normally asked through email and phone.

Tables 5.3 and 5.4 summarize the characteristics of the sample. These figures have been rounded off to further ensure confidentiality. Of the 23 case study organizations, 11 were based in India and 12 in New Zealand.

We were not seeking to test any preconceived hypothesis about what drives corporate environmentalism. Instead our objective was to let the managers infer the drivers that they believed were responsible for propelling their organizations towards environmental responsiveness. Hence, we did not seek to deliberately steer the interviews towards the issue of cost savings. Thus, only after the managers had described the status of environmental responsiveness at their organization, an open ended question was asked: "so what is it that drives your organization to be environmentally responsive?" The intention of this questioning strategy was that if costs savings were viewed as a driver, the interviewees would mention that in response to this question. Accordingly, where the managers brought up the issue of cost savings, we further investigated whether or not these cost savings were viewed as being one of the drivers for the corporate environmental responsiveness.

Data Analysis

We first analysed each case individually (Eisenhardt 1989a, b; Eisenhardt and Graebner 2007; Miles and Huberman 1994; Yin 2003). Within case analysis typically

Table 5.2 Summary of environmental measures in the case study organizations in New Zealand

Organiza-tion	ISO 14000	Environ-ment policy	Environ-ment report	Distinct environ-ment division	Employee environ-ment training	Environ-ment awards	Environmental bench-marking against other organiza-tions	Pollution preven-tion and waste reduction
Atlas	√	√	√	√	√	√	√	√
Skyes	√	√	√	√	√	√	√	√
Shield	√	√	√	√	√	√	√	√
Fabio	√	√	√	√	√	√	√	√
Phoenix	√	√	√	√	√	√	√	√
Hercules	√	√	√	√	√	√	√	√
Amity	√	√	√	√	√	√	√	√
Solitaire	√	√	√	√	√	√	√	√
Sunrise	√	√	√	√	√	√	√	√
Marion	√	√	√	√	√	√	√	√
Keratin	√	√	√	√	√	√	√	√
Waite	√	√	√	√	√	√	√	√

Table 5.3 Profile of case studies in India

Organization	Sector	Revenue in US $ millions (2007)	Employees
Valiance	Petrochemicals	30,100	25,000
Cosmos	Steel	7000	39,000
ICLL	Pulp and paper	3100	21,000
Endeavour	FMCG	3000	16,000
Tripax	Pharmaceutical	1700	11,000
Pharmachem	Pharmaceutical	1000	9000
Sun	Fertilizer	900	100,000
Cottex	Textile	470	4000
Organochem	Chemical	460	4300
Mayer systems	Electronics	460	4500
Raj	Hotel chain	400	7000

involves developing detailed case histories for each of the organizations, which assists the researcher in becoming intimately familiar with each case (Eisenhardt 1989a). This facilitates the emergence of unique patterns for each individual case, without being influenced or constrained by patterns in other cases.

Accordingly, detailed individual case histories were prepared for all 23 organizations. NVivo 8 qualitative analysis software was used to corroborate and synthesize the data from the extensive field notes, the interview transcripts and archival data. To provide a check on the emerging case histories, a second researcher who was not engaged in data collection and thus had not been sensitized to the data, read the original interviews and documents and formed an independent view. This view

Table 5.4 Profile of case studies in New Zealand

Organization	Sector	Revenue in US$ millions (2007)	Employees
Atlas	Dairy	10,800	16,400
Skyes	Construction	4300	20,000
Shield	Petrochemical	2100	300
Phoenix	Electricity generation	1545	500
Fabio	Food distribution	1540	1200
Hercules	Retail chain	1300	5500
Amity	Food industry	480	1500
Solitaire	Mining	440	800
Sunrise	Chemicals and fertilizer Manufacturer	360	600
Marion	Electricity distribution	150	140
Waite	Electronic and defence Equipment	150	600
Keratin	Wool scouring	100	80

was then incorporated into each case history to provide a more accurate view of each organization. Although similarities and differences among cases were noted, no further comparative analysis was undertaken, until the detailed individual case write-ups were completed.

We then moved to cross-case analysis, comparing cases from India and New Zealand. We sought within-group similarities and differences, as well as intergroup differences and similarities. We aimed to broaden the frame of reference and systematically proceed beyond initial impressions. The analysis process was iterative and took 8 months to complete.

A second stage of coding was then done using NVivo 8. The initial free codes for each individual organization were organized into clusters based on cross-case analysis. Responses from individual cases were now coded under these categories to identify the emerging patterns. Using the matrix query function in NVivo, 2×2 cell designs were also used to compare several categories at once. This further brought out the differences in the drivers of environmental responsiveness within and across the groups.

This detailed within and cross-case analysis improved the likelihood of more accurate and reliable theory emerging from case study data (Eisenhardt 1989a). The findings and insights obtained from within and cross-case analysis, are discussed below.

Findings

The analysis revealed that although environmental responsiveness resulted in cost savings in both Indian and New Zealand case studies, in no case were cost savings viewed as a driver for corporate environmentalism.

Findings in India

Of the 11 case study organizations in India, seven did not mention cost savings at all while explaining the drivers of corporate environmentalism. The failure of cost savings to merit even a passing reference during the interview may be construed as support for the thesis that either environmental responsiveness did not lead to cost savings for these organizations, or if these organizations did achieve any cost savings, these savings were not a motivation to initiate these practices or explore other opportunities for environmental responsiveness.

The four organizations that referred to the issue of cost savings viewed them as a very welcome but unintended and additional benefit of environmental investments. None of these four organizations cited cost savings as a motivation for investing in environmental measures. As the following extracts illustrate, improvements in bottom line as a result of cost savings are seen as a very positive offshoot, but not as a driver.

At *Organochem* (a chemical manufacturing company), the environmental manager stressed that significant cost savings had resulted for their organization as a consequence of being environmentally responsive:

> For a chemical plant any pollution is a loss, so reducing the generation of pollutants will add to our bottom line as well as improve the environmental performance.

But he goes on to specify that the factors that drove Organochem to be environmentally responsive stemmed from the supply chain pressures:

> Our company is heavily into exports. We are in a major way exporting our project to about 60 odd countries and majority of them are in the developed world. Our major customers demand similar performance in the environment health and safety area as the companies out in Europe or North America. So we would like to improve our environmental performance levels so that we can have sustainable business with these valued customers.

He further clarifies that:

> Most of our valued international customers who are looking for long-term partnership come to the plant sites for detailed auditing before they finalize their long-term orders. Much of this auditing is in the area of environment health and safety.

The manager at *Endeavour* (a fast moving consumer goods company) further elaborates this *welcome but unintended consequence of cost savings* when he states that the cost savings, resulting from measures aimed at decreasing energy consumption, were all but forgotten until a few years later when an audit revealed the savings:

> We started this energy drive from 96 onwards. Towards the end of 99, an audit revealed that we were actually making savings. We were double excited about that as by that time we had started forgetting all about it.

The above response clearly indicates that although environmental responsive measures had resulted in cost savings, it was not the intention to achieve these cost savings that had prompted the measures in the first place. Endeavour had chosen to be environmentally responsive for a number of other reasons. It is a multinational (MNC) operating in India and had chosen the social and environmental responsibility platform to overcome its '*liability of foreignness*' (Kostova and Zaheer 1999). Cost savings however, did not feature as a part of the equation that drove it to protect its legitimacy.

The manager at Endeavour explains that being a MNC they have to be extra vigilant in protecting their reputation:

> A number of other (MNC) businesses have been affected by it, they have gone into red. These are big names like Coca-Cola, Pepsi and even McDonalds. So these issues [environmental and social] become global issues and they can spread like a wildfire.
>
> It can be very detrimental to the way we do the business as a MNC. It can affect the corporate goodwill and reputation and that cannot be gained.

At *ICLL* (a pulp and paper manufacturing company), it '*emerged*' that environmental efforts at recycling etc., had resulted in cost savings:

> I think one thing has emerged very clearly for us is that environment has become very profitable for us as well (laughs). I mean if you save water, if you save energy, if you have forestry you can straightaway calculate and it is very beneficial thing to do. In the solid waste we have found that actually by recycling everything that you waste, you actually make money.
>
> But to say that is a driver… well it is more the sustainability platform we have strategically chosen to be at.

The manager at ICLL strongly attributes the environmental responsiveness to the organizational commitment to sustainability to which cost savings were incidental. He elaborates that:

> This plant was set up in 1906 and towns have grown up around the factory. So in such cases especially since you are the only big unit and the employer, a lot of expectations do emerge from the society. We are known here as a 'Thali' company, which means the farmers, would say that we are a mother company. 'Thali' is the word for mother.
>
> As a corporate if you are operating on such a large scale and you are also operating in so many businesses you have to take a much larger view than just the finances.

The response from the manager at *Cosmos* (a steel manufacturing company), indicates that for Cosmos, environmental responsiveness had in some cases resulted in clear material and resource cost savings:

> At Cosmos we have a matrix to measure raw material consumption. We have been at the level of 3.90 tonne per tonne of saleable steel produced in 2000. We have come down to 3.31 tonne in 2007. So 0.59 tonnes of raw material have been used less with respect to tonnes of saleable steel. Similarly we have a benchmark regarding the raw material which gets consumed. We were at a level of 11.5 in 2000. Today we are at a level of 6.3.

However, while explaining the drivers for environmental responsiveness the manager stressed that these cost savings were incidental:

> It is not that if we invest ten rupees or ten dollars in waste management then we will get 12 dollars tomorrow. We realize that if we don't invest this ten dollar today, if we don't invest in climate change today, tomorrow we may not be there! That will be completely irresponsible.
>
> Environmental sustainability contributes to our long term bottom line. There is an obvious mutuality. It is an important effect but it is not the reason.

The manager at Cosmos makes a pertinent point when she states that:

> Our motivation comes from our values. The moment it becomes externally motivated then
> we will do things which are by selection, which will be by design not by default. To invest
> in the environmental projects that we are, it has to be an integral part of the value system

A detailed case analysis revealed that, environmental responsiveness at Cosmos could be traced to its desire to maintain the reputation that it had built for more than a century. Cosmos was set up in India towards the end of the 1800s and has over this period acquired a reputation for social (and now environmental) responsiveness.

In summary, of the 11 case study organizations in India, seven did not mention cost savings at all. In the four organizations that referred to cost savings, they were consequential, rather than intentional. The implications of this finding are significant and are very clearly articulated in the point made by the manager at Cosmos. If the theoretical notion that cost savings can be projected as a driver for environmental responsiveness is propagated then only very selective environmental initiatives can be promoted. This will be to the detriment of those environmental initiatives, which may not be able to show tangible cost savings, but may have implications for the wider business case (such as managing reputational risk).

Findings in New Zealand

Five of the 12 organizations in New Zealand did not refer at all to cost savings during the interview. Hence, either the environmental responsiveness did not lead to cost savings, or the savings did not motivate the organizations in the first instance or push them to explore other opportunities for environmental responsiveness. Seven of the 12 case study organizations in New Zealand, however, reported that the environmental measures in place at their organizations had in some (but not all) cases resulted in cost savings.

Similar to organizations in India, these cost savings were regarded as a very positive effect of the environmental measures at these organizations. However, for none of these seven organizations were cost savings a driver. As the manager at *Skyes* (a construction company) explains *compliance* has in some cases *lead* to cost savings:

> The first thing of course is compliance. However, we have observed that in some situations
> compliance has resulted in waste reduction and that has lead to cost reduction.

He further elaborates that:

> From the point of view of managing (environmental issues) we are required to do it by law.
> Law requires us, even if we had no concerns about the environmental effects.

Similarly at *Fabio* (a food distribution company) some of the environmental measures such as recycling plastic bags have *resulted* in cost savings:

> Sometimes you can achieve that win–win balance between the environmental compliance
> and achieving lower cost as well. Like, for example recycling our plastic bag; that means
> we don't have to dump it, we can recycle it. It's a win–win situation for us.

But once again the manager clarifies that:

> But for us the biggest driver would be regulation.

The response of the manager at *Atlas* (a dairy company) further underscores the importance of regulatory compliance to be able to do business in New Zealand:

> To operate within New Zealand you need to meet certain environmental standards set by the regional councils.

She further specifies that environmental investments do not always result in cost savings but when they do:

> It is very much a win–win situation **in the situations where** we can achieve that.

Similarly the response of the manager at *Amity* (a food company) indicates that environmental responsiveness is regulation driven:

> Five years ago now, at a time when the organization did not specifically have someone managing the environmental issues we had an uncontrolled release to the environment. Some of the discharges got into the storm water system.
> That prosecution certainly was a big motivator.

He further highlights that only some of these environmental measures have resulted in cost savings:

> The costs of compliance have increased over the years. 18 months ago we had a landfill increase of 40 percent So when you put that (waste reduction) across—we actually managed to reduce our total costs on solid wastes disposal.
> So while we may not have necessarily had an overall reduction of costs but we have definitely had mitigation in some areas.

The manager at *Marion* (electricity distribution) points out that although some environmental measures have resulted in cost savings that is not a driving factor:

> The effect on the financial bottom line, although it does happen positively in some cases, would not be a driver in the sense of the size of the impact on the budget. We don't tend to think about them (environmental measures) in those terms.

He also clearly points out that:

> Compliance is not optional.

The manager at *Keratin* (wool scouring) cites one incidence of having saved substantial costs:

> We were one of the first to use the 20 tonne containers rather than those that used 16 tonne containers. So we save energy. It is more common to get 100 tonnes in six containers but we now get them only in five containers.

However, he goes on to explain that this cost saving was incidental to the supply chain pressures resulting from demands of the European organizational customers who required this change.

The manager at *Waite* (electronic and defence equipment manufacturer) credits the environmental programs at his organization with costs savings:

> In a lot of our environmental programs, it has resulted in reduced costs as well.

However, he describes the drivers behind those environmental programs as being related to new regulatory pressures in their export markets:

> One of the biggest drivers we have at present is the legislation in some of our markets particularly in Europe.

Finally, although the manager at Sunrise (chemicals and fertilizers manufacturer) did not report any cost savings associated with environmental responsiveness, he provides a very interesting insight, which further helped us arrive at our thesis. He explains that, as in most organizations, every capital investment project at Sunrise had to meet the rate of return criteria. However, this normally important criterion is dispensed for capital investment involving environmental initiatives. This is because environmental investments come under the 'must do' regulatory category and are not negotiable:

> For instance we have an internal rate of return hurdle for most capital expenditures but when that expenditure is on an environment project, you cannot ignore the consent requirements. It is just in the must do category and you cannot show an economic return to it.

This response clearly indicates that cost savings was not what this organization was actively seeking when initiating its environmental responsiveness.

In summary, of the 12 case study organizations in New Zealand, five did not mention cost savings at all. In the seven organizations that referred to cost savings, these were again clearly a consequence, but not a driver.

Discussion

Proponents of eco-efficiency (DeSimone and Popoff 1997; Schmidheiny 1992) predict that cost savings are a major motivator of environmental responsiveness. They further state that organizations in developing countries are especially likely to favour environmental measures which lead to cost savings. Our research found no evidence for this. The findings of this study reveal that firstly, corporate environmental measures do not always involve cost savings. Secondly, in the cases where environmental responsiveness can be associated with cost savings, it does not serve as a motivation for organizations to be environmentally responsive, nor does it provide a platform to explore further environmentally responsive projects. These conclusions are based on findings from organizations in both developing (India) and developed (New Zealand) countries. That these findings hold true across organizations in both developing and developed countries—which are characterized by political, social, economic, and institutional differences—lends further robustness to the thesis evaluated in this study.

To ensure reliability, we rigorously examined our findings for alternative explanations. It can thus be argued that organizations which are actively pursuing environmental goals would desire to be *viewed* as responsible organizations and—by an extension of this logic—would prefer to not simply be seen as profit oriented organizations. This might explain their reluctance to admit cost savings as a driver for environmental responsiveness. Therefore, social desirability bias may lead managers in the case study organizations against admitting that cost savings were an intended outcome of an environmental program. However, in order to reduce social desirability bias, organizations in this study were promised dual screens of confidentiality. As evidence of the reduced social desirability bias, managers both in India and New Zealand ascribed profit motives to environmental responsiveness in their organizations. Thus, Organochem, in India, and Waite and Keratin, in New Zealand, clearly indicated that a desire to increase their profits (through being able to export to European markets, which demand greater environmental responsiveness), was a clear motivation for their environmental programs.

Providing these dual screens of confidentiality, we believe, helped reduce the social desirability bias. Managers in the case study organizations thus clearly admitted that profit motivation, supply chain pressures, and necessity of compliance, were amongst a range of drivers which propelled their organizations to be environmentally responsive. Propelled by these drivers, organizations in certain cases made cost savings. However, in none of the case study organizations were these cost savings viewed as the initial driver for environmental responsiveness.

We examine the study findings through the lens of resource dependence theory (Frooman 1999; Pfeffer and Salancik 1978). According to resource dependence theory, organizations are dependent on the external environment (and hence on the stakeholders) for their resource needs (Pfeffer and Salancik 1978). It is this dependence of firms on stakeholders for critical resources that gives stakeholders leverage over firms. Resource dependence thus creates differentials among stakeholders; the more dependent a firm is on a stakeholder for critical resources, the greater is the extent to which that stakeholder can influence the firm's response (Frooman 1999). Extending the resource-based logic to corporate environmental practices therefore provides a theoretical rationale for understanding stakeholder saliency. It theoretically explains which environmental stakeholders will be considered important by a firm.

Drawing on the resource dependence theory, we interpret our findings in light of the power that stakeholders yield over firms. The findings thus suggest that corporate environmental responsiveness in organizations in both India and New Zealand exhibited resource dependence at work. Thus it was pressures from powerful external stakeholders (such as regulators, supply chain pressures, media etc.) or from powerful internal stakeholders (such as a founder's vision or top management), that drove organizations to be environmentally responsive (see Table 5.5). These resource dependence dynamics propelled the extent and level of environmental responsiveness in the case study organizations and the costs savings were a welcome effect.

Paquette (2005) and Islam and Deegan (2008) highlight the role of supply chain pressures in driving organizations to be environmentally responsive and provide support for this study's thesis. Islam and Deegan (2008, p. 870) point towards MNC buying companies being the primary driver for sustainability initiatives in developing countries. Luken and Stares (2005) found that these supply chain pressures

Table 5.5 Resource dependence on powerful stakeholders and corporate environmental responsiveness

Resource dependence dynamics theme	Case study organizations
Powerful supply chain pressures	Waite (NZ)
	Keratin (NZ)
	Organochem (India)
Regulatory pressures	Atlas (NZ)
	Fabio (NZ)
	Amity (NZ)
	Marion (NZ)
	Skyes (NZ)
Top management and vision of powerful founding fathers	Cosmos (India)
	ICLL (India)
Media and societal pressures as forces that can threaten "liability of foreignness"	Endeavour (India)

from MNCs can sometimes *result* in cost savings but Paquette (2005, p. 14) advises that:"In the future, environmental pressures will require significant and pervasive changes in supply chain design and operations, changes that will *not* likely be motivated by incremental costs savings".

Therefore, based on our findings and supported by the above discussion we propose that:

> Proposition: While cost savings can sometimes **result** from environmental responsiveness, the promise of cost savings is not the **driver** for corporate environmental responsiveness.

Our findings are, however, subject to certain limitations. Our analysis is based on case analysis of large organizations and we cannot claim that our findings will be applicable to small and medium enterprises (SMEs).

Conclusions

In this paper we propose that cost savings, associated with being environmentally responsive—in the cases where they can be observed—are a welcome *effect* of environmental responsiveness. Organizations however, currently do not view these cost savings as a *driver* of environmental responsiveness. While these findings apparently challenge the prevalent view, but with reference to resource dependence theory, we argue that currently the demands of powerful stakeholders, both external (e.g., regulators, supply chain, media, etc.) and internal (e.g., top management), drives corporate environmental responsiveness. These stakeholders have the required power and influence and therefore have the ability to coerce firms into acquiescence.

Extant research in environmental accounting provides an anchor for further exploring our thesis. Thus, despite the fact that the tools for environmental accounting are now well developed (Burritt et al. 2009; Gray and Bebbington 2001; Parker 2000), yet environmental accounting researchers are currently battling with a marked unwillingness of organizational accountants to report on environmental costs (Burritt 2004; Gale 2006). Environmental accounting experts agree that a rigorous application of environmental accounting is a challenging task and organizations are currently notorious in their inability (or unwillingness) to account for environmental costs.

This is supported by Gale (2006), whose research reiterates that environmental costs are largely unrecorded or hidden in overhead accounts. Gale (2006) suggests that because of lack of accounting for environmental costs, organizations often pay three times for wastes and these hidden costs therefore represent significant lost opportunities for cost savings. He suggests that because organizations currently are not making a concerted attempt to account for environmental costs, therefore, there exists an inability to understand the true costs and benefits that result from environmental responsiveness.

This lack of interest in accounting for environmental costs has implications for our thesis. If organizations are currently not actively accounting for environmental costs of projects then it is hard to contend that cost savings are a driver of corporate environmental responsiveness. We attribute this conclusion to resource dependence dynamics. According to our findings powerful external and internal stakeholder requirements govern corporate environmental responsiveness. Driven by pressure from these stakeholders, organizations adopt the required environmental responsiveness programs which are demanded by these stakeholders. These environmental measures may sometimes *result* in cost savings. However, organizations, at least currently, have not started to focus on cost savings as drivers of corporate environmental responsiveness.

References

Arora, S., & Cason, T. N. (1995). An experiment in voluntary environmental regulation: Participation in EPA's 33/50 program. *Journal of Environmental Economics and Management, 28*(3), 271–286.

Banerjee, S. B. (2002). Corporate environmentalism: The construct and its measurement. *Journal of Business Research, 55,* 177–191.

Banerjee, S. B. (2011). Embedding sustainability across the organization: A critical perspective. *Academy of Management Learning and Education, 10*(4), 719–731.

Burritt, R. L. (2004). Environmental management accounting: Roadblocks on the way to the green and pleasant land. *Business Strategy and the Environment, 13*(1), 13–32.

Burritt, R. L., Herzig, C., & Tadeo, B. D. (2009). Environmental management accounting for cleaner production: The case of a Philippine rice mill. *Journal of Cleaner Production, 17*(4), 431–439.

Cairncross, F. (1994). The challenge of going green. *Harvard Business Review, 72*(4), 40–41.

Clemens, B. (2006). Economic incentives and small firms: Does it pay to be green? *Journal of Business Research, 59*(4), 492–500.

Crawford, D., & Scaletta, T. (2006). The balanced scorecard and corporate social responsibility: Aligning values for profit. *The Financial Management Institute Journal, 17*(3), 39–42.

D'Souza, C., & Peretiatko, R. (2002). The nexus between industrialization and environment: A case study of Indian enterprises. *Environmental Management and Health, 13*(1), 80–97.

DeSimone, L. D., & Popoff, F. (1997). *Eco-efficiency: The business link to sustainable development*. Cambridge: MIT Press.

Dutton, J. E., & Dukerich, J. M. (1991). Keeping an eye on the mirror: Image and identity in organizational adaptation. *Academy of Management Journal, 34*(3), 517–554.

Eisenhardt, K. M. (1989a). Building theories from case study research. *Academy of Management Review, 14*(4), 532–550.

Eisenhardt, K. M. (1989b). Making fast strategic decisions in high velocity environments. *Academy of Management Journal, 32*(3), 543–576.

Eisenhardt, K. M., & Graebner, M. E. (2007). Theory building from cases: Opportunities and challenges. *Academy of Management Journal, 50*(1), 25–32.

Frooman, J. (1999). Stakeholder influence strategies. *Academy of Management Review, 24*(2), 191–205.

Gale, R. (2006). Environmental management accounting as a reflexive modernization strategy in cleaner production. *Journal of Cleaner Production, 14*(4), 1228–1236.

Graebner, M. E., & Eisenhardt, K. M. (2004). The seller's side of the story: Acquisition as courtship and governance as syndicate in entrepreneurial firms. *Administrative Science Quarterly, 49*(3), 366–403.

Gray, R., & Bebbington, J. (2001). *Accounting for the environment* (2nd ed.). London: Sage.

Hart, S. L. (1995). A natural resource based view of the firm. *Academy of Management Review, 20*(4), 986–1014.

Hart, S. L. (1997). Beyond greening: Strategies for a sustainable world. *Harvard Business Review, 75*(1), 67–76.

Hart, S. L. (2007). *Capitalism at the crossroads: Aligning business, earth, and humanity*. New Jersey: Wharton School Publishing.

Hart, S. L., & Ahuja, G. 1996. Does it pay to be green? An empirical examination of the relationship between emission reduction and firm performance. *Business Strategy and the Environment, 5*(1), 30–37.

Holliday, C. O., Schmidheiny, S., & Watts, P. (2002). *Walking the talk: The business case for sustainable development*. Sheffield: Greenleaf.

Islam, M. A., & Deegan, C. (2008). Motivations for an organization within a developing country to report social responsibility information: Evidence from Bangladesh. *Accounting, Auditing and Accountability Journal, 21*(6), 850–874.

Kostova, T., & Zaheer, S. (1999). Organizational legitimacy under conditions of complexity: The case of the multinational enterprise *Academy of Management Review, 24*(1), 64–81.

Luken, R., & Stares, R. (2005). Small business responsibility in developing countries: A threat or an opportunity. *Business Strategy and the Environment, 14*(1), 38–53.

Malhotra, N., Hall, J., Shaw, M., & Oppenheim, P. (2006). *Marketing research: An applied orientation* (3rd ed.). French Forests: Pearson Education Australia.

Menguc, B., & Ozanne, L. K. (2005). Challenges of the 'green imperative': A natural resource based approach to the environmental orientation-business performance relationship. *Journal of Business Research, 58*(4), 430–439.

Miles, M. B., & Huberman, A. M. (1994). *Qualitative data analysis. An expanded sourcebook* (2nd ed.). London: Sage.

Paquette, J. R. (2005). The supply chain response to environmental pressures (Discussion Paper). Massachusetts Institute of Technology, Engineering Systems Division.

Parker, L. D. (2000). Environmental costing: A path to implementation. *Australian Accounting Review, 10*(22), 43–51.

Pfeffer, J., & Salancik, G. R. (1978). *The external control of organizations*. New York: Harper & Row.

Porter, M. E. (1991). America's greening strategy. *Scientific American, 264*, 96.

Porter, M. E., & Linde, C. v. d. (1995a). Green and competitive: Ending the stalemate. *Harvard Business Review, 73*(5), 120–134.

Porter, M. E., & Linde, C. v. d. (1995b). Towards a new conception of the environment: Competitivenes relationship. *Journal of Economic Perspectives, 9*(4), 97–118.

Porter, M. E., & Reinhardt, F. L. (2007). A strategic approach to climate. *Harvard Business Review, 85*(10), 22–26.

Russo, M. V., & Fouts, P. A. (1997). A resource based perspective on corporate environmental performance and profitability. *Academy of Management Journal, 40*(3), 534–559.

Sandhu, S., Ozanne, L., Smallman, C., & Cullen, R. (2010). Consumer driven corporate environmentalism: Fact or fiction? *Business Strategy and Environment, 19*(6), 356–366.

Sandhu, S., Smallman, C., Ozanne, L. K., & Cullen, R. (2012). Corporate environmental responsiveness in India: Lessons from a developing country. *Journal of Cleaner Production, 35,* 203–213.

Schendler, A. (2002). Where's the green in green business? Harvard Business Review, *June,* 28–29.

Schmidheiny, S. (1992). *Changing course: A global business perspective on development and the environment*. Cambridge: MIT Press.

Sharma, S., & Henriques, I. (2005). Stakeholder influence on sustainability practices in the Canadian forest products industry. *Strategic Management Journal, 26*(2), 159–180.

Sharma, S., & Vredenburg, H. (1998). Proactive corporate environmental strategy and the development of competitively valuable organizational capabilities. *Strategic Management Journal, 19*(8), 729–753.

Siggelkow, N. (2007). Persuasion with case studies. *Academy of Management Journal, 50*(1), 20–24.

Walley, N., & Whitehead, B. (1994). It's not easy being green. *Harvard Business Review, 72*(3), 46–52.

Weick, K. E. (1993). The collapse of sensemaking in organizations: The Mann Gulch disaster. *Administrative Science Quarterly, 38*(4), 628–652.

Yin, R. K. (2003). *Case study research: Designs and methods* (3rd ed.). Thousand Oaks: Sage.

Chapter 6
Extending Sustainable Practices Beyond Organizations to Supply Chains

Claudine Soosay, Andrew Fearne and Mohsen Varsei

Introduction

Over the past few decades, the concept of sustainability has emerged as a focus within the business management domain mainly pertaining to environmental issues. The history and definition of the term sustainability have emanated from an intergenerational transcendent viewpoint to a multi-dimensional approach and multi-stakeholder concern today. "The inter-generational philosophy focuses on making sure that future generations are not negatively impacted by decisions made today" (Seuring et al. 2008, p. 1546), whereas the multi-dimensional focus stems from the 'triple bottom line' of balancing economic, environmental and social dimensions of sustainability, as popularized by Elkington (1999). One of the biggest challenges is that there is no rulebook for sustainability in terms of measuring and reporting sustainability. Although laws and regulations provide guidance on some issues, organizational sustainability is about identifying the optimum mix of strategies and practices to produce sustained, superior performance. This performance can be expressed in both financial and non-financial terms, and needs to be resilient in the face of turbulent markets and uncertainty. Given that sustainability cannot be measured absolutely, an organization's performance in sustainability is assessed on whether balanced and equitable progress is being made continuously on the full range of issues and regularly compared to the performance of other organizations of similar industry characteristics and size (Global Reporting Initiative 2012). Given the growing media publicity and heightened awareness of

C. Soosay (✉) · M. Varsei
School of Management, University of South Australia Business School,
GPO Box 2471, 5001 Adelaide, Australia
e-mail: Claudine.Soosay@unisa.edu.au

A. Fearne
Centre for Value Chain Research, Kent Business School,
University of Kent, CT2 7PE Canterbury, Kent, England
e-mail: A.Fearne@kent.ac.uk

© Springer Science+Business Media Dordrecht 2014
S. Sandhu et al. (eds.), *Linking Local and Global Sustainability,* The International Society
of Business, Economics, and Ethics Book Series 4, DOI 10.1007/978-94-017-9008-6_6

sustainable practices, many firms also realize that sustainability plays a significant role in enhancing not only their financial performance, but also in fulfiling the broadening demands of customers, stakeholders and society. As businesses operate in environments that are increasingly dynamic and challenging, we see new business models emerging over time, where competitive advantage is dependent on flexible and rapid response to market changes, and where new capabilities are based on collaborations with customers, suppliers, shareholders, employees, government and even with competitors (Walters and Rainbird 2007).

As a result, it is established that sustainability can be more effectively implemented with collaborative efforts of firms at the supply chain level. Over the past few decades, the concept of sustainable supply chains has received much attention in the literature. Many organizations see the importance of effectively managing supply chain operations, resources, information and funds in order to maximize profitability, while concurrently minimizing environmental impacts and maximizing the social well-being (Hassani et al. 2012). The literature on sustainable supply chain management highlights the need to incorporate economic, environmental and social dimensions concurrently (Andersen and Skjoett-Larsen 2009; Gimenez and Tachizawa 2012). While there have been many published works in this area, very few studies have actually examined all three areas simultaneously—hence resulting in an appeal for future research to adopt this holistic approach (Abbasi and Nilsson 2012; Boloori Arabani and Farahani 2012; Gupta and Palsule-Desai 2011; Matos and Hall 2007; Pishvaee et al. 2012; Seuring 2012; Seuring and Müller 2008). Additionally, we argue that it is also necessary to discern end consumers' perception of sustainable products and services, since supply chains exist to meet customer needs and demand (de Barcellos et al. 2011). Therefore, the importance of what consumers associate with sustainability and resulting purchase decisions are paramount not only to businesses, but also supply chains.

This chapter seeks to address the gap in the literature by illustrating the sustainability initiatives of Yalumba Wine Company's supply chain in Australia by using an iterative process of data collection conducted over 36 months and adopting a value chain approach. We examine the economic, social and environmental aspects of sustainable operations and how these could further be enhanced by realizing the dynamics of the chain's operations in an integrated manner. The remainder of the chapter is organized as follows. First, we review the literature on sustainable supply chain management, highlighting the economic, social and environmental considerations. Second, we review existing frameworks and guidelines for sustainable supply chains as prescribed by non-governmental and international organizations, particularly the New Zealand Business Council, United Nations and Global Reporting Initiative (GRI). Third, we synthesize the literature which underpins the considerations for sustainable supply chain management, and in determining the scope and objectives of our study. Thereafter the methodology used to generate data from the examined case is described followed by the findings and our conclusions.

Literature Review

Supply Chains and Sustainability

The Council of Supply Chain Management Professionals defines a supply chain as "a system of organizations, people, technology, activities, information and resources involved in moving a product or service from supplier to customer" (CSCMP 2012). The concept of supply chains comprises three basic stages—procurement, production and distribution—with each stage consisting of several interrelated activities. It is a complex and sometimes fragile endeavor, which relies on a network of independent yet interconnected organizations. Supply chains commence activities upstream with suppliers of components or raw materials, who then send these to other organizations for manufacture, processing and transformation into finished products. Thereafter such products flow downstream to distributors, wholesalers, agents and retailers, who finally sell them to end users for consumption (Thomas and Griffin 1996).

The traditional supply chain management view is that a firm's competitive position is based on effectively managing operations and resources so as to maximize profits. Abdullah et al. (2004) highlighted that supply chain management focused on effective downstream flows in their operations for the end customer through quality delivery in an expedient and frugal manner, implying the ultimate objectives of cost reduction and profit maximization in various activities. With this notion, it was found that firms competed with each other in their supply chain in order to maximise their own interests (Wernerfelt 1984), often neglecting environmental and social concerns at the broader level. However, over the past few decades, supply chains have transformed significantly, as business leaders came to understand that to remain competitive and sustainable, all activities and processes of the supply chain need to be integrated in order to achieve shared goals and ethical practices. Similarly, sustainability should be viewed as a shared vision and a core business paradigm in the supply chain with extensive participation, coordination and commitment of all firms.

In this way supply chain management plays a key role since it affects the extraction, transportation, production and consumption of materials and products, which all have major impacts on the environment and society. For instance, around 70 % of fossil fuels in the United States are consumed in industrial and transportation activities (Gupta and Palsule-Desai 2011). Likewise, all aforementioned activities are considerably concerned with social issues as a result of interacting with people and communities inside or outside of the supply chain. Therefore, a supply chain must be managed not only in terms of optimizing economic objectives, i.e., costs, quality and lead times (Sameer and Jayavel 2003), but also in terms of minimizing the environmental effects and social impacts at the supply chain level. In this way all three dimensions of sustainability can be viewed as a shared vision of those firms involved in the supply chain: refereed to as 'sustainable supply chain management'.

Sustainable Supply Chain Management

Sustainable supply chain management is a new, rapidly growing and highly important field for both research and practice (Ashby et al. 2012; Ramudhin et al. 2010). Following Elkington's triple bottom line conceptualization of sustainability, sustainable supply chain management (SSCM) is defined as "the strategic, transparent integration and achievement of an organization's social, environmental, and economic goals in the systemic coordination of key inter-organizational business processes for improving the long-term economic performance of the individual company and its supply chains" (Carter and Rogers 2008, p. 368). In sustainable supply chains, the social and environmental impacts need to be enhanced by the members to remain in the supply chain, while the overall economic feasibility is maintained (Seuring and Müller 2008). In fact, growing environmental issues such as greenhouse gas (GHG) emissions (Gupta and Palsule-Desai 2011) and social concerns such as the use of forced labor and child labor (Andersen and Skjoett-Larsen 2009) have invoked many organizations to consider a wider range of objectives rather than just economic objectives both at organizational and supply chain levels. Furthermore, pressure from various stakeholders, including consumers, shareholders, governments, non-governmental organizations (NGOs), public authorities and trade unions have compelled organizations to manage more sustainable supply chains (Andersen and Skjoett-Larsen 2009). The introduction of various environmental legislations (e.g., carbon tax), standards (e.g., ISO 14000), and also corporate social responsibility standards (e.g., SA 8000) would mean that companies at the chain level must now move beyond the single economic objective and incorporate a balance of all three dimensions of sustainability, which could often be conflicting for decision-makers since a complex trade-off exists among these dimensions. This is a common problem faced by organizations during the supplier selection process, where not all suppliers can meet all three objectives of lower operating costs, and reduced social and environmental risks simultaneously. As a result, the decision on which supplier to employ becomes a dilemma.

The aforementioned point highlights that sustainability issues could impact decisions at the supply chain level. While some sustainability decisions can pay for themselves and add value in supply chains, as, for example, recycling materials in reverse logistics or managing energy usage efficiently, there are some choices that undermine environmental, social and financial performances directly or indirectly (Ross et al. 2012). Despite this fact, the implications of social and environmental impacts in decision-making are now more essential than before. That is why "93 % of CEOs believe that sustainability issues will be critical to the future success of their business" according to the United Nations Global Compact report (2010, p. 13). Since organizations seek strategic alliances with their supply chain partners to reap the benefits of the pivotal role of supply chain management in business success (Cousins et al. 2006; Shapiro 2007; Tan et al. 2002), they increasingly aim to implement sustainability at the supply chain level. Likewise, the area of sustainable supply chain management has been considerably researched and publicized, particularly in the last decade, to provide insights for enhancing sustainability.

While the current comprehension of sustainability is the consideration of social, environmental and economic dimensions (Seuring and Müller 2008), the relative proliferation of literature and research has predominantly dealt with one or two dimensions in isolation (Pagell and Wu 2009; Ashby et al. 2012). Moreover, sustainability has been misinterpreted as green or environmental practices by some researchers and businesses, leading to the neglect of the ethical aspects or social dimension of sustainability (Carter and Easton 2011). Based on a comprehensive review of the literature spanning over 13 years from 1994 to 2007, Seuring and Müller (2008) identified that only 31 published articles have really addressed and discussed all three dimensions, thereby resulting in an appeal for future research to adopt this integrated approach (Boloori Arabani and Farahani 2012; Pishvaee et al. 2012; Seuring 2012; Seuring and Müller 2008).

Economic Dimension

Economic sustainability in supply chain management has been largely researched in the literature and is often the starting point in establishing supply chains (Seuring 2012; Seuring and Müller 2008). There are four core elements including supply, operations, logistics and integration (Wisner 2012). Each of them embraces important issues which impact economic sustainability of the chain. Supplier strategic alliances in the supply element, product design in the operations element, marketing issues and global network in the logistics element and finally performance measurement in the integration element are just some examples of those important issues that must be dealt with by decision-makers to managing supply chains (Wisner 2012).

Supply chain management traditionally focuses on economic based performance indicators with the main intention to minimize total costs in the supply chain while meeting market demands (Chaabane et al. 2008; Shapiro 2007). This requires an optimised balance between both sub-objectives of costs and responsiveness (Chopra 2010). Supply chain costs, which can be classified as fixed and variable costs, cover raw material and other acquisition, production and facility investment costs as well as raw material, intermediate and finished product transportation within supply chain tiers, i.e., from suppliers to plants, from plants to distribution centres and finally to retailers (Pishvaee et al. 2012; Ramudhin et al. 2010). While it is believed that cost reduction may affect market responsiveness, there are other measures and strategies adopted in supply chain management which help overcome this paradox and enable long-term financial prosperity and overall economic sustainability. These include effective demand planning, inventory management, capacity management, lean approaches, facility location and supply chain network design (Amit and Subhash 2005; Boloori Arabani and Farahani 2012; Melo et al. 2009; Ross et al. 2012; Shen 2007).

Social Dimension

The ethical and social considerations in businesses today require firms to consider issues beyond organizational boundaries and include supply chain practices (Brammer et al. 2011; Dreyer et al. 2006). The commercial and reputational risks (Carter and Rogers 2008), which arise from social violations not only threaten product brand image, but also impact on consumer confidence and loyalty. The publicized cases of Nike, Gap, H&M and Mattel (Frost and Burnett 2007) in their oversight of supply chain operations has sparked public concerns about ethical practices, union rights, and use of underaged workers (Andersen and Skjoett-Larsen 2009) particularly by upstream suppliers. For example, the design flaws in Mattel's toys comprising small, high power magnets which could come loose and be swallowed by infants and children (Lyles et al. 2008) caused a worldwide product recall in 2007 and ultimately loss of consumer confidence in Mattel.

The social impacts of the supply chain must not only envisage legislative issues pertaining to human rights, working conditions or product safety, but also ascertain the impacts on communities and the larger society as a whole. The intersection of social and environmental sustainability implies links in human activity to the ethical and natural consequences of the ecosystem (from the extraction and transportation of raw materials to the deposit or recycling of waste of products) and the well-being of society (Sanders 2012). There are various approaches and standards established to support social sustainability in supply chains such as Social Accountability 8000 (SA 8000), codes of conduct, supplier development and also social life cycle assessment (SLCA), which integrate social impacts into life cycle assessment approach (Hutchins and Sutherland 2008; Seuring and Müller 2008). Additionally, Dreyer et al. (2010) proposed a framework which incorporates those social issues related to human dignity, human health and basic needs fulfilment.

Environmental Dimension

Supply chain activities also include extracting raw materials, purchasing, manufacturing, packaging, transporting and recycling products; all of which present a considerable threat to the environment (Wisner 2012). This threat encompass GHGs, such as carbon dioxide and methane, hazardous materials, toxic chemicals and other pollutions as well as land use and resource depletion issues (Sanders 2012). This has led to the recent surge in government intervention in mitigating such environmental problems such as the European Union and Australian carbon pricing scheme and China's import restrictions on cadmium and mercury (Wisner 2012). Nevertheless many supply chains have introduced various initiatives to comply with environmental legislations and regulations. This includes Timberland, a US-based company that deals with personal and household goods, which adopted the Green Index environmental rating system in its supply chain. The objective was to minimize the harmful impacts, particularly in resource consumption, climate and chemical use. Timberland believes that this index will help its supply chain members to use less harmful chemicals and carbon-intensive materials, thereby enhancing environmental sustainability (United Nations Global Compact 2012).

Over the past two decades, the environmental aspect of supply chain management has been a prominent research area with the terms 'green supply chain management', 'green operations' and 'green design' emerging (Carter and Easton 2011;

Srivastava 2007, p. 57). While waste management, reverse logistics, network design and remanufacturing are some of the key challenges of green operations, the literature emphasizes both 'environmentally conscious design (ECD)' and 'life cycle assessment/analysis (LCA)' approaches to address environmental sustainability. LCA, often called 'cradle to grave' analysis, is a comprehensive analytical tool in quantifying the environmental impacts related to the production, processing, packaging, distribution, use and disposal of a product. The focus of LCA is on the intensity of resource utilization (e.g., energy, water) and the environmental impact of outputs (e.g., by-products, waste and emissions) at each stage of the supply chain, with the aim of identifying opportunities for improving resource use, reducing environmental impacts and targeting parts of the life cycle where improvements can be made (ISO 2006; Matos and Hall 2007; Rebitzer et al. 2004; Thoma et al. 2012; Tsoulfas and Pappis 2006). Additionally, the ISO 14000 provides guidance on environmental management standards for establishing a green supply chain (Carter and Rogers 2008; Seuring and Müller 2008; Srivastava 2007; Wisner 2012).

Guidelines for Sustainable Supply Chains

Various media, NGO campaigns, regulatory frameworks, customers and consumers advocate for guidelines and tools in implementing sustainable practices in supply chains. Although individual chain members provide differing products, services and functions at various stages, there are a number of consistent themes which could guide sustainability at the chain level. In 2003, the New Zealand Business Council for Sustainable Development introduced a business guide for sustainable supply chains as a "catalyst for change toward sustainable development and to promote eco-efficiency, innovation and responsible entrepreneurship" (Sustainable Business Council 2003, p. 2). It embraced a view where sustainable development must extend from an individual company to both upstream and downstream partners in the supply chain. The espoused framework stems from a process management approach and addresses three main areas concerning procurement (particularly monitoring external suppliers and setting codes of conduct), internal operations (considering the impact of product transformation and forward and reverse logistics) and product development and stewardship (which entail the effective collaboration with chain partners in the design, manufacture and distribution of products) (Sustainable Business Council 2003). While building this chain of custody requires a cogent approach, the framework also suggests complying with various systems such as ISO14001, SA8000, AA11000 and Enviro-Mark which could be incorporated into existing HACCP, OHS or quality management systems.

The United Nations Global Compact Management is another model, which is deemed a comprehensive approach for firms to embed sustainability in their supply chains. The model, which was introduced in 2010, prescribes ten principles that address the four main areas of human rights; fighting corruption, environmental management and sustainability. Due to the widespread concerns about poor social and environmental conditions of supplier practices in developing economies, this model streamlines various regulations and encourages firms to embrace such issues. The global compact model was suggested as a framework for continuous improvement and mainstreaming into strategies and operations for supply chains as a collective unit. It defines supply chain sustainability as the "management of environmental, social and economic impacts, and the encouragement of good governance practices, throughout the lifecycles of goods and services" (BSR 2010, p. 7). It prompts firms to evaluate a business case for action and understand all the steps involved in the entire supply chain operations. Thereafter, firms can translate their sustainability expectations into a set of guidelines for suppliers such as abiding with relevant regulation and being proactive in minimizing environmental and social harm (BSR 2010).

A shortcoming of the Global Compact Model is the heavy focus on engaging mainly with upstream members in the chain to address the ten principles (pertaining to human rights, corporate governance and environmental issues). It fails to detail the downstream considerations for supply chains, such as dealing with distributors, retailers and consumer use of products or end of life issues. This is acknowledged as a limitation in the current guide and acknolwdeges that subsequent versions will consider the downstream impacts. Nevertheless, the Global Compact guide for supply chains advocates the need for firms to understand the expectations of their stakeholders and to seek input from them as well as downstream customers. By launching a website as a one-stop shop, businesses are able to not only obtain information about supply chain sustainability, but also to share information about their initiatives, activities and issues during implementation. This website initiative serves as an online assessment and learning tool for firms in their implementation of sustainability throughout the chain.

Another notable guideline for supply chains is the Global Reporting Initiative (GRI) protocol. The GRI is a non-profit, multi-stakeholder, network-based organization that works towards a sustainable global economy by pioneering and developing a comprehensive Sustainability Reporting Framework adopted globally. The GRI realized the increasing importance of sustainability reporting faced by multinational corporations to manage sustainability risks and to build collaborative relationships with their suppliers and customers. Thereafter in 2009, the GRI launched a working group and a set of guidelines to establish a global action network for transparency specifically in supply chains. A draft version of the fourth generation (G4) of reporting guidelines was released in mid-2012. It includes the application levels, boundary disclosure on management approach, governance, and reporting for supply chains. It offers standard disclosures and guidance for organizations when preparing sustainability and disclosure reports. The GRI's indicators are categorized into the three dimensions of sustainability as depicted in Table 6.1.

The GRI guidelines also document the role of a supplier and the differences between adopting a supply chain and value chain approach. According to the GRI, a supplier is an organization or person that provides materials, products or services directly or indirectly to another organization including brokers, consultants, contractors, sub-contractors, distributors, home workers, primary producers and wholesalers (GRI 2012, p. 314). A value chain refers to all parties upstream and downstream

Table 6.1 Categories and aspects of sustainability. (Source: GRI 2012)

Category	Economic		Environmental	
Aspects	Economic performance Market presence Indirect economic impacts Procurement practices		Materials Energy Water Biodiversity Emissions, effluents and waste Products and services Compliance Transport Overall Screening and assessment Remediation	
Category	Social			
Sub categories aspects	*Labor practices and decent work*	*Human rights*	*Society*	*Product responsibility*
	Employment Labor/management relations Occupational health and safety Training and education Diversity and equal opportunity Equal remuneration for women and men Screening and assessment Remediation	Investment Non-discrimination Freedom of association and collective bargaining Child labor Forced and compulsory behavior Security practices Indigenous rights Screening and assessment Remediation	Local communities Corruption Public policy Anti-competitive behavior Compliance Screening and assessment Remediation	Customer health and safety Product and service labelling Marketing communications Customer privacy Compliance

that are linked by the organization's activities, products, services and relationships, and may therefore impact and be impacted by the organizations; whereas the supply chain is only the part of the value chain which consists of the sequence of suppliers and activities upstream that provides materials, products or services to the reporting organization (GRI 2012, p. 316). The GRI protocol instigates firms to adopt the value chain method in assessing and reporting sustainability because this extensive approach encompasses all processes, activities, organizations and relationships in the entire chain, and because it includes both forward and reverse logistics flow of products and services. Therefore, depending on where the focal organization is located in the chain, all tiers of suppliers and customers must be considered (see Fig. 6.1). Take the case of Zara as an example of one of the largest international fashion companies which belongs to the Inditex Group. Although known globally for their ubiquitous retail stores, and for their commitment to sustainable practices, the firm would need to take into account upstream and downstream supply chain partners in growing organic cotton, supply of fabric, manufacture of clothing, transportation and distribution worldwide, retail activities and after sales services for consumers.

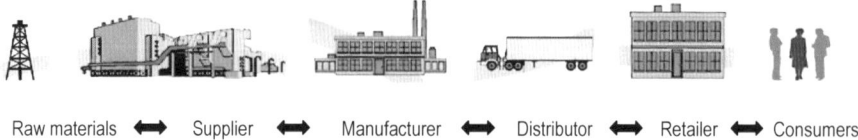

Raw materials ⬌ Supplier ⬌ Manufacturer ⬌ Distributor ⬌ Retailer ⬌ Consumers

Fig. 6.1 Value chain approach encompassing all firms in the chain

Additionally, by using a value chain approach, firms would subsequently need to determine both the boundary (i.e., range of value chain elements) and scope (i.e., extent of economic, social and environmental dimensions) of reporting as it relates to the relevant members in the chain. The wide range and scope of areas to be assessed (as depicted in Table 6.1) may seem challenging, time consuming and costly for organizations to discern. However, firms are recommended to select relevant indicators that may judiciously be considered critical in "reflecting the economic, social and environmental impacts, or in influencing the decisions of stakeholders" (GRI 2012). This can be illustrated in Fig. 6.2.

Organizations will need to evaluate the various scope and boundaries of supply chain sustainability in order to ensure an equitable and modest representation of the impacts and performance of its supply chain members. Sustainability assessment should cover at least the elements or areas in the chain where the organization has or experiences significant impacts. While the GRI protocol and guidelines serve as a useful tool for assessing and reporting sustainability, it can also be used as a learning mechanism to understand the processes, activities and parties involved in the supply chain and which codes of conduct would be deemed most appropriate for various firms' operations and practices. Similar to the New Zealand sustainable development guide, such practices and codes of conduct could be incorporated into overall quality management systems and regular supplier evaluation. Once firms begin to understand the guidelines, requirements and various mechanisms, they are then able to exercise and enforce sustainable practices at the supply chain level.

Based on the literature review, the area of sustainability has received considerable attention in the literature as a topic of enquiry from various disciplines. The established notion of the triple bottom line in enabling economic benefits through improving social standards and preserving the environment for future generations is well accepted and gradually pervading the business arena, including supply chain management. At the strategic level, the long-term objectives of sustainable supply chains would be planning and optimizing the best configuration of suppliers, manufacturers, distribution centres and logistics providers to enhance overall performance of the chain. The strategy of sustainable supply chain management is to obtain competitive advantage for the focal company and its supply chain while meeting consumer and stakeholder needs. We establish that these economic, social and environmental features of sustainability are interrelated and interdependent. Similarly, achieving a balance of all three dimensions of sustainability could

E.g. reporting the entire value chain

E.g. reporting greenhouse gas emissions for the environmental dimension

E.g. reporting child labor for the social dimension

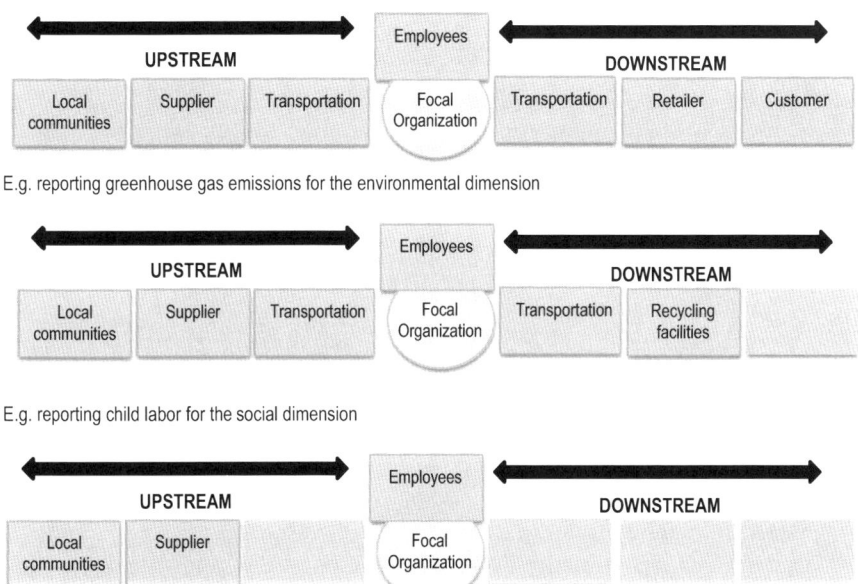

Fig. 6.2 Scope and boundary of reporting. (Source: GRI 2012)

often be challenging for supply chains due to the complex trade-offs involved. The paradox of environmental management and cost effectiveness implies greater pressure on the procurement of products and services; achieving a fully sustainable supply chain is not an easy task as there are often complex structures dealing with multiple products and various parties in global markets. This poses challenges in defining the supply chain scope and boundaries where significant impacts might occur.

In an effort to examine the sustainability initiatives of a supply chain, we selected the Yalumba wine company located in South Australia as the focal organization and its supply chain. The objective of the study was to examine how the three dimensions of sustainability could be further enhanced and to what extent the chain's operations are convergent with consumers' perception of sustainable production of products and services. The empirical study involved examining the value creation (economic dimension) at all stages in the supply chain, the information flow and relationships between supply chain members in enabling a shared vision of ethical practices and corporate social responsibility (social dimension), and the environmental impacts in terms of GHG emissions at each phase of the chain's operations. We also gathered empirical data from consumers in understanding the value they placed in sustainable production of wine.

Case Study of a Sustainable Supply Chain

Methodology

The study adopted an iterative process involving several data collection methods over 36 months in total. However, the bulk of data were collected during 6 months in Australia and the UK. Yalumba's supply chain was mapped using a substantial amount of primary research. This comprised interviews with 57 people from various organizations upstream and downstream in the chain (including secondary chain members). This was further supplemented by an online survey of 77 chain members. In addition, six focus group interviews and an online survey were conducted with 1100 consumers in the UK to perceive the value placed in sustainable production of wine. Consequently, the methodology focuses on these key issues:

- The creation and flow of value at each stage in the chain looking at the efficiency in production and operations, and if investments in such activities provide value and reasonable economic returns. Additionally the value of sustainable wine products from the consumer perspective was also assessed.
- The dynamics of information in the chain from upstream primary production to final consumption as well as the nature of relationships, trust, communication, organizational commitment, and the risks and rewards shared in the chain so as to provide a clearer indication of how social aspects of sustainability could be administered.
- The GHG emissions in each stage of the chain as representing the environmental analysis. The collection and analysis of this data was undertaken at Yalumba as part of their "commitment to sustainable winemaking" (Camilleri 2009) by their senior environmental manager in accordance with environmental management standards, auditing procedures and guidelines. We acknowledge that this study only reports the aggregate emissions at various stages in the chain so as to protect the commercial and confidential issues of those organizations involved in the study.

The supply chain comprises six main stakeholders. One, grape growers in the Riverland, South Australia. This region produces half of South Australia's grapes and a quarter of Australia's wine, the bulk of which is exported. Two, the focal organization i.e., Yalumba Wine Company, which is Australia's oldest family-owned winery and one of the country's largest exporters of wine. It operates two wineries, both in the Barossa Valley at Angaston and Moppa in South Australia. Three, Amcor, one of the world's largest packaging solution providers and a major supplier of glass and corrugated packaging and bottle closures to the Australian and New Zealand wine industry. Four, Tarac Technologies, a company that adopts technologies for reprocessing the residuals from the wine-making processes. Five, Tesco UK, the world's fourth largest supermarket responsible for 25 % of all UK wine sales, making it the single largest overseas buyer and retailer of Australian wine. Six, consumers of wine in the UK (Soosay et al. 2012, p. 70).

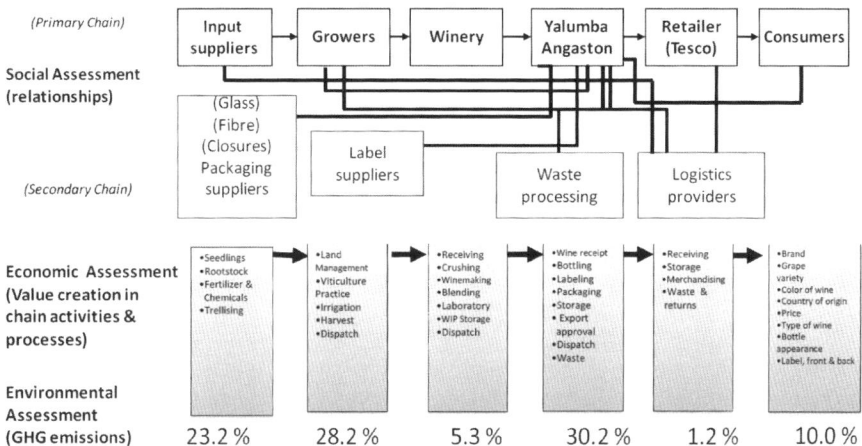

Fig. 6.3 Assessment of the three dimensions of sustainability in the supply chain

Findings

Operating for over 150 years, this family-owned organization specializes in grape growing and wine making. Apart from economic objectives, the company also acknowledges the need to integrate the broader dimensions of environmental and social matters into the firm's strategy and operational decision-making processes. The values of Yalumba have evolved through the years from addressing business and lifestyle demands to including a commitment to the conservation and long-term sustainability of the environment (Camilleri 2009). Yalumba's sustainability initiative required identifying innovative ways to remain profitable whilst simultaneously expanding business goals to include environmental and social concerns. The firm engages with its stakeholders, particularly upstream supply chain members who provide goods and services to the value creation of its quality wine brands. It also adopts the life cycle paradigm with a commitment to expand the concept of cleaner production and sustainability throughout the chain, decrease the resources and emissions to the environment, improve the firm's socio-economic performance, and facilitate links between the economic, social and environmental dimensions (Camilleri 2009).

The analysis of the supply chain is illustrated in Fig. 6.3. The economic assessment entailed mapping all activities and walking through the chain to understand the processes undertaken in every supply chain node. A significant aspect of the supply chain operations is grape growing. The growers are advised on viticulture practice prior to purchasing seedlings and agricultural inputs such as fertilizer, chemicals, rootstock and trellising materials. This is to enhance the economic viability of grapes and wine produced. During viticulture practice, grape growers are encouraged to maximize the opportunities for using ethical and best practices, economies of scale and efficiency in the procurement and use of inputs, machinery, irrigation, harvest and despatch of grapes. The bottling and packaging of wine are carried out at the Yalumba Angaston plant. At this stage, the wine is differentiated into its final packaging where these processes entail different input suppliers; glass and cardboard packaging, closures, labels and consumables amongst other issues (labeled as secondary chain members) (Fearne et al. 2009).

Overall, the processes and operations in the chain appear to be efficient and economically sustainable. We suggest that there is further scope for supply chain members upstream, particularly growers, to improve and engage in best practices. For instance, there are various opportunities to access information on benchmarking, which allows them to compare their efficiency with that of other growers overseas. This assists growers to identify areas for more productive and sustainable practices, particularly in reducing input costs, adopting new technologies, reducing chemical use and dealing with environmental factors such as salinity and water quality. The viticultural and business management capacity of Yalumba's chain could be enhanced to overcome competition from emerging production countries, especially in volume wine. This is because of the increasing emphasis on export markets for wine as there is little room for expansion in the domestic market. As a result, Australian growers must be competitive in the production of quality wine grapes.

Information flow and the nature of relationships were evaluated using data from the semi-structured interviews. The interviewees comprised personnel at various levels in organizations who managed different functional activities in the chain. Overall, we established that relationships in the chain are strong and argue that in order to establish guidelines for ethical and socially responsible practices in the supply chain, Yalumba and its stakeholders within the network will need to the overcome the complexities caused by different cultures, business norms, regulatory environments and economic situations facing each organization (and consumers). It is acknowledged that establishing partnerships and collaborations can be time consuming and demanding. Consequently, as the focal organization, Yalumba needs to invest in those suppliers that can create value, meet their guidelines and also embody sustainable practices. The supply chain mix would be determined by various factors such as "equitable sharing of risk and rewards; degree and type of communication; degree of joint investment and co-innovation; level of trust and commitment; metrics and joint operating controls; scope of activities undertaken by the stakeholders; style, level and content of planning; and the type of contracts used in the relationships" (Camilleri 2009, p. 13). These partners would subsequently then be able to reap equitable profit sharing, reputation, resilience, trust and goodwill in the chain.

The environmental assessment shows upstream activities as generating higher emissions, particularly from growers in viticulture practices and adopting trellising systems; and during the production (bottling and packaging) phase at the winery. These activities represent a high percentage of overall carbon emissions in the chain, while downstream activities, particularly transportation (export), retail and consumption constitute relatively lower emissions. What is notable is that our findings dispel the myth of 'wine miles' where the significance is not about the distance the products travel, but the transportation mode adopted because sea freight

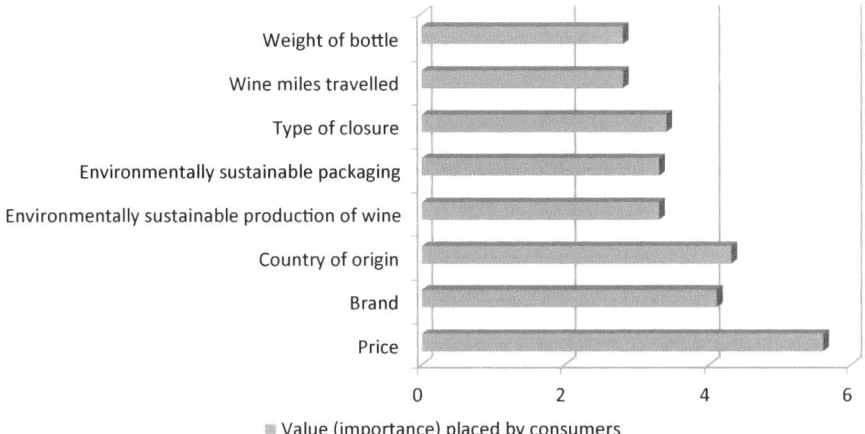

Fig. 6.4 Consumer value for wine

facilitates bulk shipments and is far more eco-friendly than air freight. Therefore the carbon emission per bottle is not significant during export. GHG emission analysis provides substantial input to management decision-making. For example, our findings indicate that although trellises are essential to good grape production, in the sense that they help control vigorous vines, sunlight penetration, spray penetration and air flow, they unfortunately contribute to significant emissions in the chain due to the high CO_2 emission involved in the production of timber posts. (Most posts for grapevine trellising systems are timber posts—either pine or hardwood posts.) Similarly, the high emission during viticulture relates to nitrous oxide and methane (which traps heat in the Earth's atmosphere) released during decomposition of biomasses and carbon sequestration by the vines' growth as well as sugar production in the grapes. Additionally, land management refers to emissions associated with farming practices, particularly from power and fuel combustion with the use of machinery and vehicles during harvest and freight movement within the supply chain. This might therefore advocate for organizations to proactively reduce the chain's carbon footprint in such areas.

In order to supplement our findings from the value chain mapping and to include consumer perspectives, we also conducted six focus group interviews and an online survey with 1100 consumers in the UK. The objective was to understand their perception of (economic) value in the product and if sustainability (environmental dimension) was a factor affecting their purchase. The survey entailed a seven-point Likert scale ranging from 1 (not at all important) to 7 (extremely important) and covered various attributes of the wine product, particularly relating to sustainability. Figure 6.4 summarizes the mean scores of importance placed by consumers pertaining to their purchase of wine.

UK consumers tend to place much confidence in Australian wine as a product of acceptable standard and quality. However, our results depict that consumer value and purchase are determined primarily by price, where in the case of a reputable brand is hard to dispute. Whilst Tesco has encouraged their suppliers to reduce their carbon footprints through sustainable production, packaging and carbon labeling, the results from our survey showed that not many UK consumers perceived sustainability as a highly valued attribute in the wine they purchased. The two most important aspects relate to price and where the wine originated, whilst the lowest mean scores were in wine miles and the weight of the bottle. Similarly during the focus group interviews, very few participants perceived any link between the concept of sustainability and wine production. This was poorly understood generally, where many of them believed it to be mostly associated with bottle recycling.

Discussion and Conclusion

Understanding consumer behavior and purchase patterns is a complex process. While most consumers recognize the importance of environmental and ethical production of goods and services, their discernment and resultant purchase vary according to the type of purchase. We establish that sustainability is only one factor affecting consumer's choice of products; where the decision to buy is more importantly determined by price, quality and availability of the product as "the biggest deterrents to buying green products or services are price, a suspicion of deceptive marketing, and availability" (Sustainable Index 2010b, p. 3). However, it is established that those organizations who are committed to offering products and services with low environmental impacts are more likely to win customer loyalty in the long run (Anuwichanont et al. 2011; Gadeikiene et al. 2012; Sustainable Index 2010a). This needs to be supplemented with more initiatives and campaigns designed to encourage more sustainable consumption behavior, and to influence consumer decision-making at the point of purchase. Based on this, we argue that organizations will need to address a myriad of factors to ensure reasonable price, quality and availability, in addition to environmental sustainability of products. Therefore, by focusing on all three dimensions of economic, social and environment sustainability, this can be achieved within a streamlined manner in the supply chain.

Similarly, the paradox of environmental management and cost effectiveness implies greater pressure on the procurement of products and services. The highly dynamic wine industry requires Yalumba to be proactive in the area of social and environmental responsibility if it is to continue to enhance its competitiveness and market position. Achieving a fully sustainable supply chain is not an easy task as there are often complex structures dealing with multiple products and various parties in global markets. This poses challenges in defining the supply chain scope and boundaries where significant impacts might occur. This study has mapped Yalumba's entire value chain from South Australia to the UK by adopting an iterative, complex and time-consuming process in order to identify the various processes, activities and parties involved. What has emerged from our findings is that there are trade-offs between the activities that create value in terms of economic sustainability, the GHG emissions from various activities and the administration of socially responsible practices. We establish that this supply chain is adept to overcoming such challenges, given the established favorable relationships that exist between the partners in the chain. In order to reap commercial returns in a socially and environmentally sustainable way, organizations must proactively recognize relevant issues within the chain and establish appropriate strategies to address them. This may effectively require a set of guidelines, principles and agreed codes of conduct at the chain level with the main objective of generating values of sustainable production of products and services for customers. Additionally, sustainable supply chain management can be implemented through environmental-led, strategic purchasing and supply, supply chain capabilities, product-based green supply, and greening the supply process (Kang et al. 2012). This requires more flexible interaction between all firms involved, long-term and culturally grown partnerships and cross-organizational cooperation strategies between companies. These could then serve as a catalyst for change toward sustainable development, eco-efficiency, innovation and responsible business practices in order to benefit the supply chain as a whole.

References

Abbasi, M., & Nilsson, F. (2012). Themes and challenges in making supply chains environmentally sustainable. *Supply Chain Management: An International Journal, 17*(5), 517–530.

Abdullah, S., Zairi, M., & Ahmed, A. (2004). Extending the concept of supply chain: The effective management of value chains. *International Journal of Production Economics, 87,* 309–320.

Amit, S., & Subhash, D. (2005). Review of supply chain management and logistics research. *International Journal of Physical Distribution and Logistics Management, 35*(9), 664–705.

Andersen, M., & Skjoett-Larsen, T. (2009). Corporate social responsibility in global supply chains. *Supply Chain Management: An International Journal, 14*(2), 75–86.

Anuwichanont, J., Mechinda, P., Serirat, S., Lertwannawit, A., & Popaijit, N. (2011). Environmental sustainability in the Thai hotel industry. *International Business and Economics Research Journal, 10*(11), 91–100.

Ashby, A., Leat, M., & Hudson-Smith, M. (2012). Making connections: A review of supply chain management and sustainability literature. *Supply Chain Management: An International Journal, 17*(5), 497–516.

Boloori Arabani, A., & Farahani, R. Z. (2012). Facility location dynamics: An overview of classifications and applications. *Computers & Industrial Engineering, 62*(1), 408–420.

Brammer, S., Hoejmose, S., & Millington, A. (2011). Managing sustainable global supply chains- a systematic review of the body of knowledge. Network for business sustainability, business. Thinking. Ahead. www.nbs.net/knowledge/supply-chains. Accessed 19 Sept 2012.

BSR. (2010). The business case for supply chain sustainability: A brief for business leaders. www.bsr.org. Accessed 10 Oct 2012.

Camilleri, C. S. (2009). *The life cycle paradigm as an intrinsic component of supply network and value analysis.* Proceedings of the 6th Australian Conference on life cycle assessment: Sustainability tools for a new climate, 16–19 Feb, Melbourne, Australia.

Carter, C., & Easton, P. (2011). Sustainable supply chain management: Evolution and future direction. *International Journal of Physical Distribution and Logistics Management, 41*(1), 46–62.

Carter, C., & Rogers, D. (2008). A framework of sustainable supply chain management: Moving toward new theory. *International Journal of Physical Distribution and Logistics Management, 38*(5), 360–387.

Chaabane, A., Ramudhin, A., Paquet, M., & Benkaddour, M. A. (2008). *An integrated logistics model for environmental conscious supply chain network design*. Proceedings of AMCIS Paper 175. http://aisel.aisnet.org/amcis2008/175. Accessed 1 Aug 2012.

Chopra, S. (2010). *Supply chain management: Strategy, planning, and operation* (4th ed.). Upper Saddle River: Prentice Hall.

Council of Supply Chain Management Professionals (CSCMP). (2012). SCSMP supply chain management definitions. http://cscmp.org/aboutcscmp/definitions.asp. Accessed 6 June 2012

Cousins, P. D., Lawson, B., & Squire, B. (2006). Supply chain management: Theory and practice—the emergence of an academic discipline? *International Journal of Operations and Production Management, 26*(7), 697–702.

de Barcellos, M. D., Krystallis, A., de Melo Saab, M. S., Kugler, J. O., & Grunert, K. G. (2011). Investigating the gap between citizens' sustainability attitudes and food purchasing behaviour: Empirical evidence from Brazilian pork consumers. *International Journal of Consumer Studies, 35,* 391–402.

Dreyer, L., Hauschild, M., & Schierbeck, J. (2006). A framework for social life cycle impact assessment. *The International Journal of Life Cycle Assessment, 11*(2), 88–97.

Dreyer, L., Hauschild, M., & Schierbeck, J. (2010). Characterisation of social impacts in LCA-Part1—development of indicators for labour rights. *The International Journal of Life Cycle Assessment, 15*(3), 247–259.

Elkington, J. (1999). *Cannibals with forks: The triple bottom line of 21st century business*. Oxford: Capstone.

Fearne, A., Soosay, C., Stringer, R., Umberger, W., Dent, B., Camilleri, C., Henderson, D., et al. (2009). *Sustainable value chain analysis: A case study of South Australian wine*. A report to the Primary Industries and Resources, Government of South Australia. http://www.pir.sa.gov.au/__data/assets/pdf_file/0003/93225/V2D_Final_Report.pdf. Accessed 3 Jan 2012.

Frost, S., & Burnett, M. (2007). Case study: The Apple iPod in China. *Corporate Social Responsibility and Environmental Management, 14*(2), 103–113.

Gadeikiene, A., Banyte, J., & Kasiuliene, I. (2012). The development of long-term relationships with green consumers in the context of sustainability trends in Lithuanian textile market. *Eurasian Business Review, 2*(2), 71–95.

Gimenez, C., & Tachizawa, E. (2012). Extending sustainability to suppliers: A systematic literature review. *Supply Chain Management: An International Journal, 17,* 531–543.

Global Reporting Initiative (GRI). (2012). Global reporting initiative second G4 public comment period: Overview, global reporting organisation. https://www.globalreporting.org/reporting/latest-guidelines/g4-developments/Pages/G4-Development-Process.aspx. Accessed 15 Mar 2012.

Gupta, S., & Palsule-Desai, O. D. (2011). Sustainable supply chain management: Review and research opportunities. *IIMB Management Review, 23*(4), 234–245.

Hassani, E., Surti, C., & Searcy, C. (2012). A literature review and case study of sustainable supply chains with a focus on metrics. *International Journal of Production Economics, 140*(1), 69–82.

Hutchins, M. J., & Sutherland, J. W. (2008). An exploration of measures of social sustainability and their application to supply chain decisions. *Journal of Cleaner Production, 16*(15), 1688–1698.

International Organisation for Standardisation (ISO). (2006). ISO 14040:2006 environmental management: Life cycle assessment- principles and framework. www.iso.org. Accessed 11 Mar 2013.

Kang, S. H., Kang, B., Shin, K., Kim, D., & Han, J. (2012). A theoretical framework for strategy development to introduce sustainable supply chain management. *Procedia-Social and Behavioral Sciences, 40,* 631–635.

Lyles, A. M., Flynn, B. B., & Frohlich, T. M. (2008). All supply chains don't flow through: Understanding supply chain issues in product recalls. *Management and Organization Review, 4*(2), 167–182.

Matos, S., & Hall, J. (2007). Integrating sustainable development in the supply chain: The case of life cycle assessment in oil and gas and agricultural biotechnology. *Journal of Operations Management, 25,* 1083–1102.

Melo, M. T., Nickel, S., & Saldanha-da-Gama, F. (2009). Facility location and supply chain management: A review. *European Journal of Operational Research, 196*(2), 401–412.

Pagell, M., & Wu, Z. (2009). Building a more complete theory of sustainable supply chain management using case studies of 10 exemplars. *Journal of Supply Chain Management, 45*(2), 37–56.

Pishvaee, M. S., Torabi, S. A., & Razmi, J. (2012). Credibility-based fuzzy mathematical programming model for green logistics design under uncertainty. *Computers & Industrial Engineering, 62*(2), 624–632.

Ramudhin, A., Chaabane, A., & Paquet, M. (2010). Carbon market sensitive sustainable supply chain network design. *International Journal of Management Science and Engineering Management, 5*(1), 30–38.

Rebitzer, G., Ekvall, T., Frischknecht, R., Hunkeler, D., Norriydberg, T., Schnidt, W. P., Suh, S., Weidema, B. O., et al. (2004). Life cycle assessment part 1: Framework, goal and scope definition, inventory analysis and applications. *Environment International, 20,* 701–720.

Ross, A., Parker, H., & Benavides, M. (2012). Sustainability and supply chain infrastructure development. *Management Decision, 50*(10), 1891–1910.

Sameer, P., & Jayavel, S. (2003). Factors influencing global supply chain efficiency: Implications for information systems. *Supply Chain Management: An International Journal, 8*(3), 241–250.

Sanders, N. R. (2012). *Supply chain management: A global perspective.* Hoboken: Wiley.

Seuring, S. (2013). A review of modeling approaches for sustainable supply chain management. *Decision Support Systems, 54*(4), 1513–1520.

Seuring, S., & Müller, M. (2008). From a literature review to a conceptual framework for sustainable supply chain management. *Journal of Cleaner Production, 16*(15), 1699–1710.

Seuring, S., & Sarkis, J., Müller, M., & Rao, P. (2008). Sustainability and supply chain management—an introduction to the special issue. *Journal of Cleaner Production, 16*(15), 1545–1551.

Shapiro, J. F. (2007). *Modeling the supply chain.* Australia: Thomson Brooks/Cole.

Shen, Z. J. M. (2007). Integrated supply chain design models: A survey and future research directions. *Journal of Industrial and Management Optimization, 3*(1), 1–27.

Soosay, C., Fearne, A., & Dent, B. (2012). Sustainable value chain analysis—A case study of Oxford Landing from vine to dine. *Supply Chain Management: An International Journal, 17*(1), 68–77.

Srivastava, S. K. (2007). Green supply chain management—A state of the art literature review. *International Journal of Management Reviews, 9*(1), 53–80.

Sustainable Business Council. (2003). Business guide to a sustainable supply chain: A practical guide, New Zealand council for sustainable development. http://www.sbc.org.nz/supplychain/. Accessed 11 Nov 2011.

Sustainable Index. (2010a). Consumer attitudes and perceptions on sustainability. The Guardian: Sustainable business, June. http://image.guardian.co.uk/sys-files/Guardian/documents/2010/06/11/GSiJun2010.pdf. Accessed 14 Aug 2012.

Sustainable Index. (2010b). Consumer attitudes and perceptions on sustainability. The Guardian: Sustainable business, March. http://image.guardian.co.uk/sys-files/Environment/documents/2010/07/06/Consumer-attitudes-and-perceptions-on-sustainability-March-2010.pdf. Accessed 14 Aug 2012.

Tan, K. C., Lyman, S. B., & Wisner, J. D. (2002). Supply chain management: A strategic perspective. *International Journal of Operations and Production Management, 22*(6), 614–631.

Thoma, G., Popp, J., Nutter, D., Shonnard, D., Ulrich, R., Matlock, M., Kim, D. S., Neiderman, Z., Kemper, N., East, C., et al. (2013). Greenhouse gas emissions from milk production and consumption in the United States: A cradle-to-grave life cycle assessment circa 2008. *International Dairy Journal, 31*(1), S3–S14.

Thomas, J., & Griffin, P. (1996). Coordinated supply chain management. *European Journal of Operational Research, 94,* 1–15.

Tsoulfas, G. T., & Pappis, C. P. (2006). Environmental principles applicable to supply chains design and operations. *Journal of Cleaner Production, 14,* 1593–1602.

United Nations Global Compact. (2012). Sustainable supply chains: Resources and practices. http://www.unglobalcompact.org/. Accessed 15 Dec 2012.

United Nations Global Compact Office and Business for Social Responsibility. (2010). Supply chain sustainability: A practical guide for continuous improvement. United Nations. http://supply-chain.unglobalcompact.org/site/article/68. Accessed 12 Jan 2013.

Walters, D., & Rainbird, M. (2007). *Strategic operations management: A value chain approach.* New York: Palgrave Macmillan.

Wernerfelt, B. (1984). A resource-based view of the firm. *Strategic Management Journal, 5,* 171–180.

Wisner, J. D. (2012). *Principles of supply chain management: A balanced approach* (3rd ed.). Mason: South-Western, Cengage Learning.

Chapter 7
Life Cycle Analysis and Sustained Organisation Change in Auto Repair Shops

Barbara Resta, Paolo Gaiardelli and Anna Pistoni

Introduction

No other sector has had an impact so relevant on human life than the automotive sector, since Karl Benz registered the patent for his 'Motorwagen' in 1886. Indeed, the invention of the car has changed not only the idea of transportation around the world, affecting the way people live and relate to each other, but it has also created the condition for the growth in our economy. This, in turn, has influenced our society in many ways and has introduced a wide array of environmental consequences and challenges (Orsato and Wells 2007). In particular, the positive contributions to the world's economy and society are offset by significant environmental impacts.

While the introduction of automobile transportation represents a revolution in mobility, a statement of welfare and a symbol of personal economic growth, freedom and openness, the word car can be associated with urban sprawl and decay, a rise in obesity, fatal accidents, air and water pollution, noise pollution and the depletion of natural resources. For example, traffic emissions are one of the major sources of air pollution in Western industrialized countries (Krämer et al. 2000). Exhaust fumes from cars are responsible for approximately 30 % of global atmospheric emissions and 17 % of the emissions of CO_2 (Carley and Spapens 1998). They are a major contributor to the process of climate change (SustainAbility/UNEP 2001), and they have a number of outcomes, including reduced life expectancy, respiratory diseases, allergic illnesses and symptoms, as well as various forms of cancer (Heinrich et al. 2003).

B. Resta (✉) · P. Gaiardelli
CELS—Research Group on Industrial Engineering, Logistics and Service Operations, University of Bergamo, Department of Engineering, Viale Marconi 5, 24044 Dalmine (BG), Italy
e-mail: barbara.resta@unibg.it

A. Pistoni
Department of Economics, Insubria University, Varese, Italy

Department of Accounting, Bocconi University, Milan, Italy

© Springer Science+Business Media Dordrecht 2014   91
S. Sandhu et al. (eds.), *Linking Local and Global Sustainability,* The International Society of Business, Economics, and Ethics Book Series 4, DOI 10.1007/978-94-017-9008-6_7

In addition, as mentioned by the Cleaner Vehicles Task Force (2000), the manufacture and disposal of vehicles notably influences Earth's resource dilapidation and environmental degradation because:

- Automobile manufacturing processes are associated with high levels of use of natural resources such as raw materials, water and energy;
- Some elements of vehicle manufacturing (such as metals and paints) result in the emission of pollutants into environment;
- The extensive geographical scale of the automotive industry involves the transportation of a significant amount of materials and goods;
- At the end of their life, vehicles represent an enormous waste stream. As mentioned by the general reports edited by the European Community, scrapped cars generate between 8 and 9 million t of waste materials every year in the EU alone (European Commission 2000).

The strategic relevance of environmental sustainability has driven car producers to look at new business models and to direct their investments towards the manufacture of goods and services with low environmental impact. Enlarging the business vision from a purely economic perspective to a wider view including environmental issues is therefore the unique way to maintain competitiveness in terms of financial, strategic and marketing benefits. Nevertheless, practical and theoretical literature shows that both organizational and legislative solutions adopted by the automotive industry have been implemented with a primary focus on technological innovation at the level of product development, as well as production processes. Scant attention has been devoted to sustainability, particularly with reference to network configuration and organization (e.g., partners, suppliers, service providers, recyclers), infrastructures (e.g. facilities, equipment, logistics) and related activities (e.g., distribution, sales and service).

Automotive companies seem to have devoted less effort to promoting sustainable actions for service activities, particularly after-sales such as repair and maintenance. Although these activities represent one of the most promising and attracting business opportunities, not only for their economic importance but also for the key role played in driving customers to service loyalty and repurchase intent (Mathieu 2001), sustainable empirical applications in this business are highly sporadic and are often limited to single initiatives (Castle 2001; Graedel 1998).The application of sustainability concepts in the auto repair service should represent a new fundamental way for companies to achieve competitiveness, not only in terms of process efficiency but also in terms of added value creation for the final customer, who is becoming more and more sensitive to this topic (Smith 2008).

In such a context, this chapter attempts to investigate the application of sustainability principles to after-sales service management, through the development of an empirical approach based on Life Cycle Assessment (LCA) techniques. In particular, the model refers to the auto repair industry, identifying the critical elements in managing repair processes and workshop infrastructures and proposing a set of indicators to measure and control workshop performance with a viable perspective.

The chapter is organized as follows: in the second section an overview of some initiatives related to the sustainability concepts that are currently present in the market is given; in the third section the framework developed for the implementation of sustainability in the after-sales service is described, while Sect. 4 provides a first empirical application. Finally, conclusive considerations on strengths and weakness of the proposed model are presented in Sect. 5.

Sustainability in the Automotive Industry: Evidence from the Field

In order to reduce the environmental impact associated with their products, car producers are focusing investments on designing advanced technology vehicles with a low carbon footprint and producing them with as little impact to the environment as possible.

First of all, great strides have been made at the product innovation level in improving vehicle fuel efficiency and safety and reducing exhaust emissions to decrease the environmental burden associated with the use phase through the introduction of alternative fuels, such as ethanol, biodiesel, natural gas, hydrogen and electricity and the development of new generation hybrid propulsion systems. Renault Zoe, Ford Focus Electric, Smart Electric Drive, Nissan LEAF and Citroën C-Zero are just a few examples of fully electric cars recently released onto the market, while the Toyota Prius Plug-in Hybrid (PHV) is tangible evidence of car makers' efforts towards providing effective, efficient and sustainable vehicles. Awarded the Green Car Report's Best Car to Buy 2012, the Prius PHV is based on a third generation Toyota Prius outfitted with lithium-ion batteries co-developed with Panasonic, which enables all-electric operation at higher speeds and longer distances than the conventional Prius Hybrid.

However, before manufacturers can begin selling alternative-fuelled vehicles in a given region, there must be an adequate and convenient refuelling infrastructure. With e-mobility in Italy, for example, Smart (Daimler Group) and Enel, Italy's largest power company, have developed a joint pilot project for the introduction of electric mobility which makes possible the diffusion and efficient use of electric vehicles with rapid and innovative recharge technologies, able to offer safe and intelligent services. Smart provided 100 select customers with electric vehicles on lease agreements, while Enel was responsible for the development and the management of the infrastructure that delivers only certified energy coming from renewable sources. The pilot project, active from 2010 to 2011 in three major Italian cities, has been a stepping stone for the introduction of the electric Smart in the official product offering. Analogous initiatives promoted by other car makers exist in several European cities.

Additionally, automakers are working with industry partners on material selection and management to eliminate the remaining trace amounts of mercury in automobiles, increase the use of recyclable content, and to expand the use of renewable materials presently used, as well as to develop new materials and applications for other renewable materials.

With regards to the production process, car makers have focused their efforts on the efficient utilization of input, reducing energy consumption at manufacturing plants and logistics sites, using renewable energy and promoting an efficient use of resources. They are also working on the generation of outputs, working on waste management, and on the development of smart solutions for employee mobility (e.g., promoting green travel plans). For example, at the BMW Group, named the automotive industry's Super Sector Leader for the seventh time in the Dow Jones Sustainability Index in 2012, corporate sustainability is firmly entrenched throughout the entire value chain: from the development of fuel-saving and alternative vehicle concepts through clean production processes to green recycling practices.

The attention to environmental sustainability of the automotive industry is not only linked to product innovation and manufacturing and logistic process reengineering by automakers. The whole business model and many other actors are involved in this unavoidable shift towards a more sustainable vision. For example, the introduction of solutions based on the principle of satisfying mobility needs rather than purely owning the vehicle represents a further application of environmentally sustainable approaches. Proposals like the long-term lease, car-sharing or car-pooling, besides the generation of other business opportunities, favour better control of a vehicle's reliability, facilitating their accessibility, allowing a greater level of utilization, and having benefits in safety and quality of life. It has been estimated that the diffusion of such new service solutions can reduce the number of cars by about 40 % and distances driven by up to 60 % (Steininger et al. 1996) and will play an important role in 'smart cities' of the future. For example, Car2go is a new mobility concept launched by Daimler in several cities in Europe and North America. The subsidiary makes available Smart vehicles for leasing on a pay-as-you-go scheme within the city 24/7. Similarly, Mu by Peugeot is an innovative mobility solution that mixes aspects of regular car hire and car clubs, and rents out bikes, scooters and even accessories using a prepaid card that can be topped up online at any time.

Still, though much has already been done, a great deal remains. In fact, within this big picture, very little attention has been paid to service, repair and maintenance activities that have environmental impacts through the use of natural resources, and the release of harmful workshop emissions. Sustainable initiatives in this area often appear limited to a single repair and maintenance activity rather than to a specific workshop equipment or infrastructure. For example, Toyota Motor Italy (in cooperation with Lifegate) has been promoting the Eco check-up since 2008. This offering consists of a car maintenance service, aimed to guarantee car availability aligned with full respect for the environment. Thanks to advanced technologies and spare parts, it is possible to reduce fuel consumption and travelling costs, increase the performance and the life of mechanical components, whilst at the same time balancing CO_2 emissions. Another initiative devoted to the introduction of sustainability principles in after-sales services have been launched by the Volvo Truck Corporation, which is working to build CO_2 neutral dealerships, carrying our environmental ideas through its entire operations. The first CO_2 neutral dealership was built in Verona, Italy, in 2008. With the help of solar panels on the roof of the building, more energy is produced than used and the surplus is sold as green energy.

Whilst on the one hand sustainability has gained high relevance in the corporate strategy of car manufacturers, on the other hand there has been less attention paid towards sustainability in repair and maintenance activities and generally even less in the service sector. The presence of norms that regulate the environmental impact of vehicles has pushed manufacturers to direct investments towards the development of environmentally friendly cars, as well as towards the communication of their positive impacts on the environment to society. Limited attention is paid to the after-sales service world, which is also reflected in the distribution and repair network. In fact, the dealers tend to pay higher attention to the new products, instead of the after-sales activities. Another reason for such a low level of interest is the difficulties that are encountered by companies when attempting to involve all of the suppliers and partners, including the repair workshop network, and diffusing the sustainability culture undertaken by the company.

In such a context, providing specific tools based on the evaluation of empirical evidence may help managers in applying sustainability principles within their own companies and in communicating the benefits to the stakeholders, paving the way towards a greater environmental awareness of the automotive service sector. The next section introduces and describes a framework that has been developed for supporting repair workshops to assess and improve their sustainability levels.

Implementation of Sustainability in the Automotive After-Sales Service: Model Construction

The previous section has shown that car makers have been promoting various applications to reduce their environmental impact. However, environmentally friendly projects for after-sales activities, and in particular for maintenance and repair services, are still scarcely implemented. In order to fill this gap, this section introduces a closed-loop model that is conceived to support auto repair managers in improving the environmental performance of their workshops with a viable perspective. The model, which is based on a set of green indicators, relies on a standard approach to measure and reduce workshops' environmental impacts, save money in the short- as well as in the long-term, and increase a sustainable image of the firm.

In particular, it allows:

- Classifying all processes and activities of an auto repair workshop as well as identifying its main facility features;
- Detecting process inputs (materials and energy provided by external suppliers), outputs (environmental releases in the form of air emissions, water emissions or solid waste) and resources (tools and equipment that support the processes execution), of an automotive repair workshop;

- Linking each process input and the adopted resources with the generated outputs properly, both at process and facility feature levels;
- Calculating the environmental impacts of each process, activity or facility feature using a set of green Key Performance Indicators (KPIs);
- Ranking the 'environmental criticality' of each process and facility feature as well as each input/output or adopted resource, to establish an 'intervention priority list';
- Assessing, selecting and testing the best sustainable solution.

The model is built on the LCA framework. LCA is defined as a "compilation and evaluation of the inputs, outputs, and potential impact of a product system throughout its life cycle" (ISO 14040). It aims at specifying the environmental consequences of a product or a service 'from cradle-to-grave' (Rebitzer et al. 2004), including raw material acquisition, processing and manufacturing, distribution and transportation, use, reuse and maintenance, recycle and waste management (SETAC 1991).

LCA has been selected for three main reasons:

- It is based on an international standard, ISO 14040, which is recognized all over the world;
- It adopts a methodological approach considered as the best available for quantitative and differentiated environmental analysis of products and services;
- It can be used not only to consider the overall product lifecycle, from the resource extraction ('cradle') to the product disposal ('grave'), but also to assess a specific phase of the product lifecycle ('gate to gate'), as repair and maintenance;
- Literature suggests that automotive services might be evaluated by comprehensive LCA techniques (Curran 1996), even if the applications in this field are scarcely explored, since the majority of practical and theoretical research dealing with LCA application refers to vehicle body components (Franze et al. 1995; Franze and Neumann 1995; Makuta et al. 2000; Saur et al. 2000), components for engines and transmission (Keoleian and Kar 2003), vehicle concepts such as recycling (Schmidt et al. 2004), design options (Prendi and Tam 2008), painting (Papasavva et al. 2001), innovative technologies (McCleese and LaPuma 2002) and alternative fuels (MacLean et al. 2000).

In accordance with the LCA framework, development of the model has been carried out in four phases as described in the following.

Phase 1: Project Goal and Scope

The goal of an LCA is to compare a set of environmental effects assignable to a product or a service in order to support the adopted environmental strategy and provide a sound basis for strategic decisions. In this project the goal is the transformation of a traditional auto repair workshop into a sustainable organization whose business model is founded on three pillars at the same time: financial and economic results, environment, and competitiveness. By making the workplace healthier and working activities safer, also social sustainability can be obtained as a direct consequence.

The scope phase of an LCA defines the system boundaries that should include all upstream and downstream processes associated with the production and use of a vehicle. Nevertheless, as previously indicated, an LCA can be also adopted to analyze the environmental impacts of a single product lifecycle phase ('gate-to-gate' option). Based on this assumption the purpose of this project is to evaluate and improve processes and facility features of a repair and maintenance workshop.

Phase 2: The Inventory Analysis (LCI)

Life Cycle Inventory (LCI) analysis gathers data on the environmental burdens associated with a product or a service, listing how much energy or materials are used during the product life cycle and how much waste is generated. In order to fulfil this goal, two separate steps that deal with data retrieval and management have been developed: the first one refers to the analysis of workshop facility features and to process mapping, while the second consists of the construction of an inputs-outputs-resources matrix.

Phase 2.1 Facility Features Analysis and Process Mapping

First of all a panel of experts was formed. It consisted of two academic senior researchers, experienced in LCA and sustainable performance measurement systems, a practitioner in LCA and two auto repair workshop managers. At the time at which the project was launched, none of the experts were involved in any project concerning LCA application in the automotive sector. This choice was made to ensure an independent and neutral evaluation.

Once the team was made, five automotive workshops were selected and an audit campaign was carried out to identify the main processes and features that characterize an auto repair workshop. Data was collected through semi-structured interviews. This format (which does not utilize a fixed array of questions), was chosen in order to reflect the different processes and features of the investigated workshops.

Three main facility features characterizing a generic auto repair workshop were identified: lighting, heating, and water distribution systems.

Moreover, adapting the value chain concept proposed by Porter (1985), four primary and four secondary (cross-supporting) macro-processes were identified. The primary macro-processes, which directly contribute to the value creation are: body repair and maintenance; mechanical and electrical repair and maintenance; tyre replacement, and car washing. The secondary (cross-supporting) processes are: workshop administration, marketing and communication, waste management and cleaning services.

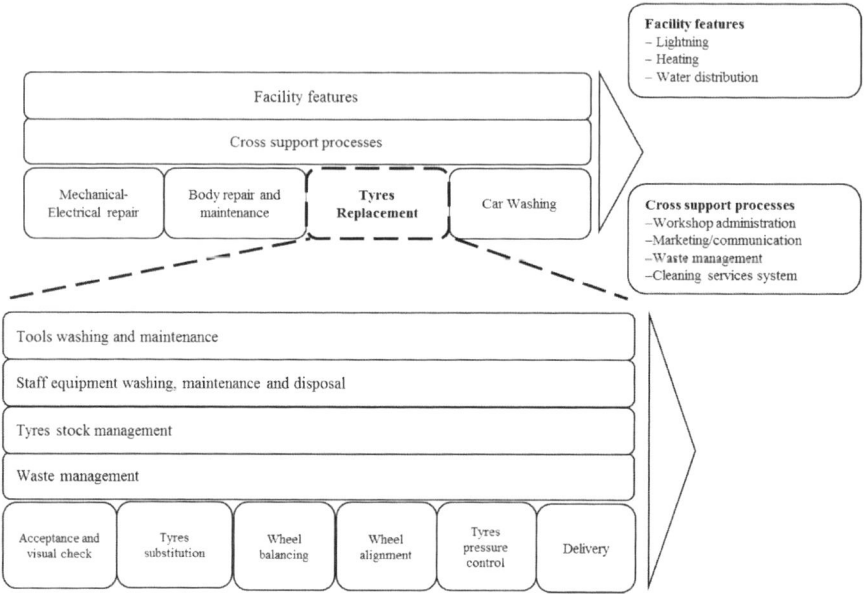

Fig. 7.1 Auto repair workshop processes description: Tyre replacement (general scheme)

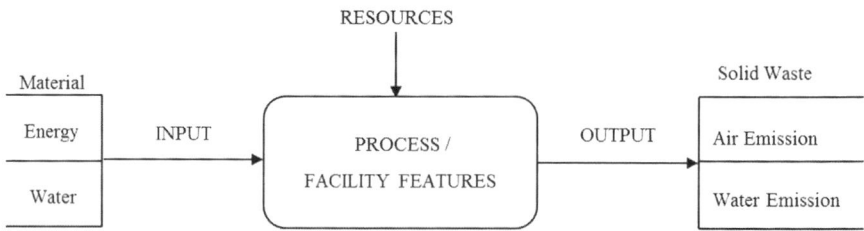

Fig. 7.2 Elements related to each single process/facility feature—general scheme and coding

Afterwards, each single macro-process was broken down into further primary and secondary processes using the same logic indicated above, as shown in Fig. 7.1. The figure illustrates, as an example, the list of processes constituting the tyre replacement macro-process.

Phase 2.2. Construction of an Input-Output-Resources Matrix

Once the process and facility feature mapping was completed, for each single process/facility features, inputs, outputs and resources were identified and coded as shown in Fig. 7.2.

The main result of this process mapping was a comprehensive inventory matrix, containing 87 different inputs, 96 outputs and 45 resources. This matrix can be further extended by detailing and associating each of the single inputs, outputs and resources to each workshop process and facility feature, with relevant values. In such a way, each matrix column can support managers in identifying the input consumption, the output generation and the resource utilization of each process and/or facility feature. Figure 7.4, reported in the Appendix, shows an extract of the matrix, specific to the tyre replacement macro-process (left-hand side of the figure) and workshop facility features (right-hand side of the figure).

Phase 3: The Impact Assessment Phase

The output of Phase 2 was then used to assess the environmental burdens associated with workshop processes and facility features. In order to reach the goal, sustainable performance areas and indicators were identified and a synthesis index enabling the prioritization of sustainable actions was created.

Phase 3.1. Performance Areas and Green KPIs Identification

First of all, environmental performance areas were identified, considering an operative perspective as well as strategic and economic. This analysis was carried out in accordance with the GRI standards (Global Reporting Initiative 2006). Then for each area a set of green KPIs was proposed. The selected indicators were chosen to be simple, precise and easy to calculate and use. They can be used as a basis for a *Workshop Scorecard*, enabling managers to clarify their sustainable vision and and translate them into action as well as to provide feedback about the internal business processes and the external outcomes. A performance target can also be defined for each indicator and used as a benchmark reference to sustain continuous improvement. Table 7.1 reports the detailed list of selected KPIs.

Phase 3.2. Definition of a Synthesis Index

A prioritization is needed to assess the workshop environmental impacts and to decide upon the most important category on which to base the assessment. Such a prioritization could also be useful for external benchmarking, for example to compare the environmental performance of different workshops. For this reason the different input/output values must be weighted, and then added up to develop a Global Warming Index, referring to a specific process, facility feature, input or output.

This index, which has been judged as a unique and most representative eco performance category of a repair and maintenance workshop, has been created through

Table 7.1 Workshop scorecard

Perspective	Performance area	Main KPIs
Operative	Material consumption	Total material consumption
		Consumption of eco-friendly materials
		Consumption of recycled materials
	Energy consumption	Gas consumption
		Electric power
		Electric power from removable
	Water consumption	resources
		Total water consumption
		Non potable water/total
	Waste production	% of generated polluted water
		Total waste production
		% of generated recyclable waste
		% of generated toxic waste
		% of generated differed waste
Strategic &economic perspective	Environmental protection expenses	Total expenses for environmental activities
		Total investments in environmental protection
	Innovation and training	Total costs for waste dismantling
		Training hours on sustainability/training hours
		N° of project on sustainability
		Technical training courses LEV o ZEV

the application of the characterization formula proposed by Heijungs et al. (2004), and adapted by Forster et al. (2007):

$$CC_i = \sum_S GWP_S * V_{si}$$

$$CC_S = \sum_i GWP_S * V_{si}$$

GWPs is the global warming potential (characterization factor) for substance S (input or output) calculated in terms of carbon dioxide (CO_2) equivalent, and V_{si} is the quantity of substance S included in the process/facility feature i. CC_i is the result for climate change of the process/facility feature i, while CC_S is the overall environmental impact of substance S. The characterization factors, quantifying the contribution of each selected indicator to the CO_2 emissions are calculated in accordance to the Clean Planet Standard Protocol (Asja Market 2008). The amount or volume of each substance used in each process or facility feature is available from the inventory and each substance can be characterized by its global warming potential calculated in terms of its carbon dioxide (CO_2) equivalent. Thus it is possible to calculate the contribution to climate change for each substance used in the workshop by summing the individual contributions from that substance in each of the activities. Similarly the contribution to climate change by each process/facility feature can be calculated by summing the contributions from each substance used in that particular process/facility feature. The adopted approach is shown in Fig. 7.5, reported in the Appendix.

Then, the operative KPIs can be assessed in terms of CO_2 emissions using the following formula:

$$CC_{KPI} = \sum_{S \in KPI} CC_S = \sum_{S \in KPI} \sum_i GWP_S * Q_{si}$$

where CC_{KPI} is the KPI result for climate change.

Phase 4: Interpretation of Results

Throughout an LCA, it is necessary to revise the scope of the study by considering the results that emerge from the inventory analysis and impact assessment. Interpretation is used to identify gaps in the data, redirect stages and modify initial goals and system boundaries. An "intervention priority list" can then be created by ranking the 'environmental criticality' of KPIs, processes, facility features or inputs/outputs, identified at the previous step through a brainstorming approach (Osborn 1967) and matched with a weighted scoring method (Charnes et al. 1978).

The relevant outputs delivered can be used to define a set of solutions to be implemented that can decrease the environmental impact, focusing on the most critical activities or infrastructures of a workshop. In particular, three different types of solutions have been identified:

- Facility structure and equipment, such as the installation of a solar plant that allows a green production of electricity and/or of hot water for the heating system;
- Organizational solutions to drive processes towards sustainability, such as the application of lean manufacturing principles that can be adopted to optimize the workshop efficiency in using resources;
- Material supply management and waste disposal, including reuse, recycling and recovery.

The chosen solutions are then assessed with financial tools, to evaluate their investment returns and cash flow impact (Schweitzer et al. 1991; Mishan and Quah 2007; Shrieves and Wachowicz 2001). By constantly collecting data and calculating the indicators defined in Phase 3 and reviewing the results, the development of new indicators may eventually be required, and new solutions could be proposed by applying a continuous improvement approach.

Finally, the model developed for the application at the workshop level can be replicated in all the workshops of an assistance network. Similarly, the specific solutions adopted in a single workshop can be adopted by other companies of that network, exponentially increasing its potential gains.

Table 7.2 Body repair shop inputs, outputs and resources

Inputs		Outputs	
(I1) Distilled water	200 L	(O1) Waste water	150 L
(I2) Scotch tape	1200	(O2) Scotch tape	1200
(I3) Anti silicon additive	25 L	(O3) Waste (metal)	10 Kg
(I4) Gas cylinder (welding)	1	(O4) Gas cylinder (welding)	1
(I5) Blotting paper	35	(O5) Other bottles	0
(I6) Masking paper	150 kg	(O6) Bottle spray (oil/paint)	10
(I7) Seat covers	0	(O7) Distilled water (plastic bottle)	150
(I8) Floor mats	0	(O8) Blotting paper	35
(I9) Steering wheel covers	0	(O9) Paper	0
(I10) Noise proof headphone	0	(O10) Masking paper	150 kg
(I11) Detergent/cleanser	25 L	(O11) Plastic component	300
(I12) Floor cleaner	30 L	(O11) Metallic components	250
(I13) Abrasive disks	1500	(O12) Anti silicon additive bins	5
(I14) Filters	10	(O13) Paint can	70
(I15) Thinner	60 L	(O14) Varnish can	20
(I51) Gas	5000 m^3		
(I52) Electricity	12 MWh		
(I53) Water	750 m^3		
Resources			
(R1) Extractors	2		
(R2) Electric screwdriver	2		
(R3) Car bench	1		
(R4) Scales (for paint)	1		
(R15) Painting oven	1		

An Empirical Application

In this section the application of the model to an Italian body repair shop is presented. Data was gathered through semi-structured interviews and several audits performed by the authors. Then, the collected information was discussed with a panel of experts, who supported the scholars in the application of the model to the real case and in the definition of the potential solutions to implement in order to reduce the body shop's impact on the environment.

Firstly, the 31 processes associated to the body repair macro-process (22 relevant to operational activities and 9 relevant to supporting activities) were selected from the comprehensive inventory matrix. Moreover, all of the main facility features (such as the lighting, heating and water distribution systems) were considered. For each process, inputs (including electricity and gas), outputs (disposed wastes), and resources (adopted tools and equipment) were measured. Altogether, 53 inputs, 65 outputs and 15 resources were considered. An excerpt is presented in Table 7.2.

Afterwards, the operative KPIs were assessed in terms of CO_2 emissions, as shown in Table 7.3.

The 'Gas consumption' KPI was recognized as the most critical, since it was causing major CO_2 emissions (9946 kg). As shown in Fig. 7.3, the input/output/

Table 7.3 KPIs measurement and assessment

Performance area	Performance KPI	Inputs/Outputs/Resources and KPIs connection			Global warming index CO_2 emissions (kg)
Material consumption	Total material consumption	/	I1→I50	/	5,673
Energy consumption	Gas consumption	/	I51	R15	9,946
	Electric energy consumption	/	I52	R1→R14	6,984
Water consumption	Water consumption	/	I53	R13, R14	218
Waste production	Total waste production	O1→O65	/	/	5,432

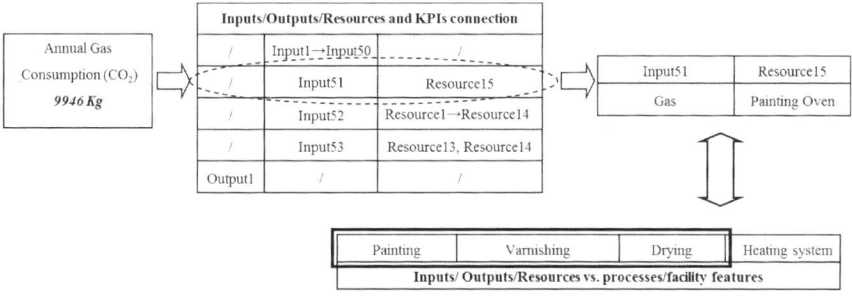

Fig. 7.3 Identification of unsustainable processes/facility features

resources, which were directly linked to gas consumption, were 'Gas' (Input 51) and 'Painting oven' (Resource 15). Consequently, the analysis was then focused on three operative processes (Painting, Varnishing and Drying) and on one facility feature (Heating System), which were directly connected with the aforementioned inputs and resources.

Since 95 % of the total gas consumption was imputable to operative processes, while only 5 % to the heating system, the solutions proposed were addressed to improve the environmental sustainability of painting, varnishing and drying. In particular, the substitution of a traditional painting oven with a combined system (a traditional oven with an infrared lamp system) was evaluated through an environmental assessment and economic analysis.

As shown in Table 7.4, the technical solution under analysis was characterized by lower gas consumption, but higher electricity consumption. However, the drying cycle provided by a traditional oven lasts 1 h, while the combined system requires only 10 min. As a consequence, a significant reduction could be gained both in terms of gas consumption (from 20 to 2 m^3 per drying cycle) and electricity consumption (from 23 kWh per drying cycle to 5.8 kWh per drying cycle), resulting in an equivalent CO_2 emissions saving of around 86 %.

Table 7.4 Combined system: environmental analysis

	Traditional oven	Combined system	Savings (%)
Drying time	1 h	10 min	83
Gas consumption	20 m^3	2 m^3	90
	39.8 kg CO_2 eq	4 kg CO_2 eq	
Electric energy consumption	23 kWh	5.8 kWh	75
	13.4 kg CO_2 eq	3.4 kg CO_2 eq	
Total CO_2 emissions (per drying cycle)	*54.2 kg CO_2 eq*	*7.4 CO_2 eq*	*86*

Table 7.5 Combined system: economic analysis

	Traditional oven	Combined system
Investment cost		50,000 (€)
Maintenance costs		
Filters	2.90 (€/h)	2.90 (€/h)
Ordinary maintenance	1.25 (€/h)	1.25 (€/h)
Burner maintenance	0.60 (€/h)	0.60 (€/h)
Extraordinary maintenance	1.50 (€/h)	1.50 (€/h)
Amortisation	4.00 (€/h)	5.67 (€/h)
Total overhead (per hour)	*10.25 (€/h)*	*11.92 (€/h)*
Drying time	1 h	10 min
Total overhead (per drying cycle)	10.25 (€/drying cycle)	2.00 (€/drying cycle)
Total cost of energy (per drying cycle)	14.09 (€/drying cycle)	1.78 (€/drying cycle)
Total cost (per drying cycle)	24.34 (€/drying cycle)	3.78 (€/drying cycle)
Saving cost (per drying cycle)	24.34−3.78=20.56 (€/drying cycle)	
Break even point	50,000 €/20.56 (€/drying cycle)=2432 drying cycles	

The economic analysis, which aims at quantifying the achievable advantages in monetary terms, is reported in Table 7.5. It shows that the required investment in this new technology (around 50,000 €) can be recovered in approximately 2400 drying cycles, due to lower operative costs.

The introduction of a scheduling procedure for the painting, varnishing and drying activities was also suggested in order to improve the environmental impact of the body shop through a better planning process. In particular, every day the worker involved in the painting activities and the workshop manager jointly plan the body components to be treated the day after. The components are then clustered based on their dimension and colour in order to better exploit the oven capacity. As a result, the number of drying cycles per day can be reduced by around 8 %, allowing a better usage of the resource and resulting in lower CO_2 emissions and a lower total cost of energy per car.

Apart from economic and environmental benefits, the adoption of new solutions allowed the workshop to significantly improve its green image in the market, at the same time bringing about the acquisition of new customers and the improvement of sustainability awareness of its loyal customers.

The application of the model has also highlighted a positive relationship between business and individual attitudes towards sustainability. The employees of the body repair workshop involved in the pilot case have acquired and developed a better awareness of sustainability issues, bringing home the adoption of simple measures in their daily life to protect the environment.

Conclusions

Sustainability is gaining more and more relevance on the manager's agenda since it can positively contribute to the firm's value creation process. The benefits are numerous and range from cost reduction, through risk management and business innovation, to revenue and brand value growth. In the automotive industry, several companies are starting to pave the way towards sustainability through a number of different approaches. Firstly, car makers are implementing programs to improve efficiency in manufacturing and logistics processes. Secondly, high investments are being allocated to product innovation, on the one hand reducing the carbon emissions of traditional combustion engines, whilst on the other hand developing alternative powertrain technologies. Some companies are also rethinking the value proposition offered to the customers and redefining the mobility concept through the promotion of new services such as car-sharing, car-pooling and pay-as-you-go solutions. However, after-sales services have received little attention within such a debate. Only a few programs exist to decrease the negative impact of service activities on the environment.

In such a context, this chapter proposes a model to support the auto repair industry in the development of a sustainable network, in order to fulfil long- and short-term environmental, economic and competitive benefits. The model, which has been built on the LCA framework, supports the identification of opportunities for preventing pollution and for reducing resource consumption through a systematic analysis. In particular, the model is a powerful decision-making tool which may help managers of auto repair workshops to quantify environmental interventions and evaluate the improvement options throughout the life cycle of their processes. Besides direct environmental benefits deriving from the introduction of selected solutions, the model allows for easier, clearer, and better workshop management. It enables the development of a clear picture of how each process works, what needs to be changed and how the proposed changes, introduced to solve a specific criticality, affect the entire business. More specifically, the business process mapping (as output of Phase 2 The Inventory Analysis) introduces an univocal and rigorous documentation and analysis of the business that integrates different views and information, highlighting the relationships between activities, resources, consumed input and realized output, and consequently supports the validation and test of alternative solutions. Furthermore, the model provides the managers with a performance measurement system for sustainability (as output of Phase 3 The Impact Assessment Phase), characterized by an adequate set of KPIs that can be used to monitor and control the critical sustainability areas. Such a workshop scorecard is an important driver to implement a positive synergy between business and sustainability strategy and to favour a successful alignment between strategic decisions, actions and attitudes. It is possible because, while economic aspects of the decisions are not properly addressed by existing LCA tools, the developed model provides a robust framework for process design and improvement by simultaneously taking into account environmental, technical, and economic criteria. Combining the results of environmental evaluations with economic considerations broadens the domain of application of traditional LCA tools and enables the implementation of win-win solutions where both environmental and economic benefits can be realized.

Summarizing, the model provides a management system able to support an auto repair workshop to: (i) evaluate its environmental performances with a dynamic perspective; (ii) identify which activity and/or infrastructure needs to be improved or changed in order to reduce the environmental impact, enabling cost savings in both the short- and long-term; and (iii) increase a sustainable image. The model, though intended for the application at the workshop level, could also be replicated at the network level, multiplying its contributions to protect the environment.

As demonstrated by the pilot case study that has been used to illustrate and analyse the applicability and consistency of the model, the solutions proposed and implemented have enabled significant economic and environmental savings through waste elimination and more efficient resource utilization. Moreover, the model has also enabled the spread of a culture for sustainability in the market as well as in the company, both at the business and individual level.

Some directions for future research can be pointed out to overcome the limitations of this work:

- The six proposed sustainability areas and the relevant indicators can be extended to consider other relevant aspects of environmental sustainability;
- The Global Warming Index has been considered as the unique and most representative eco-performance category of a repair and maintenance workshop; in future investigations it would be of interest to analyze the introduction of other additional impact categories (such as the impact of land use, ozone depletion, human toxicity, etc.). This could be useful to represent the workshop eco-sustainability with a wider perspective;
- The proposed methods can be integrated both with a marketing perspective to further investigate how and the extent to which sustainability impacts customer satisfaction and retention, and with a social standpoint to identify how eco-improvements of workshop processes and/or infrastructures can also influence the social context where the workshop operates;
- A more in-depth investigation into workshops may provide additional insights and alignment of the application with reality and in general may prove to be a fruitful avenue for further research in the automotive industry.

Finally, since the application cannot be considered exhaustive and fully extendible to all industry areas, further developments can be carried out in order to enlarge the sample of business applications.

Appendix 1

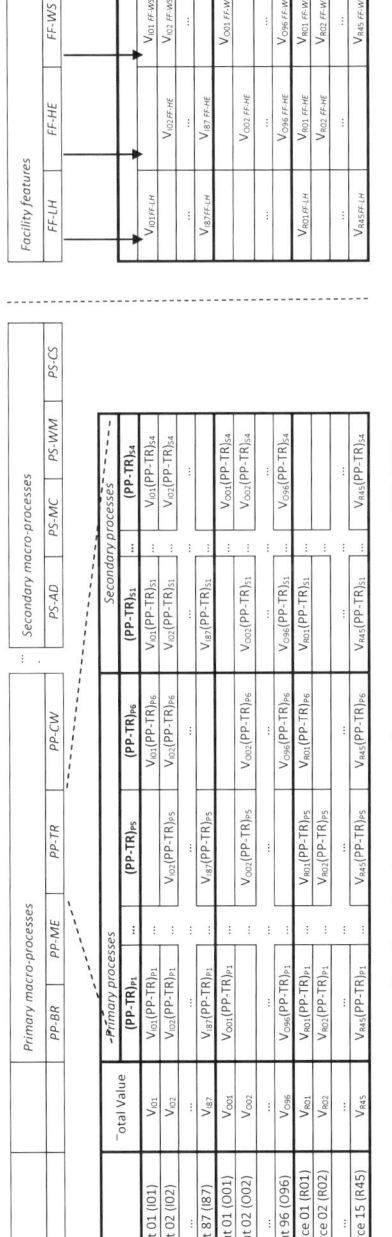

Fig. 7.4 Inventory matrix: example of application to tyre replacement macro-process (PP-TR)

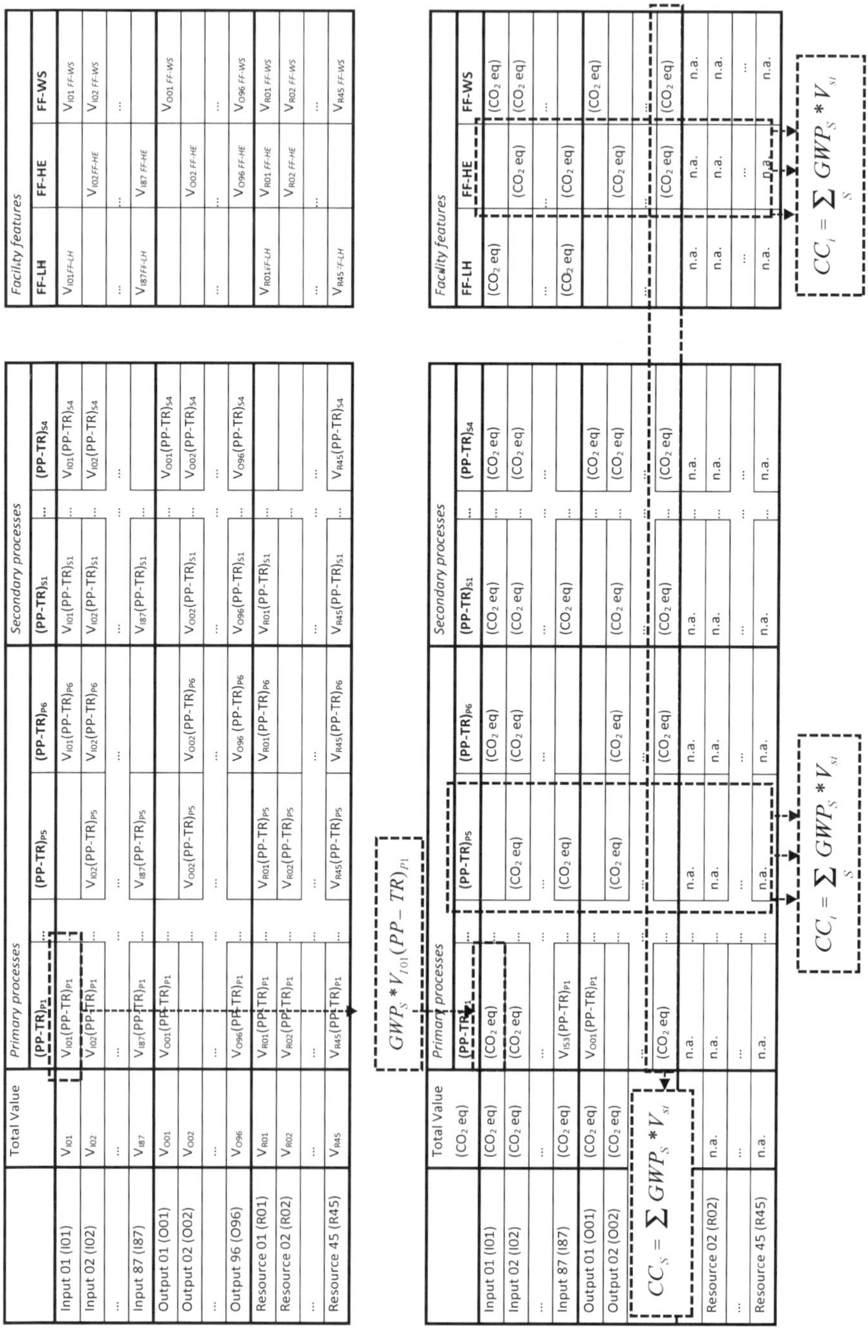

Fig. 7.5 Process and facility features impact calculation

References

Asja Market. (2008). http://www.asjacleanplanet.com/ita/protocollo.html. Accessed 19 Apr 2009.

Carley, M., & Spapens, P. (1998). *Sharing the world: Sustainable living and global equity in the 21st century*. London: Earthscan.

Castle, D. (2001). A sustainability vision for the automotive services industry. Final report prepared for Oregon Department of Environmental Quality, Oregon. New York: Charles Scribner's Sons.

Charnes, A., Cooper, W. W., & Rhodes, E. (1978). Measuring the efficiency of decision making units. *European Journal of Operational Research, 2*(6), 429–444.

Cleaner Vehicles Task Force. (2000). The environmental impacts of motor manufacturing and disposal of end of life vehicles moving towards sustainability. Technical report. London: Department of Trade and Industry (DTI).

Curran, M. A. (1996). *Environmental life-cycle assessment*. New York: McGraw-Hill.

European Commission. (2000). LIFE FOCUS/A cleaner, greener Europe: LIFE and the European Union Waste Policy. Office for Official Publications of the European Communities, Luxembourg.

Forster, P., Ramaswamy, V., Artaxo, P., Berntsen, T., Betts, R., Fahey, D. W., Haywood, J., Lean, J., Lowe, D. C., Myhre, G., Nganga, J., Prinn, R., Raga, G., Schulz, M., & Van Dorland, R. (2007). Changes in atmospheric constituents and in radiative forcing. In S. Solomon, D. Qin, M. Manning, Z. Chen, M. Marquis, K. B. Averyt, M. Tignor, H. L. Miller(Eds.), *Climate change 2007: The physical science basis*. Cambridge: Cambridge University Press.

Franze, H.A., & Neumann, U. (1995). Life-cycle optimization of car components. SAE-Papers, No 950207.

Franze, H. A., Metz, N., & Neumann, U. (1995). Environmental impact calculations of automotive parts by life-cycle analysis: The BMW approach. SAE-Papers No 951843.

Global Reporting Initiative. (2006). Sustainability reporting framework: Guidelines. http://www.globalreporting.org. Accessed 3 May 2011.

Graedel, T. E. (1998). Life-cycle assessment in the service industries. *Journal of Industrial Ecology, 1*(4), 57–70.

Heijungs, R., de Koning, A., Ligthart, T., & Korenromp, R. (2004). Improvement of LCA characterization factors and LCA practise for metals. TNO-Report, TNO, The Netherlands.

Heinrich, J., Schwarze, P. E., Stilianakis, N., Momas, I., Medina, S., Totlandsdal, A. I., von Bree, L., Kuna-Dibbert, B., & Krzyzanowski, M. (2003). Studies on health effects of transported-related air pollution. In M. Krzyzanowski, B. Kuna-Dibbert, & J. Schneider (Eds.), *Health effects of transport-related air pollution. Copenhagen* (pp. 125–183). Copenhagen: World Health Organization (WHO) Regional Office for Europe.

Keoleian, G. A., & Kar, K. (2003). Elucidating complex design and management trade-offs through life cycle design: air intake manifold demonstration project. *Journal of Cleaner Production, 11*(1), 61–77.

Krämer, U., Koch, T., Ranft, U., Ring, J., & Behrendt, H. (2000). Traffic-related air pollution is associated with atopy in children living in urban areas. *Epidemiology, 11*(11), 64–70.

MacLean, H. L., Lave, L. B., Lankey, B., & Joshi, S. (2000). A life-cycle comparison of alternative automobile fuels. *Journal of Air and Waste Management Association, 50*(10), 1769–1779.

Makuta, M., Moriguchi, Y., Yasuda, Y., & Sueno, S. (2000). Evaluation of the effect of automotive bumper recycling by life-cycle inventory analysis. *Journal of Material Cycles and Waste Management, 2*(2), 125‑137.

Mathieu, V. (2001). Service strategies within the manufacturing sector: Benefits, costs and partnership. *International Journal of Service Industry Management, 12*(5), 451–475.

McCleese, D. L., & LaPuma, P. T. (2002). Using Monte Carlo simulation in life cycle assessment for electric and internal combustion vehicles. *International Journal of Life Cycle Assessment, 7*(4), 230–236.

Mishan, E. J., & Quah, E. (2007). *Cost-benefit analysis*. London: Routledge.

Orsato, R. J., & Wells, P. (2007). The automobile industry & sustainability. *Journal of Cleaner Production, 15*(11–12), 989–993.

Osborn, A. F. (1967). *Applied imagination: Principles and procedures of creative problem solving*. New York: Charles Scribner's Sons.

Papasavva, S., Kia, S., Claya, J., & Gunther, R. (2001). Characterization of automotive paints: An environmental impact analysis. *Progress in Organic Coatings, 43*(1–3), 193–206.

Porter, M. (1985). *Competitive advantage. Creating and sustaining superior performance*. New York: Free Press.

Prendi, L., & Tam, E. K. L. (2008). Life cycle inventory of the automotive paint processes. *Journal of Coatings Technology, 5*(6), 30–37.

Rebitzer, G., Ekvall, T., Frischknecht, R., Hunkeler, D., Norris, G., Rydberg, T., Schmidt, W. P., Suh, S., Weidema, B. P., & Pennington, D. W. (2004). Life cycle assessment part 1: Framework, goal and scope definition, inventory analysis, and applications. *Environment International, 30*(5), 701–720.

Saur, K., Fava, J. A., & Spatari, S. (2000). Life cycle engineering case study: Automobile fender designs. *Environmental Progress, 19*(2), 72–82.

Schmidt, W. P., Dahlqvist, E., Finkbeiner, M., Krinke, S., Lazzari, S., Oschmann, D., Pichon, S., & Thiel, C. (2004). Life cycle assessment of lightweight and end-of-life scenarios for generic compact class passenger vehicles. *International Journal of Life Cycle Assessment, 9*(6), 405–416.

Schweitzer, M., Trossmann, E., & Lawson, G. (1991). *Break-even analyses: Basic model, variants, extensions*. Chichester: Wiley.

SETAC. (1991). *A technical framework for life cycle assessments*. Pensacola: Society for Environmental Toxicology and Chemistry Publication.

Shrieves, R. E., & Wachowicz, J. M. (2001). Free cash flow (FCF), economic value added (EVA), and net present value (NPV): A reconciliation of variations of discounted-cash-flow (DCF) valuation. *The Engineering Economist, 46*(1), 33–52.

Smith, N. C. (2008). Consumers as drivers of corporate social responsibility. In A. Crane, A. McWilliams, D. Matten, J. Moon & D. S. Siegel (Eds.), *The Oxford handbook of corporate social responsibility* (pp. 281–302). New York: Oxford University Press.

Steininger, K., Vogl, C., & Zettl, R. (1996). Carsharing organizations. *Transport Policy, 3*(4), 177–185.

SustainAbility and United Nations Environment Programme (UNEP) (2001). *Driving sustainability: Can the auto sector deliver sustainable mobility?* London: SustainAbility/UNEP Report.

Part III
Theoretical Investigations of Sustainability

These three chapters are part of the ongoing process of imagining a new discipline of sustainable decision-making.

Chapter seven heralds the coming of age of Organisations and Environment research, as a mature discipline in which both concerns can be balanced.

Chapter eight looks at Ecological Footprint analysis, and questions whether we can achieve environmental sustainability, without transforming our society.

Chapter nine calls for the unification of the different rationales for the preservation of the environment.

Chapter 8
Building the Future by Looking to the Past: Examining Research Published on Organizations and Environment

Pratima Bansal and Jijun Gao

Introduction

The anchor in any research program is the phenomenon being explained. In the field of organizations and environment (O&E) research, there are two different anchors: organizations and the natural environment. With the first, researchers see the natural environment as an important factor in determining organizational outcomes. With the second, researchers assume that the environment is an important outcome in itself and are interested in how organizations interact with the natural environment. An assumption common to both approaches is that the natural environment and organizations are related to each other and warrant research consideration. However, there is also a deep-rooted difference.

On the organizations side, we frame our work in the language, theories, and assumptions of mainstream business researchers and professionals. We assume that the audience for our research should be drawn from more traditional management disciplines, such as strategy, organizational behavior, and finance. Without such an audience, we speak only to ourselves and have very little impact on the wider field of business. The natural environment represents one variable among the many that explain organizational outcomes. So, our job is to demonstrate the efficacy of the natural environment. In doing so, we can grab wide attention from general managers and have the largest possible impact. If successful, we can move seamlessly in and out of the traditional business disciplines, with little risk of being labeled marginal or non-mainstream.

This chapter has been previously published in Organization & Environment (Volume 19, issue 4, pages 458–478). The required permissions have been obtained from Sage Publishers to republish it in this book.

P. Bansal (✉)
Ivey Business School, Western University, London, Canada
e-mail: tbansal@ivey.uwo.ca; PBansal@ivey.uwo.ca

J. Gao
Asper School of Business, University of Manitoba, Winnipeg, Canada
e-mail: Jijun.gao@umanitoba.ca

© Springer Science+Business Media Dordrecht 2014
S. Sandhu et al. (eds.), *Linking Local and Global Sustainability,* The International Society of Business, Economics, and Ethics Book Series 4, DOI 10.1007/978-94-017-9008-6_8

On the natural environment side, we see the natural environment as an important end in itself. We assume that the purpose of industrial development is to improve human health, and its success depends on a healthy planet. Business and the natural environment are inextricably linked. Consequently, researchers direct energy into investigating environmental performance, either at the organizational level of analysis or at a more macro level. Their research findings are often targeted to government policy-makers or even society, rather than primarily at business managers.

This article was motivated by our curiosity about which of these two approaches would be most pervasive and persuasive in the journals that shape organizational studies, university research ratings, and researcher promotion and tenure processes. We have focused our attention on the most heavily cited general management journals because many researchers, even those in O&E (Cohen 2006), believe that these journals house the most influential research. As well, these journals have a heavy influence on practice because of their general management focus.

At the outset of this project, we had two starting biases. First, we expected that most O&E research would be of the organizational variety. We assumed that the editors and reviewers of general management journals would be predisposed to research that looked like traditional organizational research. As well, authors would assume these biases of general management reviewers and editors and frame their research accordingly. Second, we expected that research into environmental outcomes would be the more innovative of the two, because it is not constrained by prior organizational research. The most theoretically and methodologically interesting research would likely reside in the domain of environmental outcomes.

The purpose of this paper, in part, is to assess whether these starting hypotheses are supported. By analyzing prior O&E research in the most influential general management journals, we can identify trends and biases in prior research, and use these as an opportunity to advise on research gaps. We have attempted to deliver on these objectives by organizing the paper into three parts. First, we briefly describe the analysis we undertook to ground our observations. We analyzed 79 O&E articles published in 11 general management journals. Second, we offer observations on the content of these articles, especially their approach to organizational and environmental outcomes. We find that, contrary to expectations, most research published in these general management journals explained environmental outcomes, as opposed to treating the environment as merely the empirical context or as an explanatory variable. We also describe the types of theories and methodologies used in prior research. In the final section we speculate on what these observations mean to our research domain.

Analyzing O&E Publications in Management Journals

To locate articles in the organizations and environment area, we searched ABI/INFORM (distributed by ProQuest) for the following key words: environmental performance, environmental management, environmental policy, environmental issues, natural environment, ecological, toxic, pollution, corporate sustainability, and sustainable development. A similar approach, with different key words, was used in prior reviews of the O&E field (Gladwin et al. 1995; Jermier et al. 2006). We did not analyze articles that simply included environmental performance as one dimension of a composite measure of corporate social responsibility (CSR). It is arguable that the paradigms and trends underpinning the CSR body of research are sufficiently different to warrant separate treatment (van Marrewijk 2003). As well, several comprehensive reviews of CSR research have already been published (Lockett et al. 2006; Orlitzky et al. 2003; Walsh et al. 2003).

Following the lead of Coopey (2003), we limited the search to articles published in the "top" academic journals. As a starting place, we included the eight journals on Cohen's (2006) list of highest quality journals: the *Academy of Management Journal* (AMJ), *Academy of Management Review* (AMR), *Administrative Science Quarterly* (ASQ), *Journal of Management Studies* (JMS), *Management Science* (MS), *Organization Science* (OrSc), *Organization Studies* (OrSt) and the *Strategic Management Journal* (SMJ). We also included three additional journals that we believed to be held in high esteem: the *British Journal of Management* (BJM), *Journal of International Business Studies* (JIBS), and the *Journal of Management* (JM).

Three of journals we reviewed, BJM, JMS, and OrSt are published in the UK, while the remaining eight journals are published in the US. We will refer to these journals loosely as European and US.[1] We chose these 11 journals because they influence other areas of business studies and because they are relevant in the tenure and promotion processes of most academic institutions (Bergh et al. 2006). We limited our search to the 11 years between 1 January 1995 and 31 December 2005. We did not include book reviews or dialogue articles.

Observations on Research Published in Organizations and Environment

Our analysis of the quality and quantity of O&E research published in influential management journals over the last decade leads us to make four observations.

Observation 1: O&E Research is Represented in all of the Influential Management Journals

We identified 79 O&E articles published in the influential journals from 1995 to 2005. Figure 8.1 illustrates the trend over time.

---

[1] Our analysis shows that 70% of data samples in UK journals is based on European data sources and 69% of data samples in US journals is based on North American data. Based on this evidence, one could infer that Europeans are more often targeting UK journals and North Americans more often targeting US journals.

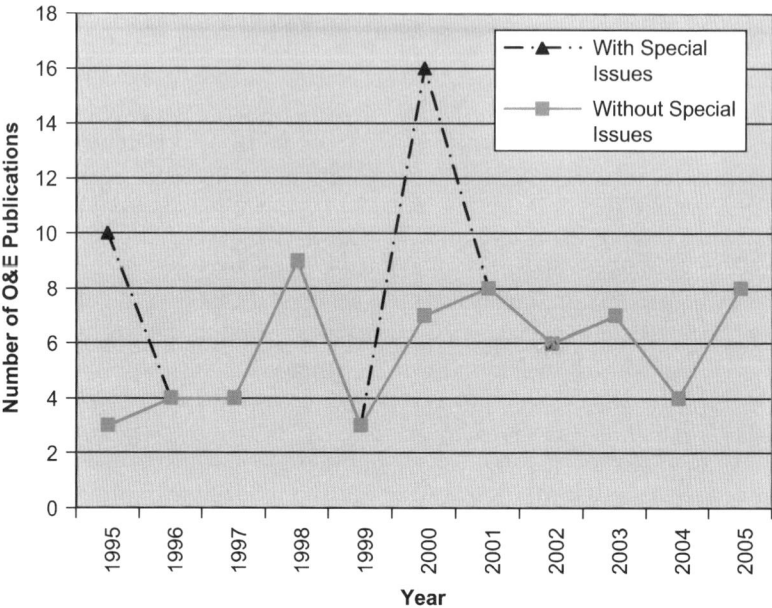

Fig. 8.1 Number of O&E articles over time

Two special issues appeared during this period. In 1995, the AMR published a special issue on "Ecologically Sustainable Organizations" which included seven articles that fit within our analytical boundaries. In 2000, the AMJ published a special issue on "Management of Organizations in the Natural Environment" which included nine articles relevant to our study. Figure 8.1 shows that when the impact of these special issues is removed, the publishing rate of O&E research has been quite stable over the past 11 years. Approximately six papers were published each year, except for a spike in 1998, in which there were nine articles published. There may be a number of reasons that explain this spike. It may be due to the increased interest in environmental issues because of the increased profile of the AMR special issue three years earlier. As well, Lockett et al. (2006) noted a similar surge in CSR research during that period, which may indicate an increased attention to social and environmental issues. There also appeared to be a larger supply of graduating doctoral students just prior to that period, who are often among the most research active (e.g. Lin and Buongiorno 1998; Nehrt 1998; Sharma and Vredenburg 1998).

A stable publishing rate is encouraging; it shows that the O&E research domain is not a fad, at least in highly influential academic journals. On the other hand, this stability is disappointing because it does not acknowledge the increasing urgency of environmental problems nor our improved understanding of O&E research issues. It is interesting to contrast this finding with that of Jermier et al. (2006) who surveyed a much larger set of journals. They discovered a dramatic increase, over 300 %, in the number of O&E related publications, in all of the scholarly journals catalogued in the ABI/Inform Global database from the period 1990–1994 to 2000–2004. Over the same period, the number of O&E articles grew by more than 2.5 times relative to the other management fields. This could imply that the growth of scholarly interest in O&E issues is not being reflected in the more influential academic journals.

It is worth highlighting the scarcity of articles in ASQ and OrSc; two US journals that are perceived to be more open to diverse research methods, such as qualitative research. There are several possible reasons why O&E articles might be under-represented in these journals. From our own experiences, we expect that ASQ remains elusive because of its rigorous and, possibly idiosyncratic, research standards. OrSc, we suspect, is not the journal of first choice for traditional organizational researchers. These researchers likely prefer comparable journals, such as the AMJ and SMJ, which appear more frequently on the 'A' lists of most North American business schools. The two O&E articles that appear in OrSc, in fact, applied non-traditional research methods (Bansal 2003; Hoffman and Ocasio 2001). The size of the sample is too small to do anything more than speculate.

It would be interesting to assess if there is a negative or positive disposition to publishing O&E research in these journals. However, making such judgments is difficult, as benchmark data are not easily available. The O&E articles we analyzed represent roughly 1.3% of the journal space in the selected influential journals, which is consistent with the findings in previous reviews (Coopey 2003; Jermier et al. 2006). If we remove the two special issues focused on O&E (AMR in 1995; AMJ in 2000), less than 1% of journal space pertains to O&E research. As a benchmark, approximately 3.4% of the members of the Academy of Management (AoM) are also members of the Organizations and Natural Environment (ONE) interest group. But, not all O&E researchers belong to this group, nor do the members of it exclusively research O&E issues. As well, most ONE members belong to other divisions. So, while 3.4% represents the percentage of AoM members who belong to the ONE division, the percentage of O&E articles appearing in journals would be expected much lower than this.

We can say something, however, about the relative representation of O&E research in European and US journals. A total of 57 articles were published in the eight US journals, about a 1.2% share of voice. The three European journals published relatively more articles with a total of 22 articles, which is about a 1.6% share of voice. Without the AMJ and AMR special issues, even fewer articles would have been published in US journals. Special issues are often an opportunity to publish ground-breaking ideas in influential journals which might otherwise overlook such research. Special issues also often motivate researchers to produce work they may not have attempted otherwise.

It is worth asking why relatively more O&E articles appear in European journals than in US journals. Once again, we can only speculate, given that we only have anecdotal evidence on which to base opinions. From our own experiences, the review process for European journals accommodates more author flexibility than US journals; the reviews are shorter and less detailed and the reviewers often give the authors more latitude in responding to their comments. Having said this, we realize that the review process for European journals has intensified in recent years. European journals, more so than US journals, may also be more receptive to environmental issues or view them as being more central to business.

Observation 2: More O&E Research Aims to Improve Environmental Performance than Organizational Performance

To determine how the natural environment was being included in prior research, we categorized the O&E articles into three groups depending on whether the natural environment was studied in terms of: (1) environmental context; (2) organizational outcomes; or (3) environmental outcomes. In the first category, O&E research uses the natural environment as context. The data are grounded in the natural environment but the theory and constructs are not. Thus, this research remains within mainstream business research, and draws the attention of a wide group of business scholars including O&E scholars. In the second category, environmental variables explain organizational outcomes, such as actions, structures, and processes, at any level of analysis. In the third category, researchers investigate whether organizational variables influence the natural environment. In these cases, the dependent variable was related to the natural environment, which was the key target of interest. Our analysis is summarized in Table 8.1. The left-hand side of the table shows the absolute numbers and percentage of O&E articles that fell into each of the three categories described above, by journal and country. The right-hand side of the table shows the absolute numbers and percentage of O&E articles across five levels of analysis, by journal and country, which is discussed in Observation 3.

Our starting position was that prior O&E research would look like other organizational research; that is, it would use environment merely as context or investigate organizational outcomes. We expected researchers to lean towards research that fit within existing paradigms and research questions, on the assumption that the gatekeepers of our profession (senior researchers, reviewers and editors) would be more receptive to these approaches. We were wrong. A full 60% of articles in US journals and 69% of articles in European journals focused on environmental outcomes.

Environmental Context

Of the 79 articles we analyzed, 12 used the natural environment as context for researching other management issues. Lewis and Harvey's (2001) study illustrates this approach most simply. They tested whether Miller's (Miller 1993) scale of business environmental uncertainty applied to the natural environment, without any additional theoretical development.

Most organizational researchers who include the natural environment as context for their research extend theory by using environmental issues for empirical

Table 8.1 Focus of research on organization and environment by journal

Journal	Journal	Explained outcome					Level of analysis				
		Context	Organizational	Environmental	Both O&E	Total	Individual	Organizational	Institutional/Industry	Paradigm	Cross-level
US-based Journals	ASQ	1 / 100%	0 / 0%	0 / 0%	0 / 0%	1 / 100%	0 / 0%	0 / 0%	1 / 100%	0 / 0%	0 / 0%
	AMR	1 / 9%	1 / 9%	9 / 82%	0 / 0%	11 / 100%	0 / 0%	3 / 28%	4 / 36%	4 / 36%	0 / 0%
	AMJ	0 / 0%	5 / 25%	14 / 70%	1 / 5%	20 / 100%	4 / 20%	9 / 45%	2 / 10%	0 / 0%	5 / 25%
	SMJ	1 / 10%	5 / 45%	5 / 45%	0 / 0%	11 / 100%	0 / 0%	6 / 55%	2 / 18%	0 / 0%	3 / 27%
	JIBS	0 / 0%	0 / 0%	2 / 100%	0 / 0%	2 / 100%	0 / 0%	2 / 100%	0 / 0%	0 / 0%	0 / 0%
	MS	2 / 22%	2 / 22%	4 / 44%	1 / 12%	9 / 100%	0 / 0%	6 / 67%	3 / 33%	0 / 0%	0 / 0%
	OrSc	2 / 100%	0 / 0%	0 / 0%	0 / 0%	2 / 100%	0 / 0%	0 / 0%	1 / 50%	0 / 0%	1 / 50%
	JM	0 / 0%	1 / 100%	0 / 0%	0 / 0%	1 / 100%	0 / 0%	1 / 100%	0 / 0%	0 / 0%	0 / 0%
Subtotal of US journals		7 / 12%	14 / 25%	34 / 60%	2 / 3%	57 / 100%	4 / 7%	27 / 47%	13 / 23%	4 / 7%	9 / 16%
Euro-based journals	OrSt	2 / 29%	0 / 0%	5 / 71%	0 / 0%	7 / 100%	0 / 0%	2 / 29%	2 / 29%	1 / 14%	2 / 29%
	JMS	3 / 26%	1 / 8%	7 / 58%	1 / 8%	12 / 100%	1 / 8%	4 / 33%	2 / 17%	3 / 25%	2 / 17%
	BJM	0 / 0%	0 / 0%	3 / 100%	0 / 0%	3 / 100%	0 / 0%	1 / 33%	0 / 0%	0 / 0%	2 / 67%
Subtotal of Euro journals		5 / 23%	1 / 4%	15 / 69%	1 / 4%	22 / 100%	1 / 4%	7 / 32%	4 / 18%	4 / 18%	6 / 28%
Total		12 / 15%	15 / 19%	49 / 62%	3 / 4%	79 / 100%	5 / 6%	34 / 43%	17 / 22%	8 / 10%	15 / 19%

Note: ASQ = Administrative Science Quarterly; AMR = Academy of Management Review; AMJ = Academy of Management Journal; SMJ = Strategic Management Journal; JIBS = Journal of International Business Studies; MS = Management Science; OrSc = Organization Science; JM = Journal of Management; OrSt = Organization Studies; JMS = Journal of Management Studies; BJM = British Journal of Management insights. Institutional analysis has been the dominant theoretical theme among studies with a natural environment context, likely because institutional forces have such a significant role in environmental issues. For example, Hoffman (1999) used the evolution of corporate environmentalism within the US chemical industry as the empirical issue to demonstrate how an institutional field takes form around issues, rather than markets or technologies. Other researchers have based empirical research on end-of-life vehicle recycling (Orsato et al. 2002), recycling programs within colleges and universities (Lounsbury 2001), and the corporate environmental policies of chemical companies in emerging economies (Child and Tsai 2005).

Some researchers in this group have focused on decision-making in the context of environmental management. For instance, Wilhelm and Srinivasa (1997) developed a mathematical model of crisis response management in the presence of oil spills; Nault (1996) developed his model under the conditions of negative production externalities. Aragon-Correa and Sharma (2003) refined the existing resource-based view by identifying its contingencies within the context of the natural environment.

Organizational processes are another important area of research in the environmental context category. Researchers in this area investigate the set of actions or events that help us understand *how* business is conducted within an environmental context. For example, Zietsma et al. (2002) examined multilevel organizational learning processes in response to environmental criticism. Mintzberg and Westley (2000) looked at the job of managing by investigating the management styles of two senior executives at Greenpeace. Bansal (2003) traced the process by which environmental issues are addressed within two computer firms, from the moment they were identified to the point of organizational action. Branzei et al. (2004) extended control theory to the formation of green strategies in Chinese firms, and Rothenberg (2003) looked at the dynamics of worker participation in environmental management programs in an automotive plant.

Organizational Outcomes

Of the 79 papers, 15 treated the natural environment as important in shaping organizational outcomes. Most research in this area had a strong pragmatic or utilitarian focus, investigating the impact of environmental actions on organizational performance (Klassen and McLaughlin 1996; Klassen and Whybark 1999; Russo and Fouts 1997), competitive advantage (Christmann 2000; Nehrt 1998; Shrivastava 1995b), and anticipated firm performance (Gilley et al. 2000). Some organizational outcomes are not directly associated with financial performance, but are critical for the continued growth or the survival of the firm. These outcomes include acquiring organizational resources and capabilities (Chan 2005; Hart 1995; Marcus and Geffen 1998; Sharma and Vredenburg 1998), integrating environmental issues and strategic planning (Judge and Douglas 1998), unsystematic stock market risk (Bansal and Clelland 2004), perceived importance of different stakeholders (Buysse and Verbeke 2003; Henriques and Sadorsky 1999), and organizational birth rates (Dean and Brown 1995).

Environmental Outcomes

More than half (62%) of the articles in our sample studied environmental outcomes, and most of the articles in the special issues of AMR and AMJ fit this category. Research that focuses on organizational outcomes attempts to demonstrate that the natural environment is relevant to organizations, but research on environmental outcomes makes no such claim. This category of research assumes that organizations impact the natural environment; thus, researchers must understand how these impacts can be reduced to alleviate environmental harm (Douglas and Judge 1995). The most ground-breaking research often appeared in this category, so it warrants considered discussion here, especially because there are many research streams in this area.

Many researchers in this field attempt to explain environmental performance using proxies such as toxic releases (King and Lenox 2000; Klassen and Whybark 1999; Russo and Harrison 2005), waste generation and waste processing activities (King and Shaver 2001), material consumption (Corbett and DeCroix 2001), environmental litigation (Kassinis and Vafeas 2002), and the adoption of ISO 14001 (Christmann and Taylor 2001; Gonzalez-Benito and Gonzalez-Benito 2005; Jiang and Bansal 2003). Others have taken a more holistic view of environmental performance (e.g., Bansal and Roth 2000). Meanwhile, much research in this stream rates environmental performance by the degree to which organizational actions exceed environmental regulations (Aragon-Correa 1998; Aragon-Correa and Sharma 2003; Buysse and Verbeke 2003; Hart 1995; McKay 2001; Sharma 2000; Winn and Angell 2000).

Another group of researchers has examined the role of regulation in shaping environmental performance (King and Lenox 2000; McKay 2001; Nehrt 1998; Newton and Harte 1997; Rugman and Verbeke 1998a, 1998b). Their underlying interest is in the relative efficacy and influence of voluntary policy measures versus mandatory regulations. Another stream of related research shifts the conversation from government regulators to a wider group of stakeholders. These researchers often argue that different stakeholders lead to different types of organizational strategies and actions with respect to the natural environment. And, some stakeholders are more effective in shaping environmental performance than others (Buysse and Verbeke 2003; Christmann 2004; Fineman 1996, 1997; Fineman and Clarke 1996; Henriques and Sadorsky 1999; Sharma and Henriques 2005).

Not all researchers have focused on measuring or explaining environmental performance; another group has considered different types of outcomes. For example, some have investigated alternative environmental solutions (Tenbrunsel et al. 2000) and the optimum timing for environmental technology investment (Cortazar et al. 1998). At the systems level, some have tried to model the effectiveness of different environmental management processes within different ecosystems, such as forest management (Lin and Buongiorno 1998) and fishery management (Meester et al. 2004). Still others have focused on the individual, investigating managerial decision-making (Cordano and Frieze 2000; Flannery and May 2000) or the tendency for employees to spearhead environmental initiatives (Andersson and Bateman 2000; Egri and Herman 2000; Ramus and Steger 2000).

Recently, some researchers have moved beyond environmental performance to the wider construct of sustainable development, which includes social and economic dimensions in addition to the environmental ones. They have explored both the concept of sustainable development (Bansal 2005; Starik and Rands 1995) and its physical manifestation (Bansal 2005; Russo 2003; Sharma and Henriques 2005; Shrivastava 1995c). Some of the research in this domain has taken novel approaches. For example, Whitman and Cooper (2000) conducted an ethnographic study of indigenous managers embedded in local ecological systems. Banerjee (2003) has drawn on perspectives from colonialism and imperialism to argue that the current discourse in sustainable development may be a reflection of the colonization of developing countries and rural regions to sustain the well-being of dominant regions.

Finally, a group of researchers has examined the underlying paradigm of corporate greening by extending the innovative theories that view the environment an important outcome in itself. Most of these corporate greening studies discuss the presence of a different set of underlying values, beliefs, and cognitions associated with environmentalism, such as 'technocentrism', 'sustaincentrism', 'ecocentrism', and, 'deep ecology', and contrast them with the more utilitarian and pragmatic framing of mainstream business practices (Banerjee 2001; Crane 2000; Fineman 1996; Gladwin et al. 1995; Newton 2005; Prasad and Elmes 2005). Researchers within this tradition argue that our dominant business paradigm disassociates humans from nature, and that environmental management can be viewed more inclusively when the natural environment is integrated with business (Gladwin et al. 1995; Jennings and Zandbergen 1995; Prasad and Elmes 2005; Purser et al. 1995; Shrivastava 1995a).

Observation 3: O&E Research Crosses all Levels of Analysis

Environmental issues apply at all levels of analysis: individual, organizational, industrial, and institutional. As a result, we anticipated that research would span these levels and that considerable attention would be paid to cross-level analysis. These expectations were confirmed.

To evaluate the levels of analysis, we assigned articles to five categories: industrial/institutional, organizational, individual, cross-level, and superordinate paradigm. The paradigm level addressed the theoretical and philosophical foundations of research in O&E, without empirical analysis.

Organizational-level analysis dominated the sample (43% of the total), and many were at the institutional/industry level of analysis (22% of the total). These findings were not surprising given that environmental problems (and solutions) are inextricably tied to societal pressures and expectations. For example, researchers in this group have investigated industry dynamics and response to constraints (Aragon-Correa and Sharma 2003; Dean and Brown 1995; Fineman and Clarke 1996; Hoffman and Ocasio 2001; McKay 2001), institutional evolution and forces (Jennings and Zandbergen 1995; Lounsbury 2001), ecological or social systems (Lin and Buongiorno 1998; Starik and Rands 1995), and the effectiveness of regulation relative to voluntarism (Newton and Harte 1997).

We were most surprised by the relatively small number of individual-level studies (5). This may be a promising direction for future research; several cross-level studies have argued that the personal attributes of managers are important to a firm's environmental strategy (Bansal 2003; Sharma 2000). The individual-level studies examined environmental champions and leaders (Egri and Herman 2000; Flannery and May 2000), environmental managers (Cordano and Frieze 2000; Whiteman and Cooper 2000), and employee participation in environmental management (Rothenberg 2003).

We were pleased to see a healthy amount of cross-level research (19%). Three studies explained organizational outcomes with organizational-level factors and individual or industrial determinants (Andersson and Bateman 2000; Bansal 2003; Marcus and Geffen 1998). Ten studies focused on environmental outcomes at the organizational level of analysis, modeling industry factors (King and Lenox 2000; Sharma and Henriques 2005), organizational and field factors (Bansal and Roth 2000), individual factors (Banerjee 2001; Fineman 1996, 1997), and both individual and organizational factors (Crane 2000; Sharma 2000). One even modeled all major levels, including analysis at the group level (Bowen 2002). Another three studies were exceptional because either their dependent variable was at the individual level (Ramus and Steger 2000) or they fell within the environmental context category (Branzei et al. 2004; Child and Tsai 2005). However, most of the cross-level research introduced different levels of analysis, but did not investigate their interactions.

We found that paradigm-level research challenged the status quo most effectively (Gladwin et al. 1995; Newton 2002; Purser et al. 1995; Shrivastava 1995a). These studies push readers to evaluate what is truly unique about the natural environment. European journals seemed especially responsive to paradigm-level research (Banerjee 2003; Halme 2002; Newton 2005; Prasad and Elmes 2005). The only paradigm-level articles that appeared in US journals were in the AMR special issue. This raises the question of whether these articles would have been accepted into regular issues of these journals, or whether the authors were inspired to pen their thoughts because of the opportunity afforded by the special issue.

Observation 4: Most Research uses Mainstream Organization Theory; The Research Methodologies, However, are Diverse

Most of the papers published (71%) are empirical (Table 8.2) and this pattern does not appear to have changed over time (Table 8.3). It is interesting to contrast this observation with that made by Lockett et al. (2006), who reviewed CSR research published in influential academic journals and found that theoretical papers increased, and empirical papers decreased, over time. One would expect that most new research domains would typically grow through a theory building process, followed by a theory testing process. Neither O&E nor CSR research reflected this pattern.

Table 8.2 Type of research on organization and environment by journal

	Journal	Conceptual	Empirical	Analytical/Simulation	Total	Qualitative	Quantitative	Total empirical
US-based journals	ASQ	0	1	0	1	0	1	1
		0%	100%	0%	100%	0%	100%	100%
	AMR	11	0	0	11	0	0	0
		100%	0%	0%	100%			
	AMJ	0	20	0	20	2	18	20
		0%	100%	0%	100%	10%	90%	100%
	SMJ	1	10	0	11	2	8	10
		9%	91%	0%	100%	20%	80%	100%
	JIBS	1	1	0	2	0	1	1
		50%	50%	0%	100%	0%	100%	100%
	MS	0	3	6	9	0	3	3
		0%	33%	67%	100%	0%	100%	100%
	OgSc	0	2	0	2	2	0	2
		0%	100%	0%	100%	100%	0%	100%
	JM	0	1	0	1	0	1	1
		0%	100%	0%	100%	0%	100%	100%
Subtotal of US journals		13	38	6	57	6	32	38
		23%	67%	10%	100%	16%	84%	100%
Euro-based journals	OrSt	1	6	0	7	6	0[a]	6
		14%	86%	0%	100%	100%	0%	100%
	JMS	3	9	0	12	6	3	9
		25%	75%	0%	100%	67%	33%	100%
	BJM	0	3	0	3	2	1	3
		0%	100%	0%	100%	67%	33%	100%
Subtotal of European journals		4	18	0	22	14	4	18
		18%	82%	0%	100%	78%	22%	100%
Total		17	56	6	79	20	36	56
		21%	71%	8%	100%	36%	64%	100%

[a] Winn and Angell (2000) used a two-study design, containing both quantitative analysis on survey data and qualitative case study. We count its methods as qualitative overall, for convenience

The empirical articles used both qualitative and quantitative methods, but it seems that there is a higher propensity of qualitative methods in O&E papers (36%), relative to papers in other business fields. This is likely a testimony to the emergent nature of the field and the desire of researchers to build theory that is grounded in data. However, it is noteworthy that qualitative methods were far more common in European journals than US journals. Only 16% of O&E articles in US journals used qualitative methods; compared to 78% of articles European journals. For example, all six empirical papers in the European-based OrSt were based on qualitative methods. This outcome may reflect the emphasis on positivist science in North America (Ghoshal 2005), so that US-based journals receive relatively more quantitative papers and are more likely to accept them.

Most studies emphasized economics-based theories, such as the resource-based view and dynamic capabilities, agency theory, industrial organization and competitive

Table 8.3 Type of research on organization and environment by year

US vs Euro	Year	Conceptual	Empirical	Analytical/ Simulation	Total	Qualita-tive	Quanti-tative	Total empirical
US-based journals	2005	0	3	0	3	0	3	3
	2004	0	3	1	4	0	4	3
	2003	1	3	0	4	1	2	3
	2002	1	2	0	3	0	2	2
	2001	0	4	1	5	1	4	4
	2000	0	13	0	13	2	11	13
	1999	0	3	0	3	0	3	3
	1998	3	3	2	8	1	4	3
	1997	0	1	1	2	0	2	1
	1996	0	1	1	2	0	2	1
	1995	8	2	0	10	1	1	2
Subtotal of US journals		13	38	6	57	6	32	38
		23%	67%	10%	100%	16%	84%	100%
Euro based-journals	2005	2	3	0	5	1	2	3
	2004	0	0	0	0	0	0	0
	2003	1	2	0	3	2	0	2
	2002	0	3	0	3	3	0	3
	2001	0	3	0	3	2	1	3
	2000	0	3	0	3	3	0	3
	1999	0	0	0	0	0	0	0
	1998	0	1	0	1	0	1	1
	1997	1	1	0	2	1	0	1
	1996	0	2	0	2	2	0	2
	1995	0	0	0	0	0	0	0
Subtotal of Euro journals		4	18	0	22	14	4	18
		18%	82%	0%	100%	78%	22%	100%
Total		17	56	6	79	20	36	56
		21%	71%	8%	100%	36%	64%	100%

dynamics, and stakeholder theory. Sociology-based theories also made a strong appearance, including institutional theory, social network theory, and social cognition. A few researchers used more macro-level theories, such as political ecology and postcolonial theory (Banerjee 2003; Orsato et al. 2002). Psychology-based theories were rare; not surprising given the paucity of individual-level studies. However, we did see some applications of goal theory, Ajzen's theory of planned behavior, and control theory (Branzei et al. 2004; Cordano and Frieze 2000; Flannery and May 2000). The theory employed did not appear to vary according to the outcomes being explored.

The obvious explanation for the preponderance of strategy and organizational theories is that many O&E researchers come from these disciplines. And, strategic management and institutional theories naturally extend to the O&E research arena. There may also be some selection bias in the journals we included in our analysis; for example, the SMJ has a strong strategy bias.

What These Observations Say About Our Research Domain

At the outset of this paper, we exposed our biases. We anticipated that O&E researchers would be more focused on organizational outcomes than on environmental outcomes in general management journals. We also assumed that the truly novel theoretical insights and methodological advances would be made in research publications focused on the natural environment. This preconception was based on the assumption that the gatekeepers and audiences of general management journals are most influenced by research that speaks the same language and makes the same assumptions that they do. So, researchers with an organization bias produce research that looks and feels like prior organizational research, while researchers with a natural environment bias can break from these constraining shackles.

We were surprised by the findings. In fact, 62% of O&E research published in these influential general management journals explained environmental outcomes. In these cases, the natural environment was not merely the empirical context or an explanatory variable. Our second expectation, that the most innovative research was in the area of environmental outcomes, was confirmed. But scratching the surface, we found clear biases in what was being published. In this section, we offer our own interpretations of the problems and we muse about the solutions. Inevitably, we have introduced our own prejudices based on our researching, publishing, and reviewing experiences. However, such provocation is often necessary to generate dialogue that will allow us to have greater impact on business and the natural environment through our research.

Collaborating with Organizational Researchers

This review showed us that research involving the natural environment was reaching the most influential general management journals. Our research was often as theoretically rich and methodologically rigorous as the other research published in these journals. As well, this research often presented strong evidence that there is a business case for environmental management. Yet, if the natural environment is truly important to organizations, then the question needs to be asked: Why do only 1.5% of the articles published in these journals pertain to the natural environment?

We can only speculate on the answer. One possible reason why more O&E research does not reach general management journals is that the gatekeepers are unreceptive to it. This might be an easy explanation, but we found little evidence of its veracity in our experience. As a frequent reviewer for the US journals, the first author has, in fact, experienced just the opposite. Indeed, in 1999, Anne Tsui, a former editor of the AMJ, wrote the following on a manuscript submitted by the first author:

> All three reviewers agreed that your paper deals with an interesting topic. As you know, there is a special research forum at *AMJ* dealing with this general topic. Within the last two years, I have accepted three papers that relate to this issue. Therefore, your manuscript is certainly on a topic that is welcomed at AMJ.

As a frequent reviewer, the first author has read numerous decisions letters from editors to O&E researchers. It is clear that this same sentiment is shared widely among editors. Resistance to O&E research, then, does not appear to be the reason why more O&E research has not reached general management journals.

We believe that the issue is mainly one of supply. There are just too few O&E researchers undertaking work of a quality to reach these journals. There is no way of telling whether the supply of researchers has changed in the last two decades, but there is some evidence suggesting that the field is likely growing. Many of the doctoral students who graduated in the 1990s, who were partly responsible for the spike in publications in 1998, are now in the position to mentor O&E doctoral students. As each faculty member often mentors several students over his/her career, the supply should increase. As well, business schools are increasingly staffing for O&E researchers and many of the most prestigious universities have hired a new O&E graduate within the last five years. This increased demand will likely stimulate increased supply and the 'coming out' of environmental researchers disguised as organizational researchers.

While the supply of researchers is slow to change and difficult to manipulate, it is relatively easier to improve the quality of research. The quality of the research being published is indisputably high, but for every article accepted for publication in these journals, there are likely many more that are rejected. The high number of conference papers presented on O&E issues annually certainly supports this claim.

Part of challenge in hitting these journals is one of crafting a good research program and writing an interesting and defensible argument. Many of these skills are tacit, such as framing the arguments and contribution, building theory, and linking tightly the methods with the theory. Craftsmanship, while seemingly transparent, is often not. Many of the general management journal editors understand this challenge and have published several articles in recent years that help researchers navigate the publishing process (Clark et al. 2006; Kilduff 2006; Rynes 2006). Doctoral students and researchers having difficulty reaching these general management journals are encouraged to read these insightful articles.

But, quality is not exclusively determined by craftsmanship of the research project. It is also determined by the language and style of the manuscript. We must speak the researchers' language of organization's fluently. We must use the same vocabulary, turn of phrases and style in order to be viewed as an insider. Good training, thorough peer reviews, and strong collaborations are helpful in ironing out our own idiosyncrasies. Therefore, it is important for O&E researchers not only to mingle with their environmental peers, but also to identify their organizational counterparts and build strong liasons. The more that O&E researchers partner with folks outside of the O&E field, the easier it is to learn the language and the more the O&E field will cross-pollinate into mainstream business, and ultimately be seen as mainstream itself. It is important for O&E researchers seeking to reach the organizations audience to work intimately with that audience.

Pushing Theoretical and Methodological Frontiers

The large percentage of O&E articles addressing environmental outcomes suggests that the natural environment is now recognized as an important issue within the general management audience. However, scratching the surface revealed an anomaly. Only a small fraction of this research offered radically new insights about the empirical phenomena. The truly innovative articles that spoke to the unique aspects of the natural environment were published primarily in European journals. In the US, most of the articles appeared in the special issue of the AMR. Had this special issue not been published, most US O&E research would have used conventional organization-based theories, hypo-deductive logic, and quantitative theory testing. Very few O&E articles explored the interactions among the different levels of analyses; most simply treated the levels as independent.

These comments may be read as a failure of O&E researchers to uncover what is unique and interesting about the natural environment. But, they can also be viewed as an opportunity to explore a myriad of new research streams. Here, we offer suggestions for a few of the more obvious directions.

Starik and Rands (1995) argued that the web of multilevel and multisystem relations around ecological sustainability might be much more complex than we think. It may include political-economic, social-cultural, and ecological environment relationships, not just the typical four levels of analysis. Gladwin et al. (1995) have spoken about these relationships in terms of inclusiveness, connectivity, and equity. These attributes suggest that there is an opportunity to explore cross-level, cross-theoretical, cross-enterprise, and cross-disciplinary analysis in new and unique ways.

Much of our research focuses exclusively on a single disciplinary domain, whether it be organizational behavior, strategic management, finance, and so forth. However, environmental issues require cross-disciplinary solutions. For example, research into the base of the pyramid (Prahalad and Hammond 2002) has relied heavily on marketing theory and models. For the base of the pyramid business model to be truly sustainable, production and consumption must be connected. However, working through the production and consumption systems are not easy and lead to theoretical challenges. There is an opportunity, arguably a need, to understand the paradoxes and tensions that arise when applying two different lenses from different theoretical foundations.

Environmental issues have emotional, cognitive, and value-based elements that pertain to the individual. And environmental issues also influence production systems, offer marketing opportunities, and require measurement and management systems at the organizational level of analysis. At the institutional level, many environmental issues require coordinated responses among groups of firms and changes to formal and informal systems. O&E researchers have an enormous opportunity to explore how these various levels are nested within each other. Individuals, organizations, and institutions operate within an interconnected system of relationships. As well, such explorations will require us to apply research methodologies that are relatively new to the field of business, such as Hierarchical Linear Modeling, two-stage and three-stage least squares, and qualitative research methods. By exploring these relationships, between different levels of analysis, theories, enterprises, and disciplines, we will really start to push new frontiers that are afforded to us by the environmental domain.

Closing Thoughts

Good O&E research is being published in management's most influential journals and it is pushing new frontiers. It was heartening to write this review because we quickly learned that the O&E field has matured in important ways. Much O&E research is theoretically rich and methodologically rigorous. O&E research has clearly made significant advances in the organization's domain.

While we were encouraged by the great strides made in the O&E field, we also saw some important opportunities for growth. We are sympathetic to the need to connect with core business disciplines, but it is troubling that we have not had an even greater presence in the most influential organizations journals. We have suggested here that more O&E researchers need to partner with colleagues in core disciplines. In doing so, O&E researchers not only improve our own ability to speak to different core audiences, but we can generate new insights through these collaborations.

As well, we have argued that we have fallen short of exploring what is new and interesting about the O&E field. Some articles have taken big risks and have made huge leaps. However, most articles that attempt to explain environmental outcomes use the same theories and methodologies that have dominated the organizations field. O&E researchers have an opportunity to really push the theoretical and methodological frontiers based on insights that are unique to the natural environment.

Researchers in our field are now in somewhat more privileged times than in 1995, as there is heightened public and business awareness of the natural environment. O&E research no longer needs to establish its legitimacy. As a research community, we need to take bigger strides into organization's research and bold steps into understanding environmental outcomes. Good research takes time, and our time has come.

References

Andersson, L. M., & Bateman, T. S. (2000). Individual environmental initiative: Championing natural environmental issues in U.S. business organizations. *Academy of Management Journal, 43*(4), 548–570.

Aragon-Correa, J. A. (1998). Strategic proactivity and firm approach to the natural environment. *Academy of Management Journal, 41*(5), 556–567.

Aragon-Correa, J. A., & Sharma, S. (2003). A contingent resource-based view of proactive corporate environmental strategy. *Academy of Management Review, 28*(1), 71–88.

Banerjee, S. B. (2001). Managerial perceptions of corporate environmentalism: Interpretations from industry and strategic implications for organizations. *The Journal of Management Studies, 38*(4), 489–513.

Banerjee, S. B. (2003). Who sustains whose development? Sustainable development and the reinvention of nature. *Organization Studies, 24*(1), 143–180.

Bansal, P. (2003). From issues to actions: The importance of individual concerns and organizational values in responding to natural environmental issues. *Organization Science, 14*(5), 510–527.

Bansal, P. (2005). Evolving sustainably: A longitudinal study of corporate sustainable development. *Strategic Management Journal, 26*(3), 197–218.

Bansal, P., & Clelland, I. (2004). Talking trash: Legitimacy, impression management, and unsystematic risk in the context of the natural environment. *Academy of Management Journal, 47*(1), 93–103.

Bansal, P., & Roth, K. (2000). Why companies go green: A model of ecological responsiveness. *Academy of Management Journal, 43*(4), 717–736.

Bergh, D. D., Perry, J., & Hanke, R. (2006). Some predictors of SMJ article impact. *Strategic Management Journal, 27*, 81–100.

Bowen, F. E. (2002). Organizational slack and corporate greening: Broadening the debate. *British Journal of Management, 13*(4), 305–316.

Branzei, O., Ursacki-Bryant, T. J., Vertinsky, I., & Zhang, W. (2004). The formation of green strategies in Chinese firms: Matching corporate environmental responses and individual principles. *Strategic Management Journal, 25*(11), 1075–1095.

Buysse, K., & Verbeke, A. (2003). Proactive environmental strategies: A stakeholder management perspective. *Strategic Management Journal, 24*(5), 453–470.

Chan, R. Y. K. (2005). Does the natural-resource-based view of the firm apply in an emerging economy? A survey of foreign invested enterprises in China. *The Journal of Management Studies, 42*(3), 625–672.

Child, J., & Tsai, T. (2005). The dynamic between firms' environmental strategies and institutional constraints in emerging economies: Evidence from China and Taiwan. *The Journal of Management Studies, 42*(1), 95–125.

Christmann, P. (2000). Effects of "best practices" of environmental management on cost advantage: The role of complementary assets. *Academy of Management Journal, 43*(4), 663–680.

Christmann, P. (2004). Multinational companies and the natural environment: Determinants of global environmental policy standardization. *Academy of Management Journal, 47*(5), 747–760.

Christmann, P., & Taylor, G. (2001). Globalization and the environment: Determiants of firm self-regulation in China. *Journal of International Business Studies, 32*(3), 439–458.

Clark, T., Floyd, S., & Wright, M. (2006). On the review process and journal development. *Journal of Management Studies, 43*(3), 655–664.

Cohen, B. (2006). Journal ratings and footprints: A North American perspective of organizations and the natural environment journal quality. *Business Strategy and Environment, 15*(1), 1–14.

Coopey, J. (2003). Sustainable development and environmental management: The performance of UK business schools. *Management Learning, 34*(1), 5–26.

Corbett, C. J., & DeCroix, G. A. (2001). Shared-savings contracts for indirect materials in supply chains: Channel profits and environmental impacts. *Management Science, 47*(7), 881–893.

Cordano, M., & Frieze, I. H. (2000). Pollution reduction preferences of U.S. environmental managers: Applying Ajzen's theory of planned behavior. *Academy of Management Journal, 43*(4), 627–641.

Cortazar, G., Schwartz, E. S., & Salinas, M. (1998). Evaluating enviromental investments: A real options approach. *Management Science, 44*(8), 1059–1070.

Crane, A. (2000). Corporate greening as amoralization. *Organization Studies, 21*(4), 673–696.

Dean, T. J., & Brown, R. L. (1995). Pollution regulation as a barrier to new firm entry: Initial evidence and implications for future research. *Academy of Management Journal, 38*(1), 288–303.

Douglas, T. J., & Judge, W. Q. J. (1995). Integrating the natural environment into the strategic planning process: An empirical assessment. *Academy of Management Best Papers Proceedings, 475*–479.

Egri, C. P., & Herman, S. (2000). Leadership in the North American environmental sector: Values, leadership styles, and contexts of environmental leaders and their organizations. *Academy of Management Journal, 43*(4), 571–604.

Fineman, S. (1996). Emotional subtexts in corporate greening. *Organization Studies, 17*(3), 479–500.

Fineman, S. (1997). Constructing the green manager. *British Journal of Management, 8*(1), 31–38.

Fineman, S., & Clarke, K. (1996). Green stakeholders: Industry interpretations and response. *The Journal of Management Studies, 33*(6), 715–730.

Flannery, B. L., & May, D. R. (2000). Environmental ethical decision making in the U.S. metal-finishing industry. *Academy of Management Journal, 43*(4), 642–662.

Ghoshal, S. (2005). Bad management theories are destroying good management practices. *Academy of Management Learning & Education, 4*(1), 75–91.

Gilley, K. M., Worrell, D. L., Davidson III, W. N., & El-Jelly, A. (2000). Corporate environmental initiatives and anticipated firm performance: The differential effects of process-driven versus product-driven greening initiatives. *Journal of Management, 26*(6), 1199–1216.

Gladwin, T. N., Kennelly, J. J., & Krause, T.-S. (1995). Shifting paradigms for sustainable development: Implications for management theory and research. *Academy of Management Review, 20*(4), 874–907.

Gonzalez-Benito, J., & Gonzalez-Benito, O. (2005). An analysis of the relationship between environmental motivations and ISO14001 certification. *British Journal of Management, 16*(2), 133–148.

Halme, M. (2002). Corporate environmental paradigms in shift: Learning during the course of action at UPM-Kymmene. *The Journal of Management Studies, 39*(8), 1087–1109.

Hart, S. L. (1995). A natural-resource-based view of the firm. *Academy of Management Review, 20*(4), 986–1014.

Henriques, I., & Sadorsky, P. (1999). The relationship between environmental commitment and managerial perceptions of stakeholder importance. *Academy of Management Journal, 42*(1), 87–99.

Hoffman, A. J. (1999). Institutional evolution and change: Environmentalism and the U.S. chemical industry. *Academy of Management Journal, 42*(4), 351–371.

Hoffman, A. J., & Ocasio, W. (2001). Not all events are attended equally: Toward a middle-range theory of industry attention to external events. *Organization Science, 12*(4), 414–434.

Jennings, P. D., & Zandbergen, P. A. (1995). Ecologically sustainable organizations: An institutional approach. *Academy of Management Review, 20*(4), 1015–1052.

Jermier, J. M., Forbes, L. C., Benn, S., & Orsato, R. J. (2006). The new corporate environmentalism and green politics. In C. H. Stewart, R. Clegg, W. R. Nord, & T. Lawrence (Eds.), *Handbook of organization studies* (2nd ed., pp. 618–650). London: Sage.

Jiang, R. J., & Bansal, P. (2003). Seeing the need for ISO 14001. *The Journal of Management Studies, 40*(4), 1047–1067.

Judge, W. Q., & Douglas, T. J. (1998). Performance implications of incorporating natural environmental issues into the strategic planning process: An empirical assessment. *Journal of Management Studies, 35*(2), 241–262.

Kassinis, G., & Vafeas, N. (2002). Corporate boards and outside stakeholders as determinants of environmental litigation. *Strategic Management Journal, 23*(5), 399–415.

Kilduff, M. (2006). Editor's comments: Publishing theory. *Academy of Management Review, 31*(2), 252–255.

King, A. A., & Lenox, M. J. (2000). Industry self-regulation without sanctions: The chemical industry's responsible care program. *Academy of Management Journal, 43*(4), 698–716.

King, A. A., & Shaver, J. M. (2001). Are aliens green? Assessing foreign establishments' environmental conduct in the United States. *Strategic Management Journal, 22*(11), 1069–1085.

Klassen, R. D., & McLaughlin, C. P. (1996). The impact of environmental management on firm performance. *Management Science, 42*(8), 1199–1214.

Klassen, R. D., & Whybark, D. C. (1999). The impact of environmental technologies on manufacturing performance. *Academy of Management Journal, 42*(6), 599–615.

Lewis, G. J., & Harvey, B. (2001). Perceived environmental uncertainty: The extension of Miller's scale to the natural environment. *The Journal of Management Studies, 38*(2), 201–233.

Lin, C.-R., & Buongiorno, J. (1998). Tree diversity, landscape diversity, and economics of maple-birch forests: Implications of markovian models. *Management Science, 44*(10), 1351–1366.

Lockett, A., Moon, J., & Visser, W. (2006). Corporate social responsibility in management research: Focus, nature, salience and sources of influence. *The Journal of Management Studies, 43*(1), 115–136.

Lounsbury, M. (2001). Institutional sources of practice variation: Staffing college and university recycling programs. *Administrative Science Quarterly, 46*(1), 29–56.

Marcus, A., & Geffen, D. (1998). The dialectics of competency acquisition: Pollution prevention in electric generation. *Strategic Management Journal, 19*(12), 1145–1168.

McKay, R. B. (2001). Organizational responses to an environmental Bill of Rights. *Organization Studies, 22*(4), 625–658.

Meester, G. A., Mehrotra, A., Ault, J. S., & Baker, E. K. (2004). Designing marine reserves for fishery management. *Management Science, 50*(8), 1031–1043.

Miller, K. D. (1993). Industry and country effects on managers' perceptions of environmental uncertainties. *Journal of International Business Studies, 24*(4), 693–714.

Mintzberg, H., & Westley, F. (2000). Sustaining the institutional environment. *Organization Studies, 21*, 71–94.

Nault, B. R. (1996). Equivalence of taxes and subsidies in the control of production externalities. *Management Science, 42*(3), 307–320.

Nehrt, C. (1998). Maintainability of first mover advantages when environmental regulations differ between countries. *Academy of Management Review, 23*(1), 77–97.

Newton, T. (2002). Creating the new ecological order? Elias and actor-network theory. *Academy of Management Review, 27*(4), 523–540.

Newton, T. (2005). Practical idealism: An oxymoron? *The Journal of Management Studies, 42*(4), 869–884.

Newton, T., & Harte, G. (1997). Green business: Technicist kitsch? *The Journal of Management Studies, 34*(1), 75–98.

Orlitzky, M., Schmidt, F. L., & Rynes, S. L. (2003). Corporate social and financial performance: A meta-analysis. *Organization Studies, 24*(3), 403–441.

Orsato, R. J., Hond, F. D., & Clegg, S. R. (2002). The political ecology of automobile recycling in Europe. *Organization Studies, 23*(4), 639–665.

Prahalad, C. K., & Hammond, A. (2002). Serving the world's poor, profitably. *Harvard Business Review, 80*(9), 48–57.

Prasad, P., & Elmes, M. (2005). In the name of the practical: Unearthing the hegemony of pragmatics in the discourse of environmental management. *The Journal of Management Studies, 42*(4), 845–867.

Purser, R. E., Park, C., & Montuori, A. (1995). Limits to anthropocentrism: Toward an ecocentric organization paradigm? *Academy of Management Review, 20*(4), 1053–1089.

Ramus, C. A., & Steger, U. (2000). The roles of supervisory support behaviors and environmental policy in employee "ecoinitiatives" at leading-edge European companies. *Academy of Management Journal, 43*(4), 605–626.

Rothenberg, S. (2003). Knowledge content and worker participation in environmental management at NUMMI. *The Journal of Management Studies, 40*(7), 1783–1802.

Rugman, A. M., & Verbeke, A. (1998a). Corporate strategies and environmental regulations: An organizing framework. *Strategic Management Journal, 19*(4), 363–375.

Rugman, A. M., & Verbeke, A. (1998b). Corporate strategy and international environmental policy. *Journal of International Business Studies, 29*(4), 819–834.

Russo, M. V. (2003). The emergence of sustainable industries: Building on natural capital. *Strategic Management Journal, 24*(4), 317–331.

Russo, M. V., & Fouts, P. A. (1997). A resource-based perspective on corporate environmental performance and profitability. *Academy of Management Journal, 40*(3), 534–559.

Russo, M. V., & Harrison, N. S. (2005). Organizational design and environmental performance: Clues from the electronics industry. *Academy of Management Journal, 48*(4), 582–593.

Rynes, S. L. (2006). Making the most of the review process: Lessons from award-winning authors. *Academy of Management Journal, 49*(2), 189–190.

Sharma, S. (2000). Managerial interpretations and organizational context as predictors of corporate choice of environmental strategy. *Academy of Management Journal, 43*(4), 681–697.

Sharma, S., & Henriques, I. (2005). Stakeholder influences on sustainability practices in the Canadian forest products industry. *Strategic Management Journal, 26*(2), 159–180.

Sharma, S., & Vredenburg, H. (1998). Proactive corporate environmental strategy and the development of competitively valuable organizational capabilities. *Strategic Management Journal, 19*(8), 729–753.

Shrivastava, P. (1995a). Ecocentric management for a risk society. *Academy of Management Review, 20*(1), 118–137.

Shrivastava, P. (1995b). Environmental technologies and competitive advantage. *Strategic Management Journal, 16,* 183–200.

Shrivastava, P. (1995c). The role of corporations in achieving ecological sustainability. *Academy of Management Review, 20*(4), 936–960.

Starik, M., & Rands, G. P. (1995). Weaving an integrated web: Multilevel and multisystem perspectives of ecologically sustainable organizations. *Academy of Management Review, 20*(4), 908–935.

Tenbrunsel, A. E., Wade-Benzoni, K. A., Messick, D. M., & Bazerman, M. H. (2000). Understanding the influence of environmental standards on judgments and choices. *Academy of Management Journal, 43*(5), 854–866.

van Marrewijk, M. (2003). Concepts and definitions of CSR and corporate sustainability: Between agency and communion. *Journal of Business Ethics, 44*(2/3), 95–105.

Walsh, J. P., Weber, K., & Margolis, J. D. (2003). Social issues and management: Our lost cause found. *Journal of Management, 29*(6), 859–881.

Whiteman, G., & Cooper, W. H. (2000). Ecological embeddedness. *Academy of Management Journal, 43*(6), 1265–1282.

Wilhelm, W. E., & Srinivasa, A. V. (1997). Prescribing tactical response for oil spill clean up operations. *Management Science, 43*(3), 386–402.

Winn, M. I., & Angell, L. C. (2000). Towards a process model of corporate greening. *Organization Studies, 21*(6), 1119–1147.

Zietsma, C., Winn, M., Branzei, O., & Vertinsky, I. (2002). The war of the woods: Facilitators and impediments of organizational learning processes. *British Journal of Management, 13*(Special Issue), S61–S74.

Chapter 9
Making Sense of Local Sustainability

Don Clifton

Introduction

In this chapter, we look at how *Ecological Footprint Analysis* (*Footprint Analysis*) can help us assess behavior at a local level in terms of humanity achieving a broader global sustainability goal. The South Australian setting is used as a case study to demonstrate how this type of assessment can be undertaken.

The discussion that follows highlights a number of confronting issues concerning humanity's challenge in moving to a sustainable way of life. First, humanity's rate of exploitation of the Earth's renewable natural resource base (i.e., our *Ecological Footprint*), exceeds the rate at which this resource can regenerate itself (i.e., available *Biocapacity*) by a factor of 150% (effectively, we need the regenerative capacity of 1½ Earths to meet current renewable natural resource exploitation demands). When we allow for renewable natural resources that are not safely available for human use so that ecosystem integrity is preserved, resources are being used at the regenerative capacity of about three Earths. We only have one Earth available.

Second, exploitation of the Earth's renewable natural resources beyond their regenerative capacity (i.e., a position of ecological *overshoot*) has been evident for at least the last 50 years and, despite the mainstream notion of sustainable development having been prominent on the international stage for over 25 years, the rate of overshoot is increasing—things are getting worse, not better. The implications for future generations are disturbing. The current generation is externalizing the harms of its resource use on to those who follow, violating the intergenerational justice principle on which virtually every formulation of what it means for humanity to live sustainably is based.

Next, the 15% of the world's population living in the richest nations (about 1 billion people) are exploiting the Earth's renewable natural resources at such a rate that, if everyone lived the way this 15% does, we would need almost seven Earths

D. Clifton (✉)
International Graduate School of Business, University of South Australia,
Adelaide, South Australia, Australia
e-mail: doncmail@bigpond.net.au; Don.Clifton@unisa.edu.au

© Springer Science+Business Media Dordrecht 2014   135
S. Sandhu et al. (eds.), *Linking Local and Global Sustainability*, The International Society
of Business, Economics, and Ethics Book Series 4, DOI 10.1007/978-94-017-9008-6_9

to sustain this lifestyle. This inequitable use of the Earth's resources presents major questions of equity within members of the current generation.

Finally, an Ecological Footprint Analysis of the South Australian setting—one that fits within the '15% of richest' category—shows that its citizens are not, as a collective, living sustainably within the global context. Further, the combination of South Australia's current Ecological Footprint and population growth policies sees this unsustainable way of life and position of resource use privilege as intended to continue indefinitely.

A Sustainable World

Contested Space

What does it means for humanity to live sustainably—for there to be a *sustainable world*? This is a difficult concept to pin down. Whether talked of as *sustainability* or as *sustainable development*, and despite agreement that a sustainable world is something we need (Gould and Lewis 2009; Osorio et al. 2005; Wissenburg 2001), the concept remains pluralistic, contested, and grounded in different value systems and world views (Gladwin et al. 1995; Manderson 2006; Osorio et al. 2005). Despite this, two distinct sustainable world approaches can be identified,[1] namely a *Reformist approach* and a *Transformational approach*.

Reformist and Transformational Approaches

The Reformist approach sees the current dominant socio-economic system[2] as fundamentally sound and able to deliver the key Reformist goal of continued human development or, more commonly, sustainable development. Under this approach,

---

[1] This Reformist-Transformational characterization is acknowledged as simplistic in that it masks the variance of thought that exists within these general classifications, including approaches that sit at the extremes. For a detailed discussion on the Reformist-Transformational approaches, see Clifton (2010a).

[2] The dominant socio-economic system referred to here is that of an economic growth model encompassing free trade, globalization, a key role for multinational corporations, a focus on technological advance, and wellbeing through increased personal income and consumption. This paradigm goes under a number of tag-names in the literature including the technological social paradigm or technocentrism (Bell 2009; Gladwin et al. 1995), and liberalism (or neo-liberalism) in the sense of liberalism being "a view of order linked to material progress, endlessly stimulated through science, technology, and corporate innovation within the lax constraints of the marketplace" (Laferriere and Stoett 2006, p. 7). It also embraces ideas consistent with human exemptionalism (Bell 2009) and modernism (Gare 2000). In this sense, socio-economic system dominance can be seen in terms of the system that is currently dominant in the world by way of its economic and political power.

humanity's challenge is to pursue human development through continued economic growth and technology advance, but in ways that address the ecological and social harms that are currently being experienced—that is, to make the current system more green-and-just. For Reformism, continued economic growth is necessary to overcome poverty and promote general human wellbeing, globalization and free trade are necessary to support these economic goals, and technological advance is needed to improve resource use efficiency, maximize natural resource productivity, and to develop less polluting production and consumption processes. Reformism is the current dominant sustainable world approach (Gould and Lewis 2009; Handmer and Dovers 1996) and is consistent with the sustainable development agenda promoted by the United Nations (UN) and its related bodies, by most governments, and by the business sector.

In contrast, the Transformational approach sees the current dominant socio-economic system as a root cause of current unsustainable behaviors and, to progress a sustainable world, transformational change is needed. It sees human wellbeing as best progressed through consumptive sufficiency and a focus on wellbeing through life experiences, continued consumptive growth as unsustainable and a primary cause of both ecological problems and poverty, poverty as best resolved through resource reallocation not more global-level resource-consumptive growth, and quantitative constraints needing to be placed on the use of the Earth's natural resources to keep it within ecosystem limits (Clifton 2010a; Diesendorf 1997; Williams and Millington 2004).

The Wellbeing + Justice Common Goal

Despite their differences, the primary goal for both the Reformist and Transformational sustainable world approaches is one of human and ecological wellbeing, underpinned by principles of intergenerational and intragenerational justice (Clifton 2010a) (this will be referred to as the *wellbeing + justice* sustainable world goal). What the components of this goal are taken to mean, and how they are achieved, is where Reformism and the Transformational approach differ. This wellbeing + justice goal is of particular importance for the discussion that follows, as Footprint Analysis, which is the method used in assessing local action in terms of global sustainability, is concerned with use of the Earth's renewable natural resources, with flow-on implications for human and ecological wellbeing and application of justice principles in how these resources are shared.

The wellbeing limb of the wellbeing + justice goal is often talked of in terms of *flourishing life*. What this translates to in practice is somewhat vague, however, in the human domain it is linked to ideas of a 'good life' (Barry 2003; Daly and Farley 2004), having meaning and value in life (Naess 1988; Taylor 1989), and living healthy and productive lives (UN 1992b). In the non-human realm, the wellbeing of life covers individual organisms, ecosystems, through to the Earth as a whole. In these contexts, flourishing life refers to what is good for the organism or system in question (for more on what it means for non-human life to flourish, see Taylor

(1989) and Boyden (2001)). From a Footprint Analysis perspective, and when considering local sustainability in the global context, what is important to consider is how the use of the Earth's renewable natural resources supports or detracts from this wellbeing objective.

For the justice limb of wellbeing + justice, what matters in the human realm for both the Reformist and Transformational approaches is that flourishing life is actually achieved (Holbrook 2009). As such, justice in the sustainable world context is ultimately end-result (i.e., *consequentialist*) based. It is concerned with more than simply making sure that certain basic needs are met (e.g., in the human domain: enough food, adequate housing, the provision of health care) in an equitable way. What is important is translating the meeting of basic needs into a flourishing life. From a Footprint Analysis perspective, how Reformism and the Transformational approach address the distribution of renewable natural resources is discussed further below.

In the non-human realm, questions of justice are a little more complex. Reformism tends to focus on maintaining ecological wellbeing primarily for human interest purposes (i.e., is *anthropocentric* in its approach), and justice has more to do with how the Earth's ecosystems are protected for the benefit of all of humanity, both current and future generations (Bell 2009; Gladwin et al. 1995; Williams and Millington 2004). The Transformational approach takes things further and, in addition to the need to treat the non-human world in a way that is just towards humans, also extends the concept of justice to the non-human world itself (i.e., is *ecocentric* in its orientation) (Bell 2009; Gladwin et al. 1995; Schlosberg 2007; Williams and Millington 2004).

How can we know though if the citizens of a particular place—say, a nation, a sub-nation state, or a local community—are living in ways that support the wellbeing + justice goal in either its Reformist or Transformational form? Footprint Analysis is one approach that can be used to help do this, and the discussion will now turn to exploring how this might be done.

Footprint Analysis

Overview

Footprint Analysis follows a three-step process (Footprint Network 2010a). First, a *Biocapacity* measure is determined, which represents the regenerative and waste-sink capacity of the renewable natural resource base for the area in question (say, for a city, a nation, or the Earth as a whole). The measure is usually presented as a collective area of productive land and ocean space that is available per person, termed *global hectares per capita* (ghpc). Next, an *Ecological Footprint* measure is calculated which shows the rate at which a unit of analysis (e.g., a city, nation, or all of humanity) is using the Earth's renewable natural resources from a physical consumption and waste-sink perspective regardless of where on the planet the

Item	Value
Global average Ecological Footprint	2.7 ghpc
Global average Biocapacity	1.8 ghpc
Ecological Footprint as a % of Biocapacity	150%

Table 9.1 Current footprint analysis data. (Data source: Footprint Network 2010b)

production of consumed goods occurs, also expressed as ghpc. Finally, the Ecological Footprint and Biocapacity figures are compared to determine a measure of *ecological credit* or *ecological deficit*. A global-level ecological deficit means that humanity's use of the Earth's renewable natural resources exceeds its regenerative capacity, resulting in depletion of resource stocks—a state of ecological *overshoot*.

Footprint Analysis and a Sustainable World

Footprint Analysis is not a complete measure of what it means for humanity to live sustainably: it instead measures what is claimed to be a necessary, although insufficient, condition—that humanity lives within the Earth's Biocapacity limits (Footprint Network 2010a; Kitzes 2007). It can be likened to the idea of living off the interest of money invested rather than depleting the capital base that generates the income. The reason this claim of living within regenerative capacity is made as a necessary requirement for humanity to live sustainably is that, over an extended period, ongoing ecological deficit causes continued depletion of the Earth's renewable natural resource base, eroding the very fabric on which life depends. At some point, continued depletion of these stocks must reach a point where they are not able to sustain flourishing life as understood within the sustainable world context. Temporary states of stock depletion may not necessarily be a problem, but long term continuation is.

Data and Interpretation Issues

Before considering the detail of how Footprint Analysis can be used for local-to-global assessment, it is important to clarify a number of issues concerning the raw Footprint Analysis data in order for these data to be used in a meaningful way. In this section we look at some of these issues.

Table 9.1 shows the current global level Footprint Analysis summary data, and Table 9.2 shows this data dissected into national income groups.

Two key observations can be made from these data. First, is that, at the global level, humanity's per capita Ecological Footprint is about 150% of available Biocapacity, so humanity is not living sustainably in Footprint Analysis terms. Second, is that there is significant inequality in Ecological Footprint, with citizens of high income nations having an Ecological Footprint of approximately five times that of low-income nations.

Table 9.2 Ecological Footprint by national income. (Data source: Footprint Network 2010b)

	Population: % of global total	Actual Ecological Footprint: % of global total	Ecological Footprint per capita (ghpc)
World	100	100	2.7
High-income nations	15	38	6.1
Middle-income nations	65	52	2.0
Low-income nations	20	10	1.2

Table 9.3 Current Footprint Analysis data with modified Biocapacity values

Item	Value
Global average Ecological Footprint (see Table 9.1)	2.7 ghpc
Biocapacity—50% unavailable for human use	
Global average Biocapacity available for human use (50% of 1.8 ghpc (see Table 9.1))	0.9 ghpc
Ecological Footprint as a % of available Biocapacity	300%

These raw data are, however, somewhat misleading as they fail to account for Biocapacity that is not safely available for human use. Humans simply can't exploit all of the available Biocapacity as some needs to be set aside to maintain ecosystem integrity by meeting the needs of other species and maintaining the resilience of these ecosystems. So what allowance should we make for Biocapacity that is not available for human use? There is no clear answer to this question (for a detailed discussion on this matter, see Clifton (2010c)), but something around 50% (or more) may well be needed. Table 9.3 shows the global-level Footprint Analysis data after allowing for Biocapacity that is not safely available for human use.

What this means is that the true extent of humanity's ecological deficit is significantly greater than the standard Footprint Analysis data reveal. This deficit position is not a once off. When Biocapacity not available for human use is considered, ecological deficit is evident from at least the early 1960s—over 50 years of humanity depleting the Earth's aggregate renewable natural resource base. Worse, the deficit is increasing with no signs of a reversal of this trend. Coupled with Ecological Footprint inequity (as per Table 9.2), this persistent and worsening ecological deficit position poses some significant problems for the wellbeing + justice sustainable world goal we discussed earlier.

The first of these problems has to do with flow-on implication to the wellbeing of parties who are impacted on by current resource consumptive behaviors. Both the Reformist and Transformational approaches support a *weak anthropocentric* view to the wellbeing + justice goal, where a sustainable world has to do with the satisfaction of human interests that support flourishing life (Clifton 2010a) based on humans making considered preferences when satisfying our interests (Norton 2003). These considered preferences include things such as being concerned about the wellbeing of current and future generations, and for the cultural, spiritual, and amenity values of Nature as opposed to merely economic interests (Hargrove 2003; Light and Rolston 2003; Palmer 2003; Speth 2005; WCED 1987). Andersson and Lindroth (2001) propose that the consequences of continued global ecological deficit are born by three main parties: (a) the economically and politically weak, as the more powerful are able to better appropriate resources for their own use, (b) future generations, through the running down of renewable natural resource stocks to support current generation consumption, and (c) non-human species, through human appropriation of resources to the detriment of these species. In these respects, continued ecological deficit is in breach of the weak anthropocentric requirement—it doesn't allow for the wellbeing of these three groups that are impacted on by this continued ecological deficit problem. In addition, the Transformational approach also embraces an ecocentric life-view (as discussed earlier) which continued ecological deficit clearly breaches and has significant ramifications throughout the entire Transformational narrative.

The second key problem has to do with the challenges in sharing available Biocapacity in an equitable way. For Reformism, the key issue is equity within the human domain—both within the current generation, and between the current and future generations. The Transformational approach extends this to include equity between humans and non-human species. The core issue however is this. For humanity to live sustainably in Footprint Analysis terms, the average global Ecological Footprint needs to reduce from the current level of 2.7 ghpc to about 0.9 ghpc (based on the Biocapacity values shown in Table 9.3). Looking forward however, and based on the mid-range UN human population projection to 2050 of 9 billion, the 2050 Biocapacity value that is safely available for human use will reduce to about 0.7 ghpc (Clifton 2010c). When we look at the 152 nations listed in the most recent set of Footprint Analysis accounts (Footprint Network 2010b), only six have an Ecological Footprint value of 0.7 ghpc or less, with all of these nations fitting within a low or least-developed nation status. So in order for humanity to live sustainably by way of Biocapacity use, some form of equitable sharing of available Biocapacity needs to be achieved in a way that sees flourishing lives for all, but done so at global average Biocapacity-use levels that are currently being experienced by only a handful of the least developed nations on Earth! This is an enormous challenge but one that need to be confronted.

Assessing the Local in Terms of the Global

To live sustainably in Footprint Analysis terms, humanity needs to limit its use of the Earth's renewable natural resources to the level of Biocapacity that is safely available for human use. In this respect, for a local area to be contributing positively to a sustainable world, it needs to be using Biocapacity in a way that is consistent with this global live-within-available-Biocapacity goal, and to do so in ways consistent with the wellbeing + justice principle.

So how do we work out if a local area is meeting these Footprint Analysis requirements? Four key 'tests' are evident in the literature that can help here (Clifton 2010b), and in the points that follow each of these tests is assessed after which the tests are applied to the South Australian setting.

Consumption Ecological Footprint and Local Biocapacity

The first of these tests is that a region's *consumption-based* Ecological Footprint—that is, the Ecological Footprint measured in terms of renewable natural resources that are consumed regardless of where on the planet those resources are sourced from—remains within that region's Biocapacity limits. This argument focuses mostly on nations or other substantial regional areas (e.g., within-nation states, or multi-nation regions). If all regions met this criterion then the claim is that the global level living-within-Biocapacity-limits requirement would be met.

The main arguments against this approach are these. First is the view that linking a region's Ecological Footprint to its own Biocapacity ignores the fairness of the region's Ecological Footprint relative to broader social justice issues. As an example, Canada has an Ecological Footprint of 7 ghpc but, being a natural resource rich country with a relatively low population density, its Biocapacity is about 15 ghpc (Footprint Network 2010b). So is it right to say Canadians are living sustainability in global terms where the global average Ecological Footprint needs to be about 0.9 ghpc? In this sense, living-within-regional-Biocapacity may create a false sense of comfort that the region's Ecological Footprint is sustainable when, in the global context, it may not be (Andersson and Lindroth 2001; Footprint Network 2006). Next is a claim that regional boundaries are arbitrary human constructs that have no meaningful relationship to how population numbers are dispersed or how biologically productive regional landscapes are (Lenzen and Murray 2001; Nijkamp et al. 2004). Finally, it is claimed that how regional boundaries have been defined and how population numbers have settled over time means that not all regions can live within their Biocapacity limits or, with the ability to trade, do they need to (Dietz and Neumayer 2007; Nijkamp et al. 2004). As an example, Singapore has an Ecological Footprint of 5.3 ghpc but no material Biocapacity value. Do Singapore residents really need to live within the nation's Biocapacity limits or, with the ability to trade, can they instead import their renewable natural resource consumptive needs?

The main argument supporting this approach is that it shows whether a region could, if it chose, live off its own Biocapacity supplies and not be subject to the risks of resource competition in the global space and hence becomes a risk management and security enhancing mechanism (Footprint Network 2008; Wackernagel and Yount 1998).

Production Ecological Footprint and Local Biocapacity

The next test is that a region's *production-based* Ecological Footprint—that is, an alternate Footprint measure based on the renewable natural resources that are physically sourced from within a region's boundaries—remains within its Biocapacity limits. Following this provision is claimed to provide a way of limiting the renewable natural resource impact of production occurring within a region's borders to the resources within those borders. The outcome is that a region's own resources would be protected and, if followed by all nations, the global renewable natural resource base would similarly be protected.

The major weakness of this approach is that it ignores the magnitude and consequences of the broader consumptive behaviors of citizen in a particular region. For example, local renewable natural resources can be preserved by importing resources from other regions and possibly degrading the resources of those regions.

Despite its weaknesses, this approach has its merits. It offers a current-day measure of regional human renewable natural resource appropriation, which can help address problems of time lags in ecosystem feedback; these time lags can otherwise result in the negative consequences of human impacts on ecosystems materializing at some time in the future, well after the damage has been done (Gibson 2001; Meadows et al. 2004). It also internalizes the consequences of production activities onto the current-day regional community, which can help address possible social justice violations, such as pushing onto future generations the negative consequences of current human behavior. Finally, protecting local resources reduces the risks of local ecological degradation which, if it occurred, may also negatively impact on other regions (Handmer and Dovers 1996; WCED 1987).

Fair-Earth-Share

The third test sets aside regional specifics, and looks at the Earth's Biocapacity as a resource to be shared by all of humanity. The idea is that access to global Biocapacity should not be determined by accidents of time and place (i.e., not based on being born in a particular location or social setting, on how national borders came about, or how population numbers have settled). Rather, it claims that all of humanity has an equal right to the Earth's Biocapacity—a right to a *fair-Earth-share*—where fair-Earth-share equals the total global Biocapacity that can safely be used by humans divided by the total global population (Collins et al. 2006; Giljum et al. 2007). Application of the fair-Earth-share concept means that if the per capita Ecological Footprint of any unit of focus (a nation, sub-nation state, local community, individual, etc.) is equal to or less than the fair-Earth-share, then that unit is living sustainably in Footprint Analysis terms or, conversely, if in excess of the fair-Earth-share, then that unit is detracting from a global sustainability objective (for examples of this application, see Simpson et al. (2000) and Nijkamp et al. (2004)). This fair-Earth-share concept is a strong theme in the Transformational approach, however its application for Reformism is not so clear. Reformism is more concerned with ensuring all members of society have their needs met in order to live flourishing lives but, beyond this, narratives are not strong on equality in Biocapacity sharing; they focus instead on the equitable sharing of the benefits of continued green-and-just economic growth (WCED 1987). Despite this, it is challenging to see how under Reformism, sustainable world justice principles could support the sharing of globally available Biocapacity in any way that is substantially different to the fair-Earth-share concept.

The key advantages of this approach are, firstly, that it directly addresses issues of distributive justice where, in a world of limited Biocapacity supply such that more for some means less for others, the fair-Earth-share concept can be quite appealing. Second, it is an approach that is generalizable to all and sets clear criteria as to whether a unit of focus is living in ways consistent with a global sustainability goal. Despite these advantages, this approach has its challenges, two of which are particularly relevant to the current discussion, namely population and national sovereignty.

For population, the fair-Earth-share approach does not directly confront the question of population numbers. From a per-capita perspective, an increasing global population is per-capita Biocapacity eroding—more people means a smaller fair-Earth-share. As such, even if a region reduced its Ecological Footprint to fair-Earth-share limits, and did so with no population growth, population growth in other regions could lower the fair-Earth-share Biocapacity value making, through no fault of its own, the otherwise 'sustainable' region 'unsustainable' (Daly 1996).

For national sovereignty, the rights of nations to make their own decisions concerning how resources within their borders are dealt with is an established principle in international declarations and agreements (e.g., see UN (1992a, 1992b)). When dealing with the use of Biocapacity that is part of the global commons (e.g., the atmosphere and CO_2 emissions), the fair-Earth-share concept is relatively easy to accommodate within this national sovereignty regime. When dealing with physical resources within a nation's borders however, this becomes more challenging. It is possible, for example, to imagine a nation deliberately embarking on a low-population policy and actively protecting its resources to ensure its citizens can live flourishing lives but, in doing so, utilizing Biocapacity in excess of a fair-Earth-share. The point is that the fair-Earth-share principle can, on its own, have the effect of undermining the national sovereignty principle, turning local resources into a form of global commons, and watering down any benefits communities might expect to enjoy from taking strong local action to progress sustainable world objectives. Some fair-Earth-share proponents propose solutions to this by allocating resource rights based on population numbers at a point in time (McLaren 2003), however many challenges remain in implementing a workable fair-Earth-share Biocapacity strategy. These implementation challenges do not, however, diminish the fair-Earth-share approach as a useful local-to-global sustainable world testing method.

The Generalization Principle

The fourth test is based on the generalization principle (Daly 1996; WCED 1987). Within the Footprint Analysis context, the idea is to consider if the Ecological Footprint and Biocapacity position of a unit of focus, and how this unit's behaviors might impact on this position over time, is generalizable to all of humanity and for a sustainable world to still come about. If it is not generalizable, then the unit of focus is not living sustainably.

One way of looking at this is in terms of the $I = PAT$ formulation. $I = PAT$ (Chertow 2000; Holdren et al. 1995; York et al. 2003) presents human impact on the environment 'I' (or, for our purposes here, the Ecological Footprint), as a product of:

'P': population.
'A': affluence, represented in terms of consumption/production per capita, usually as per capita GDP.
'T': technology, in terms of the ecological impact per unit of consumption/production.

For our purposes in considering local sustainability in the global context, the generalization principle as we are applying it here would propose that, even if a region had a current Ecological Footprint that might be considered consistent with a global sustainability goal (say, by meeting the fair-Earth-share objective), that region's behavior by way of say, population and consumption aspirations—specifically, growing either or both—may apply upward pressures to that region's Ecological Footprint that cannot be generalized to all other nations.

The advantage of this approach is that, although the first three tests are based on this generalization concept, they are one dimensional. This fourth test opens for consideration other issues relevant to a local-to-global Footprint Analysis assessment, particularly in relation to behaviors that may increase renewable natural resource use, and/or erode the amount of available Biocapacity.

A Sustainable World—The Local in Terms of the Global

In this section, the various concepts discussed so far are applied to a local setting—South Australia—to assess it in terms of its contribution to, or detraction from, a global sustainability goal.

South Australia: Current Footprint Analysis Position

South Australia's (SA) current Footprint Analysis position is set out in Tables 9.4 and 9.5.

Assessing these data in terms of the four tests described above shows:

1. Consumption-based Ecological Footprint vs local Biocapacity:
   SA's citizens, with an average Ecological Footprint of 7.0 ghpc, are not living within SA's Biocapacity limits after allowance is made for Biocapacity that is not available for human use.
2. Production-based Ecological Footprint vs local Biocapacity:
   Data on SA's production-based measure is not available so no conclusions can be drawn.
3. Fair-Earth-share:

Table 9.4 South Australia—current Footprint Analysis data. (Data source: SAG 2006b)

Item	Value
Current average Ecological Footprint for SA residents	7.0 ghpc
Current average SA Biocapacity	7.5 ghpc
Ecological Footprint as a % of Biocapacity	93%
Biocapacity—50% unavailable for human use	
SA Biocapacity available for human use (i.e., 50% of 7.5 ghpc)	3.8 ghpc
SA's Ecological Footprint as a % of available Biocapacity	186%

Table 9.5 South Australia—Footprint Analysis data in the global context

Item	Value
1. Ecological Footprint comparison—SA vs global	
Current average SA Ecological Footprint	7.0 ghpc
Current average global Ecological Footprint (as per Table 9.1)	2.7 ghpc
SA's Ecological Footprint as a % of current global average Ecological Footprint	259%
2. Ecological Footprint and Biocapacity comparison—SA's Ecological Footprint vs global Biocapacity	
Global average Biocapacity at 50% of current value (as per Table 9.3)	0.9 ghpc
SA's current Ecological Footprint as % of current global Biocapacity	777%

SA's citizens, with an Ecological Footprint of 7.0 ghpc, are living well above the global average Ecological Footprint of 2.7 ghpc, and even further above a Biocapacity fair-Earth-share value which currently sits at about 0.9 ghpc (see Table 9.3).

4. Generalization test:

   Two of the South Australian Government's (SAG) strategies relevant to the generalization test, namely it population strategy and its Ecological Footprint target, raise problems for the generalization test, and are discussed further below.

The South Australian Government's Population Strategy

The SAG has a strategy to grow SA's population from the current (year 2012) figure of about 1.6 m, to 2 m by 2027 (SAG 2011). The 2 m target is not presented as an end point at which SA's population is planned to stabilize, with projections indicating it will still be growing beyond 2050 (SAG 2006a).

The SAG's justification for its population strategy include claims that an increased population is necessary to: address social and economic problems that the ageing profile of SA's population is claimed to present, prevent a decline in population at some time in the future as a result of SA's below-replacement fertility rate, underpin economic growth to promote general wellbeing and prosperity for SA's citizens, and maintain a critical population mass to give meaningful influence to SA in negotiations at the national level (SA-EDB 2003; SAG 2004a, 2007c).

To achieve this population growth, the SAG has a number of strategies in place with a focus on increasing SA's fertility rate (or at least, not allowing it to drop below a 1.7 babies-per-female level), increasing immigration, and reducing emigration (SAG 2004a, 2007c). Although SA's current fertility rate—averaging about 1.7 over much of the 2000s period, increasing to about 1.95 in 2008 (ABS 2009a; SAG 2008)—is below the long-term replacement rate of 2.1, the current SA social age structure still sees an increasing population from births alone. This is expected to change in the future as SA's population ages (ABS 2009b), where net positive immigration will be needed to achieve the 2 m target.

Whether the SAG's population policy is consistent with sustainable world objectives is an arguable point. It is not consistent with the Transformational approach which calls for long-term population reduction with all nations needing to play a part to achieve this (Bodian 1995; Clifton 2010a; Ehrlich and Ehrlich 2008; McLaughlin 1995; Naess 2003). For Reformism, the arguments are not as clear. One view is that, with SA's below-replacement fertility rate, all the SAG's population policy is doing is moving people from one place on the planet to another. As such, although in SA current total births exceed deaths leading to fertility-based population increase, a below-replacement fertility rate will see this situation change with the passage of time. The SAG's population policy may therefore be quite limited in its impacts in eroding the Biodiversity fair-Earth-share value. In this narrow sense, the SAG's approach can be interpreted as having some degree of consistency with the Reformist stabilization approach to human population numbers.[3] On the other hand, increasing SA's population, which has such a high per capita Ecological Footprint, may nonetheless increase the overall Ecological Footprint impact if immigrants come from regions with a lower Ecological Footprint value. In this respect, the net effect may be one of increasing the global aggregate Ecological Footprint even if there is no net increase in global population numbers.

It is beyond the scope of this current discussion to explore the fine detail of the SAG's population policy, but the key issue is one of a point of principle: the SAG sees population growth as a necessary condition to further the wellbeing of SA's citizens, by underpinning economic growth and, more generally, advancing the prosperity of the SA community. It is this belief in the benefits of population growth that raises concerns as to the generalization of the SAG's approach. A strategy of long term population growth to underpin human wellbeing and prosperity is challenging to reconcile with sustainable world principles, and is a strategy that is not supported by either the Reformist or Transformational population narratives (Clifton 2010a). The SAG, although acknowledging the sustainability challenges of a growing population, still presents its strategy as consistent with sustainable world objectives and, in some ways, beneficial to it (SAG 2004a, 2006a).

---

[3] The Reformist view of human population is oriented to maximizing the population that can be supported within sustainable world criteria, with a stabilization strategy based on containing very high population growth rates in some (mostly developing) countries and preventing population decline in some (mostly developed) countries (Bodian 1995; Connelly 2008; Nordhaus and Shellenberger 2007; UN 2008; WCED 1987).

Table 9.6 The South Australian Government: Footprint Analysis data projected to 2050. (Raw data source: SAG 2007c)

Item	Value
1. Base data	
SAG's 2050 Ecological Footprint target (as per the 2007 Strategic Plan objective)—average for all SA citizens	3.7 ghpc
SA's projected Biocapacity in 2050 based on population change only—average for all SA citizens	5.7 ghpc
2. SAG's 2050 Ecological Footprint target compared to SA's 2050 Biocapacity safely available for use	
SA's Biocapacity at 50% of 2050 value—average for all SA citizens	2.9 ghpc
SA's 2050 Ecological Footprint as a % of SA's 2050 Biocapacity at 50% value	128%
3. SAG's 2050 Ecological Footprint target compared to global 2050 Biocapacity safely available for use	
Global average Biocapacity at 50% of 2050 value based on global population change only	0.7 ghpc
SA's 2050 Ecological Footprint as a % of global Biocapacity at 50% value	528%

The South Australian Government's Ecological Footprint Reduction Target

The SAG is aware that SA's Ecological Footprint is unacceptably high, acknowledging that it is considerably higher than that of most other developed nations (SAG 2007b, 2007c), considerably higher than the world average (SAG 2006b, 2007c), and "3.9 times higher" than current global average Biocapacity (SAG 2006b). In 2004, the SAG released the first version of *South Australia's Strategic Plan* which, under the "Attain Sustainability" objective, included a target to "reduce our ecological footprint to reduce the impact of human settlements and activities within 10 years" (SAG 2004b). The 2007 update of the Strategic Plan included, again under the "Attain Sustainability" objective, a quantified target to "reduce South Australia's ecological footprint by 30% by 2050" (SAG 2007c). At the time of the 2007 Strategic Plan release, the population target of 2 m (referred to above) was timed for a 2050 achievement (compared to the now shortened time frame of 2027). Assuming a 2 m SA population by 2050 (as opposed to what is likely to be, on current trends, a higher population at that time), the goal to reduce SA's Ecological Footprint by 30% by 2050 translates into a per capita Ecological Footprint at that time of 3.7 ghpc (a reduction of 47% from current levels). A summary analysis of this target is shown as Table 9.6.

Two key observations can be made from the Table 9.6 data. First, compared to projected 2050 SA Biocapacity levels (adjusting SA's current Biocapacity for population changes only), achieving the 2007 Strategic Plan's Ecological Footprint target would see SA's Ecological Footprint still breach the level of local Biocapacity that is safely available for human use. Second, compared to projected 2050 global

Biocapacity, SA's per capita Ecological Footprint would still be well in excess of a fair-Earth-share. Fair-Earth-share principles indicate that the SAG's Ecological Footprint target should be about 0.7 ghpc by 2050. At 3.7 ghpc, SA's position would be far from this.

In September 2011, the SAG released a further update of the Strategic Plan which removed the Ecological Footprint as a target, the reason for this action given as:

> This target has been removed following consensus from stakeholders about the difficulty of measurement and the need to have specific measures and strategies. (SAG 2011)

Summary

Three key points can be made from the discussion concerning SA's Footprint Analysis position and the SAG's population and Ecological Footprint goals.

First, for the three tests described above for which data are available, and in stark contrast to the SAG's claim of being a sustainability leader (SAG 2007a, 2007b), SA's position is one of detracting from a global sustainability goal. The usefulness of the first test (consumption-based Ecological Footprint vs local Biocapacity) is debatable for this local-to-global analysis, although it does raise concerns of longer term resource security for SA's citizens. The third (fair-Earth-share) and fourth (generalization) tests are, however, sufficient to support this detracting-from-the-global-goal claim. The absence of data for the second test (production-based Ecological Footprint vs local Biocapacity) is not critical to the conclusions drawn, however the availability of this data would be useful to aid the SAG in its assessment of the impacts on local renewable natural resources of production activities occurring within SA's borders.

Next is that the SAG's Ecological Footprint reduction target set out in the 2007 Strategic Plan, although having a 40-year time frame set for its achievement would, by the year 2050, still have seen SA's citizens living in ways inconsistent with a global sustainability goal. The idea of SA having a 2050 Ecological Footprint in the range of 3 to 5 times greater than a fair-Earth-share Biocapacity level would not have seen SA's citizens 'achieve sustainability'. Rather, it would maintain a position of resource use privilege that is inconsistent with the core sustainable world tenets of intragenerational and intergenerational justice discussed above.

Finally is that the removal of the Ecological Footprint target form the State Strategic Plan sees no target in that Plan which now links the SA setting to the global sustainability context. Claims of measurement difficulty are unconvincing as measurement techniques are readily accessible and have reportedly been successfully applied in the sub-national setting (Bagliani et al. 2008; Collins et al. 2006; Footprint Network 2010a). Further, "the need to have specific measures and strategies" given by the SAG to justify removing the Ecological Footprint goal are instead the very things that are needed to help SA's citizens transition to a way of life that is sustainable in the global context.

Conclusion

How does any social group—such as a nation, a within-nation state, or a local community—know if it is living in ways consistent with a global sustainability goal? In this chapter we have explored this question and presented, through the use of Footprint Analysis, a series of tests to conducting such an assessment. In conducting this review, two important questions arise where further comment may be useful.

First is how much in the way of renewable natural resources are needed in order for humans to live flourishing lives? It was noted earlier that the per capita Biocapacity expected to be available for human use by 2050 will be at a level that is currently being consumed by the citizens of only a handful of the least developed nations on Earth. This begs the question as to whether the current and projected human population can really achieve flourishing lives for all within available Biocapacity limits. Unfortunately this remains a poorly researched question and one that gets little, if any, airing in public debate.

Stemming from this is the question of whether either of the Reformist and Transformational sustainable world approaches are credible pathways to addressing not only the pressing Ecological Footprint challenges humanity is facing, but also the broader set of sustainable world problems that need to be confronted. The South Australian setting is a case in point where, consistent with the approaches of most other governments, the SAG is wedded to the Reformist narrative (Clifton 2011). Even if the SAG aggressively pursued an Ecological Footprint reduction strategy from a Reformist platform, would it have any reasonable prospects of seeing SA's citizens live in a way consistent with a global sustainability outcome? Transformational advocates would say 'no' as the pressures of continued economic growth and an aversion to long-term population reduction embedded in the Reformist paradigm make the needed level of reduction in humanity's ecological impact unachievable (for a discussion on the merits of the Reformist and Transformational narratives from an Ecological Footprint perspective, and one that supports a claim that the Reformist narrative is not a credible approach, see Clifton (2010c)).

Ultimately however, and failing a collective self-extinction decision, humanity has no option but to transition to a sustainable way of life or have this imposed on us through the workings of the Earth's natural systems in ways that may be far from desirable. The Earth's ecosystems don't care about human constructs—our ideologies, our economic structures, our desire for economically viable environmental policies, or our formulations of what individual rights we might believe we should uphold. In the end, unless humanity lives in a way that sees a sustainable way of life unfold then we pay the price through forced correction. History is littered with examples of localized social collapse (Diamond 2005). The problem we face now, as the Footprint data presented in this chapter has shown, is looming ecosystem collapse on a planetary scale.

References

ABS. (2009a). *Births, Australia, 2008: State and territory—total fertility rate*. Canberra: Australian Bureau of Statistics.

ABS. (2009b). *Births, Australia, 2008; Births as a component of population growth*. Canberra: Australian Bureau of Statistics.

Andersson, J. O., & Lindroth, M. (2001). Ecologically unsustainable trade. *Ecological Economics, 37*(1), 113–122.

Bagliani, M., Gallic, A., Niccoluccic, V., & Marchettinic, N. (2008). Ecological footprint analysis applied to a sub-national area: The case of the Province of Siena (Italy). *Journal of Environmental Management, 86*, 354–364.

Barry, B. (2003). Sustainability and intergenerational justice (reproduced from "Theoria" 1997). In A. Light & H. Rolston (Eds.), *Environmental ethics* (pp. 487–499). Oxford: Blackwell.

Bell, M. M. (2009). *An invitation to environmental sociology*. Los Angeles: Pine Forage Press.

Bodian, S. (1995). Simple in means, rich in ends: An interview with Arne Naess. In G. Sessions (Ed.), *Deep ecology for the 21st century*. Boston: Shambhala.

Boyden, S. (2001). Nature, society, history and social change. *Innovation: The European Journal of Social Sciences, 14*(2), 103–116.

Chertow, M. R. (2000). The IPAT equation and its variants. *Journal of Industrial Ecology, 4*(4), 13.

Clifton, D. (2010a). Representing a sustainable world—a typology approach. *Journal of Sustainable Development, 3*(2), 40–57.

Clifton, D. (2010b). A sustainable-world—the local in terms of the global: An ecological footprint analysis perspective. *Journal of the Asia-Pacific Centre for Environmental Accountability, 16*(3), 4–30.

Clifton, D. (2010c). A sustainable world-an ecological footprint and I=PAT perspective. *Journal of the Asia-Pacific Centre for Environmental Accountability, 16*(2), 3–26.

Clifton, D. (2011). Progressing a sustainable world—a case study of the South Australian government. *Journal of Sustainable Development, 4*(1), 3–22.

Collins, A., Flynn, A., Wiedmann, T., & Barrett, J. (2006). The environmental impacts of consumption at a subnational level. *Journal of Industrial Ecology, 10*(3, Summer), 9–24.

Connelly, M. (2008). *Fatal misconception*. Cambridge: Harvard University Press.

Daly, H. E. (1996). *Beyond growth: The economics of sustainable development*. Boston: Beacon.

Daly, H., & Farley, J. (2004). *Ecological economics: Principles and applications*. Washington: Island Press.

Diamond, J. (2005). *Collapse: How societies choose to fail or survive*. Victoria: Penguin.

Diesendorf, M. (1997). Principles of ecological sustainability. In M. Diesendorf & C. Hamilton (Eds.), *Human ecology, human economy* (pp. 64–97). Sydney: Allen & Unwin.

Dietz, S., & Neumayer, E. (2007). Weak and strong sustainability in the SEEA: Concepts and measurement. *Ecological Economics, 61*(4), 617–626.

Ehrlich, P. R., & Ehrlich, A. H. (Eds.). (2008). *The dominant animal*. Washington: Island Press.

Footprint Network. (2006). *Ecological footprint standards 2006*. The Footprint Network: Global Footprint Network Standards Committees.

Footprint Network. (2008). The ecological footprint-questions and answers. http://www.footprintnetwork.org/gfn_sub.php?content=faq#rp . Accessed 29 July 2008

Footprint Network. (2010a). Ecological footprint. Footprint Network web site: http://www.footprintnetwork.org/.

Footprint Network. (2010b). Ecological footprint and biocapacity-2010 release. Footprint Network.

Gare, A. (2000). The postmodernism of deep ecology, the deep ecology of postmodernism, and grand narratives. In E. Katz, A. Light & S. Rothenberg (Eds.), *Beneath the surface: Critical essays in the philosophy of deep ecology*. Cambridge: MIT Press.

Gibson, R. B. (2001). *Specification of sustainability-based environmental assessment decision criteria and implications for determining "Significance" in environmental assessment.* Canadian Environmental Assessment Agency Research and Development Programme.

Giljum, S., Hammer, M., Stocker, A., Lackner, M., Best, A., Blobel, D., & Shmelev, S. (2007). Scientific assessment and evaluation of the indicator "Ecological Footprint". Environmental research of the federal ministry of the environment, nature conservation and nuclear safety. Research Report 363 01 135, UBA-FB 001089/E.

Gladwin, T. N., Kennelly, J. J., & Krause, T.-S. (1995). Shifting paradigms for sustainable development: Implications for management theory and research. *Academy of Management Review, 20*(4), 874–907.

Gould, K. A., & Lewis, T. L. (2009). The paradoxes of sustainable development. In K. A. Gould & T. L. Lewis (Eds.), *Twenty lessons in environmental sociology* (pp. 269–289). New York: Oxford University Press.

Handmer, J. W., & Dovers, S. R. (1996). A typology of resilience: Rethinking institutions for sustainable development. *Industrial and Environmental Crisis Quarterly, 9*(4), 482–511.

Hargrove, E. C. (2003). Weak anthropocentric intrinsic value (reproduced from "The Monist", 1992). In A. Light & H. Rolston (Eds.), *Environmental ethics* (pp. 175–190). Oxford: Blackwell.

Holbrook, D. (2009). The consequentialist side of environmental ethics (reprint of Daniel Holbrook, 'Consequentialist Side of Environmental Ethics', in *Environmental Values, 6*, 1997, pp. 87–96). In M. Reynolds, C. Blackmore, & M. J. Smith (Eds.), *The environmental responsibility reader*. London: Zed Books.

Holdren, J. P., Daily, G. C., & Ehrlich, P. R. (1995). *The meaning of sustainability: Biogeophysical aspects.* Washington, D.C.: United Nations University and The World Bank.

Kitzes, J. (2007). *A research agenda for improving National ecological Footprint accounts.* Paper presented at the International Ecological Footprint Conference: Stepping Up the Pace-New Developments in Ecological Footprint Methodology, Policy and Practice, 8–10 May 2007, Cardiff.

Laferriere, E., & Stoett, P. J. (Eds.). (2006). *International ecopolitical theory: Critical approaches.* Vancouver: UBC Press.

Lenzen, M., & Murray, S. A. (2001). A modified ecological footprint method and its application to Australia. *Ecological Economics, 37*(2), 229–255.

Light, A., & Rolston, H. (2003). *Introduction: Ethics and environmental ethics. In Environmental ethics* (pp. 1–11). Oxford: Blackwell.

Manderson, A. K. (2006). A systems based framework to examine the multi-contextual application of the sustainability concept. *Environment, Development and Sustainability, 8,* 85–97.

McLaren, D. (2003). Environmental space, equity and ecological debt. In J. Agyeman, R. D. Bullard, & B. Evans (Eds.), *Just sustainabilities: Development in an unequal world.* London: Earthscan.

McLaughlin, A. (1995). The heart of deep ecology. In G. Sessions (Ed.), *Deep ecology for the 21st century.* Boston: Shambhala.

Meadows, D. H., Randers, J., & Meadows, D. (2004). *Limits to growth: The 30-year update.* White River Junction: Chelsea Green.

Naess, A. (1988). Sustainable development and the deep long-range ecology movement. *The Trumpeter, 5*(4), 138–142.

Naess, A. (2003). The deep ecological movement: Some philosophical aspects (reproduced from "Philosophical Inquiry" 1986). In A. Light & H. Rolston (Eds.), *Environmental ethics* (pp. 262–274). Oxford: Blackwell.

Nijkamp, P., Rossi, E., & Vindigni, G. (2004). Ecological footprints in plural: A meta-analytic comparison of empirical results. *Regional Studies, 38*(7), 747–765.

Nordhaus, T., & Shellenberger, M. (2007). *Break through: From the death of environmentalism to the politics of possibility.* New York: Houghton Mifflin.

Norton, B. G. (2003). Environmental ethics and weak anthropocentrism (reproduced from "Environmental Ethics", 1984). In A. Light & H. Rolston (Eds.), *Environmental ethics* (pp. 163–174). Oxford: Blackwell.

Osorio, L. A., Lobato, M. O., & Castillo, X. (2005). Debates on sustainable development: Towards a holistic view of reality. *Environment, Development and Sustainability, 7,* 501–518.

Palmer, C. (2003). An overview of environmental ethics. In A. Light & H. Rolston (Eds.), *Environmental ethics* (pp. 15–37). Oxford: Blackwell.

SA-EDB. (2003). *A framework for economic development in South Australia.* South Australia's Economic Development Board.

SAG (2004a). *Prosperity through people—a population policy for South Australia.* Adelaide, South Australian Government, March 2004.

SAG. (2004b). *South Australia's strategic plan—summary of targets 2004.* South Australian Government, March 2004.

SAG. (2006a). *Planning strategy for metropolitan Adelaide.* South Australian Government, Aug 2006.

SAG. (2006b). *South Australia's Ecological Footprint.* SA Government: Sustainability and Climate Change Division of the Department of the Premier and Cabinet, May 2006.

SAG. (2007a). *Climate change.* Premier Rann Speech to the Business SA Climate Change Presentation. Adelaide, 5 Sept 2007.

SAG. (2007b). *Fact sheet: A summary of government of South Australia sustainability and climate change initiatives.* South Australian Government, Oct 2007.

SAG. (2007c). *South Australia's strategic plan 2007.* SA Government, Jan 2007.

SAG. (2008). South Australia's state strategic plan—target fact sheets 2008. South Australian Government, Adelaide. http://www.saplan.org.au/. Accessed 28 Feb 2009.

SAG. (2011). *South Australia's strategic plan 2011.* SA Government, Sept 2011.

Schlosberg, D. (2007). *Defining environmental justice.* Oxford: Oxford University Press.

Simpson, R. W., Petroeschevsky, A., & Lowe, I. (2000). An ecological footprint analysis for Australia. *Australian Journal of Environmental Management, 7,* 11–18.

Speth, J. G. (2005). *Red sky at morning.* Yale: Yale University Press.

Taylor, P. (1989). *Respect for nature.* Princeton: Princeton University Press.

UN. (1992a). *Convention on biological diversity.* United Nations.

UN. (1992b). *Rio declaration on environment and development.* 3–14 June 2004.

UN. (2008). *World population policies 2007.* New York: United Nations Department of Economic and Social Affairs-Population Division.

Wackernagel, M., & Yount, D. (1998). The ecological footprint: An indicator of progress toward regional sustainability. *Environmental Monitoring and Assessment, 51*(1-2), 511–529.

WCED. (1987). *Our common future: World commission on environment and development.* Oxford: Oxford University Press.

Williams, C. C., & Millington, A. C. (2004). The diverse and contested meanings of sustainable development. *Geographical Journal, 170*(2), 99–104.

Wissenburg, M. (2001). Dehierarachization and sustainable development in liberal and non-liberal societies. *Global Environmental Politics, 1*(2), 95.

York, R., Rosa, E. A., & Dietz, T. (2003). STIRPAT, IPAT and ImPACT: Analytic tools for unpacking the driving forces of environmental impacts. *Ecological Economics, 46*(3), 351–365.

Chapter 10
Greening, Root and Branch: The Forms and Limits of Environmentalism

Lisa H. Newton

Introduction: The Shocking Young Men and Their Infuriating Thesis

The purpose of the paper is to examine the roots of our obligation to preserve the land and its resources, to address in some systematic way the "So what?" response to the massive documentation of environmental deterioration and the accompanying environmentalist imperatives. We will begin with an exercise in deconstruction—the parsing of an event, just one event, to extract from its account some of the problems that environmentalism has got itself into, especially in dealing with the multiple faces of American business. From that point we will be in a position to address the central project of the paper, an elaboration of an ethic for the appreciation and protection of the natural environment, 'the land', for short, meaning the earth, all its life, all its resources.

The event in question was the presentation of a paper at a meeting of environmental funding agencies, hardly the sort of thing that normally ruffles the feathers of angels dancing on the heads of pins. The program of the meeting featured reflections from a variety of sources on the status of the nation's environmental initiatives. To the enormous chagrin of the leaders of the environmental movement, two relative youngsters, Michael Shellenberger and Ted Nordhaus, upended what had been a relatively unified forum with an argument that environmentalism, as a movement, was dead, and that it was time to 'move on'. The paper they presented at that meeting, 'The death of environmentalism', argued that the political support that had nourished the movement was tired and gone, and that liberals should be "abolishing the category" of environmentalism as part of their politics. Environmentalism, in its parochial insistence on preserving the land and the forests, had become "just another special interest"; it was simply passé, had lost its appeal to the voters, had in general overstayed its welcome in what sounded for all the world like the worn tent of the Democratic Party. It is time, they argued, to move the strategic money

L. H. Newton (✉)
Department of Philosophy, Fairfield University, Fairfield, USA
e-mail: LHNewton@fairfield.edu

© Springer Science+Business Media Dordrecht 2014   155
S. Sandhu et al. (eds.), *Linking Local and Global Sustainability,* The International Society
of Business, Economics, and Ethics Book Series 4, DOI 10.1007/978-94-017-9008-6_10

to a variety of liberal and progressive causes that had a greater chance to woo the electorate (Barringer 2005).

Needless to state, the paper set off a storm in the environmentalist movement. Some major environmentalists wrote angry answers refuting the pair. Others, including Bill McKibben, thought that they had a point. Nicholas Kristof, columnist for *The New York Times* also thought they were right; environmentalists had been alarmists, and now they were paying for it (Kristof 2005). Debates raged and positions were taken. But the event has much deeper problems buried in it than the simple question of whether it is 'time to move on'. Let us bullet a few of them.

First: The major objection that the establishment environmentalists had to this presentation was that it was given to the *funding sources*. The picture we are given, of the 'environmentalist' or 'progressive' movement of which we are supposed to be a part, is that of elegantly titled hucksters competing for funds. Have we come to this? Is this all there is? The question is not rhetorical.

Second: The young men were frankly suggesting nothing more than a 'strategy' change. We may infer from the presentation that the authors consider environmentalism to be one of several buzz-tactics, the picking up a fashionable thought to spin it with others into a certain share of the political market, or number of votes. That read imputes to the land no real value at all, in itself—the impassioned rhetoric of environmentalism was just a ploy to get liberal votes, one that isn't working any more so should be abandoned. Like, environmentalism is *so* last year. But that just can't be right. Land, above all, endures. If the catalog of deterioration is factually correct, then it is a reality that we will have to deal with. It can't be just picked up and dropped again according to judgments of political fashion.

Third: Was conservation ever a 'liberal' or progressive cause to begin with? The etymology of the word would suggest not. How might the conservation of nature figure in the politics of liberal and conservative? The only place to find an answer is in the original division of liberals and conservatives—John Locke and the Glorious Revolution, with all his liberal Utilitarian progeny, furiously opposed by Edmund Burke, the Church, and the defenders of the traditional community. Locke and Adam Smith would reduce all the wild and common places to 'wealth', monetize them into private property and the stuff of trade, commodify them. Burke would recognize them as traditional refuges and public goods to be preserved on behalf of the ancestors for the sake of the unborn, and would protect them for their traditional community uses. The fragility of the commons was recognized for centuries, and its only protection was the unbroken tradition prescribing its uses. "The Tragedy of the Commons," the progressive overuse of the commons by its clientele until it is entirely destroyed (Hardin 1968), does not happen while the traditions are intact. It happens when the new, liberal, individualistic and profit-oriented, practices are introduced into an area previously governed by tradition. Where there has been no tradition of restraint, as in the open-access grounds of the ocean fisheries, unrestrained overuse by individualistic entrepreneurs quickly destroys the resource permanently. Liberalism is no friend of the environment. Liberalism started the problem, and it is unlikely to provide the solution. (How did the land ever switch parties from red to blue, from conservative to liberal?)

Fourth: Never mind what side of the political aisle favors the land. The land is the necessary condition for our continued existence, of whatever party we may be; ultimately, we must take care of the land, or there's no real point to taking care of anything else. As far as politics and policy are concerned, the land must be an end in itself, not a means to anything else, and there is something horrifying in the decision that the efforts to increase public support for that effort are to be tested by political efficacy and promoted or discarded on the measure of political advantage. How did we ever get so far from the point of the enterprise, the moral of the story, as it were, as to rate conservation only on grounds that have nothing really to do with it? Have we succumbed to a dangerous distraction?

A Big Tent for the Land

The error made by the young men was misdirection of focus, and the adoption of narrower rather than broader grounds for the support of the environmental movement. When the factual conditions supporting those narrow grounds disappeared—when it no longer seemed that a bearded child of the forest defiantly perched in a redwood tree would reliably draw votes on Election Day to various liberal causes—the entire 'category' could be discarded. But we can think of many reasons beyond that one to defend the land, can't we? Yes, but do they go together or contradict each other? Can they be persuaded to pull in the same direction? Can they possibly be united in a single framework?

The purpose of this paper is nothing less than the unification of the rationales for preservation of the land, of the natural environment. We will try to create a framework in which an ordered series of lines of justification may co-exist, logically independent but not incompatible, theoretically distinct but able in practice to reinforce each other. The framework constructed, we will ask some more basic questions on the ultimate grounding of a land ethic, and add some observations on outliers (lines of justification that lie outside the framework). We may find at the end that the outrageous young men may not have been so far off base after all.

An Environmental Ethics Classification System

Our defense of the environment starts with the very simplest correlation of present damage to the environment and present harm to us: If we empty the used oil into the river above where the drinking water is taken out, we're going to be drinking oil for awhile. The defense concludes with a grateful recognition of our dependence on the land for every aspect of our being, and a fervent desire to protect and preserve it for all future generations. Within that range, a variety of environmentalisms jostle for ascendancy. They can be divided according to the three major sets of drivers, or motivations, which underlie them, drivers we may call the Payoff motive, the

Citizenship motive, and the Land motive. As we shall see, the Payoff motive is very easy for American business to work with; the Citizenship motive is conflict-ridden but eventually workable; and the Land motive, while perhaps more firmly grounded than either of the others, is in practice presently more aspirational than employable. A project for our time is to construct the institutions that will make it more workable in market conditions. The three levels subdivide themselves into two levels each, one generally aimed at avoiding penalties and one generally aimed at attaining some good end, and permit a certain amount of flexibility and extension.

First, some definitions. The standard against which all *environmental* damage, enhancement, or restoration is measured is the health of the ecosystem. This is a very medical model: the health of the patient, ability to function normally, ability to recover from insults, etc., is the measure. Specifically, environmental damage is damage to an ecosystem (primarily) or to some non-domestic non-human species within an ecosystem (secondarily). Damage to humans through some environmental vector will be worth notice, but not as environmental damage. Dumping oil in the river damages the environment, since the oil harms many forms of life in the ecosystem; dumping cholera germs in the river, although it certainly has the potential to harm many humans, probably does little harm to the environment, so does not cause environmental damage. Bioterrorism, therefore, other things being equal, is not an environmental attack, nor was the explosion of methyl isocyanate in Bhopal in 1984 (for instance) a case of environmental damage. We will be interested in events that harm the environment by interfering with all life, especially with the key actors and factors in an intact ecosystem (the "keystone" species, for instance, that make it possible for the ecosystem to regulate itself); harm to humans will be measured on a different scale, as interfering not just with the lives and health of human beings but also with their prosperity, income, freedom, power, and quality of life.

Payoff Level One: Avoiding Harm

We ought to protect the natural environment from damages that will also hurt human beings. The point of this rule is the prevention of immediate self-injury, like pouring the oil into the water upriver. (It amounts to the suggestion that it is not a good idea to get rid of a rock by throwing it straight up; you might get hit by it on the way down.) Nor is it a good idea to have a garbage dump uphill from good farmland, unless it has a very good liner. Simple prudence, and an alert department of Public Health, operate at this level to protect us and the environment from simple negligence. As our levels of analysis become a bit more sophisticated, we are able to expand Level One beyond the immediate and obvious to the more distant and probable: if it turns out that burning trash in the back yard produces a very large amount of dioxin, a ferociously toxic chlorine compound, harmful to all higher fish and mammals and carcinogenic to humans (Foderaro 2005),[1] then it would seem

---

[1] It is estimated that the dioxin production from a few dozen trash burn barrels in normal use equals the output of a 200-ton-a-day modern incinerator.

the better part of valor to confiscate the barrels and provide a good public trash disposal plan. The further in the future the expected harm is predicted, and the less certain that it will come about, the harder it will be to justify the expense of protection. While the dangers of ingesting motor oil are perfectly clear, the effect of the dioxins is disputable; while the oil will contaminate the water immediately, it isn't clear when the cancer that is caused by the dioxin will manifest itself in any human. Pouring the oil somewhere else than the river might actually be cost-free; creating a municipal trash disposal plan is not.

Payoff Level Two: Seeking Advantage

We ought to adopt all those measures that will protect or restore the environment and produce an immediate profit. Discovering that organic food, food that can be labeled and advertised as raised without the use of chemical pesticides or herbicides, genetically unaltered and ripened in the field, commanded significantly higher prices than food from crops raised with the usual chemical entourage, many farmers in areas close to sophisticated markets promptly began organic farming. Similarly, in 1975 the 3M company, distressed by the high costs in remediation required by government regulation that would be incurred if its plant's heavy level of emissions were to continue, it undertook a program called "Pollution Prevention Pays (3P)" to eliminate the problem at its source. It reconstituted its products and modified its manufacturing processes to cut the toxic waste as close to zero as possible, and in the process saved money on raw materials: about $ 827 million just between 1975 and 1999, eliminating 0.8 million t of pollutants at the same time (Elkington 1998).[2] As with Level One, Level Two easily extends into the middle range of certainty and immediacy. It makes sense to design the plant buildings and processes in such a way as to minimize the use of energy and consumption of raw materials generally, even if they cost more to build up front; it makes sense on the farm to preserve wildlife corridors and woodland habitats, if they'll shelter the pollinators and predator insects that help the crops.

Payoff Levels One and Two should be familiar enough to veterans of the Environmental Economics literature; they are generally referred to as 'industrial ecology', or 'green business strategy'. They are known and accepted. They should also be familiar to students of the Ethics literature: they correspond, rather neatly, to Lawrence Kohlberg's first two stages of moral development. In this 'preconventional' stage, an act is wrong if it produces foreseeable punishment and right if it produces foreseeable reward (Kohlberg 1981).[3] The ethical framework is straightforward act utilitarianism. While we're on that subject, it is worth remembering that Jeremy

---

[2] See "Pollution Prevention," http://www.bsdglobal.com/tools/bt_pp.asp 3M was not the last company to do this; between 1988 and 1991 Nortel eliminated the use of a million kg. of CFC-113, saved $ 4 million for an investment of $ 1 million, and saved the ozone layer at the same time.

[3] Apparently his theory of the stages of moral development had been worked out about 10 years earlier.

Benthan intended his ethical theory, hedonism, the Pleasure Principle, or Utilitarianism, as it came to be called, to be usable with mathematical accuracy. Utilitarian calculations set up equations among the various options for a decision for action, finding the results of each act in terms of pleasure and pain—duration, intensity, purity, fecundity, and don't forget the major factors in the "extended" cases above—propinquity (how long before the effect occurs?) and certainty (how likely is the effect?) The more uncertain and distant the effect, the less the weight in any ethical decision. Not only is a bird in the hand worth two in the bush, but if we're in the birdselling business, a bird now is worth two birds later. This kind of reasoning is also familiar to corporate decision makers, charged with maximizing good (income rather than pleasure) and minimizing pain (costs and losses), and more or less easily justifiable to Boards of Directors, more if the reward (or avoidance of cost) is sooner, larger and more certain, less if it is later, smaller and less certain. But business motivation can be more complex than the simple Payoff, just as can individual motivation. The corporation must carry on its activities within a society, within a legal system, within shared understandings of right and wrong, within a local community. There is much that the corporation does which is only explicable in terms of its felt obligation to be a good citizen in its communities. The Citizenship driver permits us to elaborate two more levels of corporate environmentalism:

Citizenship Level Three: Compliance

We live in a complex society governed by Rule of Law, upon which every corporation depends for its existence. (Those who would like a proof of that are referred to Thomas Hobbes, *Leviathan,* the part about mean, poor, nasty, brutish and short (Hobbes 1962)). Whatever else we may think about our duties to our fellow members of society, we have at least the obligation to obey the law. It is within the power of the electorate, acting through their duly elected representatives (and the duly appointed officers of government agencies established by the legislature) to enact legislation to protect our natural heritage for the sake of all the citizens, of this generation and of those to follow. Citizenship requires at least obedience to the law—compliance with existing law in the letter. Does it also require obedience in spirit?

Ordinarily we distinguish easily between law and ethics. Law, on the ordinary acceptance, consists of definitions and instructions that proceed from the legitimate authority, at whatever level, is written down, obedience to which is monitored, breach of which will incur punishments. (The first two parts of the definition are from St. Thomas Aquinas (*Summa Theologiae,* I, 2), the second two are from John Austin (*The Province of Jurisprudence Determined*) and Bix (2005); I hope those familiar with legal theory will enjoy the meld of Natural Law Theory and Legal Positivism.) Ethics, however, beyond the law, indicates what people might like other people to do, preferences, beliefs about what is right and wrong. It is not law. But there is a third element of the law, beside what is written down and what is enforced. The problem is, that much of our legal experience is in a gray area at the edges of what is written down; it consists in the penumbra of legal expectations that attend civil behavior in a civil society. When the courts of law find one of these gray-area cases before them, especially in an area relatively new to the law, subject to change and to interpretation—in short, an area very like the field of environmental regulation—often the only rule of interpretation available to them is to follow the intent and the spirit of the law. So the extension of the "legal" obligation into the range of "ethics" may be where the courts come down—and as the Legal Realists always claimed, what the courts will decide in fact is (for the practicing business person) the best definition of "law." (Holmes 1897)[4] If avoiding unfavorable court decisions is part of "compliance" (and if I were part of a corporation's legal staff, I would certainly think it so to be), then simple compliance requires that the manager take into account the purpose and spirit of the law in plotting the corporation's path.

Citizenship Level Four: Contributions

Beyond complete (and willing) compliance with all applicable legal provisions, the corporation often cultivates and satisfies community expectations of a higher standard of citizenship, or neighborliness. Beyond anything the law requires, the corporation has a certain amount of leeway in deciding neighborly courses of action, all of which may commend it to its community, and redound to its advantage in terms of customer loyalty, community support for expansion plans, and all other benefits summarized as goodwill. The record of corporate contributions, at least from about the 1950s until fairly recently, is impressive: major corporations have sponsored the weekly broadcasting of the Metropolitan Opera performances, funded concert series, public radio, built libraries, art museums, hospitals, concert halls, and please let us not forget, universities. The United States has possibly the most powerful 'third sector' in the world: The area of not-for-profit enterprise, serving an astonishingly large variety of health-related, cultural and educational institutions. The huge fund of voluntary contributions that supports these interests comes in part from individuals, but also in large part from corporations. Among the community-oriented contributions that a company might make are many that help the natural environment: companies have dedicated portions of their sprawling grounds to conservation as nature preserves (a move that is easier to sell to the Board of Directors if that part of the property has wetlands on it and the tax write-off is substantial), have sponsored beach cleanups and wildlife preservation plans, and have contributed to innumerable environmental educational programs, especially for children.

Why do they do this? Part of the explanation may lie at the Payoff level—the company wants the good will of its neighbors for the sake of a variety of possible future advantages, just as it does not want to risk the fines consequent on non-compliance with the law. But what is interesting is the part of the motivation that goes beyond Payoff, to the strong social bonds that bind humans into communities,

---

[4] "The prophecies of what the courts will do in fact, and nothing more pretentious, are what I mean by the law."

regardless of the roles they play in their institutions. We evolved as a social species, a point worth remembering. We need no elaborate reasons to justify our concern for the welfare of other human beings (especially those close to us), or our indignation at manifest injustice in the social structures that govern their lives. These orientations to our fellow humans are as much part of our wiring as our ligaments and arteries. The corporation, to be sure, is not a human, and by the terms of its charter, its officers are under a fiduciary duty to that corporation to concern themselves only with increasing wealth for the owners, the shareholders. But in the fluid perceptions of persons, fictive and real, corporations assume personalities, manifested by the behavior of the corporate officers, and managers and neighbors alike will expect that corporation not only to act within the bounds of the law but also to entertain near-human concern for the community in which it resides.

Citizenship, the equivalent to 'conventional thinking' in the work of Lawrence Kohlberg, has one more task before we leave it. Post-conventional thinking goes beyond what the world expects of the individual or corporation, explicitly or implicitly. It summons as justification for actions not what the world expects, but what is right. Corporate officers, given their fiduciary duties, can rarely do this sort of thing on their own; initiatives not required by law on penalty of fine or rewarded in the tax structure are very difficult to justify to the owners of the company. Our job as citizens, then, is to create the tax incentives and where necessary, the laws, so that corporations can do the right thing and prosper. Essentially, what we will be doing is creating structures of cooperation on behalf of the land.

We have tried, in the articulation of these four levels to this point, to show two natural and worthwhile sets of motivations for protecting the environment. We have tried to lose, forever, the charge of 'hypocrisy', slung at corporations that act out of good citizenship, the charge that insists that corporations 'only' act on behalf of the natural environment in order to get payoffs. First, Payoff is not a bad motive; given the structure of the corporation, as a matter of fact, it's a very good one. Second, it isn't the only one; there are lots of things we do just to be good citizens. Third, there may be no clear way to distinguish between the motivations in the actor's mind, even by the actor himself—human motivation is notoriously shifting and complex, and the owner of the motivation may be in the worst position to say exactly what it is.

But motivations can go further still. Beyond being a good citizen, a corporation, through its officers, might aspire to do what is right, to save the land for the sake of the land. In the next section, we will seek some further grounding for that aspiration. Meanwhile, what would it look like? What must we do for the land? Apart from the economic structures of profit, the Payoff level, and the social structures of cooperative action within a social setting with its own intangible structures of reward and punishment, the Citizenship level, how may any corporation view its obligations to the land itself?

Here a variety of structures present themselves, none of them indisputable, in fact none of them currently undisputed. We will divide the general obligations into two categories, as with the other levels, the first emphasizing the need to avoid evil, the second emphasizing the need to do good. These will raise, and in the next section we will go on to confront, the more fundamental question: on what ethical structure can a true land ethic be based? How do we ground the human obligation to the land?

Land Level Five: Sustainability

The general definition of sustainability is well known, derived from the 1987 report of the World Commission on Environment and Development (WCED), *Our Common Future* (also known as the Brundtland Report, after Gro Harlem Brundtland, Prime Minister of Norway and Chair of the Commission).[5] The Report defines sustainability as "meeting the needs of the present generation without compromising the ability of future generations to meet their own needs," or in very short, to do what you're doing in such a way that you can do it indefinitely without running out of something you need for it. Simple prudence will carry you through Payoff Level One and Citizenship Level Three—don't poison your own well, and don't run afoul of the law. But the prudence that attends Level Five is earth-centered, very long-term, and anything but simple.

The net environmental effect that any enterprise has on the natural environment is called its 'footprint'; the requirement that must be met in order to satisfy Level Five is Zero Footprint, or Net Footprint Zero. The requirement means that the ecosystem must exist around your enterprise as if you were not there. More realistically, no demands must be made on nature, either in its role of supplying resources or its role in absorbing wastes, that cannot be repaid in the course of a normal year. This condition is not only theoretically obtainable, it has been obtained in fact in numbers of institutions.[6] Recall, the human race lived completely without footprint, in Europe and the Americas, for at least 40,000 years, and in Africa for several millennia prior to that. Not until the development of agriculture did the forests, and then the land, start to disappear, and it is possible (we now know) to conduct some sorts of agriculture in such a way that it will leave no footprint indefinitely.

The grounds for the requirement of sustainability rest on simple aversion to extinction. If we wear out the land, we cease to eat. If we diminish, below a certain point, the carpet of green that originally covered the earth, by unrestricted logging in the Amazon (Ponting 1993) and in the deep rainforests of the Congo (*The New York Times* 2003), for instance, we will cut off the oxygen supply to creatures that need oxygen to live, like us. We have had the warnings, large and small. We know that individual civilizations, from small island communities like Easter Island to the entire Mayan civilization of Mesoamerica have collapsed, horribly, because they have overstressed the natural resources that they were given (Diamond 2005). We know that agricultural practices in the "Fertile Crescent," stretching along the Tigris

---

[5] For short summary and interesting commentaries, see the UNESCO website: http://www.unesco.org/education/tlsf/theme_a/mod02.

[6] See, for an inspirational set of possibilities, the home page of Rocky Mountain Institute: www.rmi.org.

and Euphrates rivers, north of the great desert and west to the Mediterranean Sea, destroyed the most fertile farmland in the world over the course of a few thousand years, and that it will take at least that to reclaim that land from its present condition as a desert (Ponting 1993). We have had sufficient warnings on the perils of climate change, 'global warming'—from the ultra-serious, like Gus Speth's *Red sky at morning* (Speth 2004) to the vastly entertaining, like the blockbuster movie, *The day after tomorrow*—to recognize the formation of a small industry of knowledge and communication. There is a sense in which the very volume of the warnings is counter-productive, judged by the usual standards for judging warnings: people tend not to pay attention after awhile (more on this point when we get back to the outrageous young men, below). That does not make the predictions false.

But aversion to extinction cannot explain the whole of the duty to the land at this level. After all, not only will the final failure of oxygen occur very far in the future, but it will probably hit others, less fortunate and healthy than our descendants, before our family is touched. Simple fear cannot govern a decision to change a factory's waste systems in order to stop harmful emissions and slow down global warming. The effect is too far from the action. There is another duty, here, a duty not to harm the earth, even when the ultimate results of the injuries are too far to contemplate. On what might that duty be based?

Land Level Six: Recovery of Harmony

At the last level of stewardship for the land, the enterprise becomes one of restoring the balances that have been lost in the last destructive 10,000 years of human history (starting with the last 200!) The retreat from technology suggested in the last level reverses itself; we need more technology, new and better technology, to get us the life we want at a vastly lower cost to the biosphere.

The key to this level is simplicity, and the workings out of the simple life. The move to simplicity must begin, of course, with human consumption. First as individuals (later as a business community and as a nation) we need to interrogate everything we do or buy, asking: do we need this? If we need this, how can it be done or obtained more simply, more economically? (On occasion, How would nature do it?[7] We know, for example, that spider silk is stronger, pound for pound, than steel, and would make us sails and body armor stronger and lighter than Kevlar (Hawken et al. 1999). Are we as smart as the spiders?) How can it be done to make the maximum use of renewable energy, especially solar and wind energy, renewable materials, while encouraging and appreciating the work and life of the ecosystem native to the region?

Simplicity, as a way of life, is what we call 'normatively overdetermined'—that is, there are too many good reasons to pursue it to know which one is primary. For centuries, saints and sages have urged us to adopt the simple life just for the sake

---

[7] See the literature on biomimicry, most famously, Benyus (1997).

of the health of our individual souls and bodies and for the sake of happiness in our own lives. For our unsimple society—the morbidly obese, overconsumption society—is not new: Greek philosophers knew it and rejected it, Roman philosophers, Stoic and Epicurean, knew it at the height of material frenzy in imperial Rome and rejected it, and most famously, Christian religious leaders, epitomized by St. Francis of Assisi, rejected it and lived the rejection in lives of voluntary poverty. Sometimes the Christians wrote as if we should live simple lives in order to please God, in a variant of Divine Command theory, but for the most part Christians and pagans alike urged the simple life for the sake of happiness, our happiness. The overconsumption life is one of constant frustration, since the satisfaction of a material desire does nothing except multiply more of its kind—the more you have the more you want, as our mothers used to say. The key to a good life is early discipline of desire, an ordered life in which sufficiency guarantees happiness and, freed from the constant clawings for 'more', the human can direct his or her attention to personal fulfilment in work and in learning.

A second determination of the value of simplicity is captured in the bumper sticker (why do we think more and more in bumper stickers?) 'Live simply that others may simply live'. We live in an unjust world, one where poverty, not the voluntary kind, rules the lives of most of the human inhabitants. This poverty kills. "Currently, more than 8 million people around the world die each year because they are too poor to stay alive." (Sachs 2005) The next level of poverty, 'moderate poverty', means living on between $ 1 and $ 2 per day, hardly munificence. We know we can stop this, can end poverty all over the world in our generation. Jeffrey Sachs, star economist from Columbia University, shows us how. It's easy; all wealthy countries like the US have to do is raise the proportion of foreign aid to 0.7 % of GNP. Right now the US donates at a level of 0.15 % of GNP, 15 cents for every $ 100. Why don't we give more? We're too busy getting fat, apparently.

So far, that gives us two sufficient reasons to live the simple life: we will be happier ourselves and there will be much more of the world's resources left over for the poor of the world. The third reason is the one we came in for: if, as individuals and as a society, we live in simplicity, we will put less of a strain on the world's ecosystems. We have been operating for centuries—millennia, better—as if the natural world were nothing but an endless source of usable stuff (a huge Wal-Mart's, but free), and a bottomless sink for discarded waste. That has to change: We must learn, or re-learn, how to live and work in harmony with nature and natural processes—in short, how to be part of the ecosystem. The immediate implication for us as individuals is to govern our personal lives by simplicity. The implication for American business is simplicity in process and product. The effort to simplify—to reduce the use of raw materials and energy altogether, to create every product so that it can be completely reused or reassembled and recycled, to leave absolutely no footprint on the ecosystem in which the enterprise is carried on—must pervade the entirety of the enterprise, root and branch.

The Grounding of the Land Ethic

All of the above devolves into one simple proposition: For our own health and the health of the human race we will have to preserve the health of the ecosystems in which we live, and that work will require of us a radical change in technology, economic understandings, political alliances and lifestyle. Throughout, the grounds presented have been prudential, utilitarian in the largest sense of the word, derived from consequences, evil and good, foreseen with more certainty or less. The arguments seem to be powerful enough to carry the day. Still, it would be good to complete the account with an overview of a deontological ethic of the land; a derivation of the duty to treat the land, the ecosystems individually and the biosphere as a whole, with respect and care. This attempt has been made, several times. Let me go briefly through three accounts that I know will work, that is, if we accept the worldview presented as premise, they will logically support strong obligations of environmental care. Specifically, they will justify the adoption of the unfamiliar goals of zero footprint and harmonious cooperation. We will say in advance that one of them we find powerful, sufficient, but not available to everyone; one of them we have a great deal of difficulty accepting; and the third we think is largely right.

Justification One: The Earth as God's Creation

On Divine Command theory, the all-sufficient word of God, in Whom we live, and move, and have our being, determines our obligation to the land. Christians have a clear text, Genesis Chap. 2 Verse 15, in which God sets the original humans in the Garden, the created world, to tend and to keep it. Adding complementary passages as a gloss on that one, we may start with the testimony that God created all Nature, enumerated as waters, green plants, and all animals, and saw it all, and announced that it was good. In that case the Garden we have been given to take care of includes the entire world and every living thing that is in it, and God thought it was good just as it proceeded from His hand and was given to us. (That thought will ground the attribution of 'inherent worth' to Nature.) We are therefore God's stewards of the earth, which remains His, and was never ours. (The implications of the act of Creation are made clearer in Psalm 24: "The Earth is the Lord's, and the fullness thereof, the world, and they that dwell therein, *for He hath founded it* upon the seas and established it upon the floods.") It is clearly God's will that in caring for the earth, we should try to preserve its original condition, and return it to Him at the end of days in a condition as close as possible to its condition at Creation.

Of course that only raises more questions than it answers. Why, centrally, should we care what God wants us to do? Christians are given a variety of reasons. Elsewhere in Scripture, for starters, we find out that God intends to hold us accountable for every action or failure to act in every field in which he has given laws or statutes or instructions of any kind, and the punishments that God has in mind for those who fail to act as faithful stewards dwarf any that Federal judges might be able to come up with. To complete that thought, God also has powerful rewards available for those who carry out his instructions faithfully. Simple prudence, as with the original Payoff levels, would suggest careful preservation of the earth. The major difference is that on Divine Command Theory, no payoff is available until after death.

More powerful reasons, though, have nothing to do with reward or punishment. As with the Citizenship level of secular motivation, 'solidarity with humanity', especially with the poor, is one of the central commands. We are commanded, in the central tradition that grounds all Abrahamic religion, to love God with all our heart and soul and mind and strength, and to love our neighbor as ourselves. (On these two commandments hang all the law and the prophets.) For information on who is to count as 'neighbor', we are referred to the parable of the Good Samaritan: our neighbor is anyone who is in trouble, and we act as a neighbor ought to act when we minister to that person. We don't have to look far for people in trouble; all over the world humans suffer from poverty caused at least in part by environmental degradation, and we are urged to develop all our policies at home and abroad with a "preferential option for the poor"—with special attention to the way the poor of the world will be affected by them. We know for a fact that the poor are hurt most when environmental damage is done; we are therefore under special obligation from God to prevent and remedy that damage.

On a third level, as with the secular reasoning, Divine Command Theory's implications do not depend on the needs of other humans any more than they depend on personal payoffs. They have a great deal to do with this beautiful Earth, and with our love and gratitude to God for giving it to us. God has given us our lives, our potential for happiness and fulfilment, and a promise of everlasting love and eternal life, and it is only fitting for us to show gratitude for all God's gifts. How might we do this? "If you love me, keep my commandments," said Jesus, and Christians, at least, strive to do that. Among the commandments, not mentioned specifically by Jesus who was concerned with other matters, is the imperative to preserve the natural world in the condition in which it was created (as far as possible). We should do this not only on the assurance that we will be held to account for our stewardship at the Last Day, not only for the sake of our fellow pilgrims through this time of trial, but also out of sheer love for its beauty and thankfulness for its fruitful generosity, translated into love for its Creator and a burning desire to do His will.

Is Divine Command a sufficient basis for a duty to protect the natural environment? Certainly yes, for a person of sufficient faith; consider that faith was a sufficient motivator for Mother Teresa to devote her life to service to the very poorest people in the world, and she was not the first, nor will she be the last. But just as clearly, certainly not, for one who does not share the theistic worldview required. For a nonbeliever, "God commanded it," is completely irrelevant, whether the subject be adultery, taking the name of the Lord in vain, saving the trees, tithing to the Church, or abstaining from flesh on Good Friday. And there are other limitations to the Divine Command approach. As we have seen in our generation, there are sects of evangelical Christianity that hold to a rigid timetable determining the end of the Time itself and the heavens and the earth (when a new heaven and earth shall be created), and believe that that end, the Apocalypse (preceded, of course, by the

Rapture!), is coming soon. Adherents to those sectarian views hold the natural environment to be of little worth, since it's about to be destroyed anyway. (Imagine our surprise when the Secretary of the Interior under President Ronald Reagan announced himself to be part of such a sect. Rather like putting a vegetarian in charge of the meatpacking inspections, or an avowed pacifist as Secretary of Defense.) (That, on the other hand, might not be a bad idea.)

For those who believe strongly that God has appointed us as stewards of Creation, to return it in as good shape as we found it for God's sake, Divine Command Theory works as motivator, justification, and its own reward. But as we see, even Christianity is dicey on the subject of stewardship, split among several traditions of interpretation, and the theory is useless in talking with others not of the faith about the duty of stewardship. (The purpose of secular ethics is at the least to enable people of widely different traditions of faith and morals to engage in reasoned discussion about right conduct in difficult situations.) The Divine Command line of justification is then broadly inadequate or inapplicable, but it retains one virtue: It is one of the very few frameworks that can continue to justify right conduct in the course of a lifetime without visible or tangible sanctions or rewards. For this reason, no environmentalist will want to see it abandoned.

Justification Two: The Earth as a Living Organism

In 1961, by his own account, in the course of developing the science of the first exploration of the moon in search of alien life, James Lovelock and a few of his companions, as part of that investigation, came to consider the necessary conditions for any life to live anywhere. They soon realized that atmosphere and oceans, indeed the entire crust of a planet alive, would have to be part of the transport and maintenance mechanisms of whatever life was there (Lovelock 1988).[8] This led to the realization that in many ways, our planet, this earth as a whole, is very much alive—that it is one life, self-regulating, self-adjusting, a very complex system of chemical balances in reaction to the interactions of the living beings within it. The fascinating part of the discovery was the fact that life itself, all life, seems to run counter to the trend of the universe, where all energy is lost in general entropy.

> Life is the paradoxical contradiction to the second law, which states that everything is, always has been, and always will be running down to equilibrium and death. Yet life evolves to ever-greater complexity and is characterized by an omnipresence of improbability that would make winning a sweepstake every day for a year seem trivial by comparison. (Lovelock 1988, p. 23)

We, then, are living parts of that improbable living life, as our tissues are to our body, and our bond to the earth, and to its service, is perfectly obvious, whether or not it is written down anywhere or part of any accepted Western ethic. Reverence and love for the earth as the organism of which we are the tissues, the organs, is

---

[8] For the background of the hypothesis, see Lovelock (1979).

associated with a variety of Native American cultures, possibly with that movement in environmental philosophy known as 'deep ecology'. Without delving further into these origins, the general implication is perfectly clear:

> In Gaia we are just another species, neither the owners nor the stewards of this planet. Our future depends much more on a right relationship with Gaia than with the never-ending drama of human interest. (Lovelock 1988, p. 14)

We are cells within the body of the Earth, the body of Gaia. Given the effect that human activities have on Gaia, what kind of cell might we be? In light of our clear potential to make wise decisions about the future of the earth, we might want to think of ourselves as brain cells. But that's not the way we act. What else might we be? Possibly cancer. The difference between a normal cell and a cancer cell is subtle and not immediately evident; if the difference were clearer, cancer would not be a problem. Ordinarily when a cell mutates into a different and harmful state, the body's immune system recognizes it as different, seizes it and kills it before it can do any damage. But the cancer cell does not appear foreign. It grows like all other cells in the body, apparently harmless, but then begins to participate in very strange patterns. It divides, and divides again, growing large clumps of cells known as tumors, displacing all healthy cells in its area, interfering mightily with the health and function-ing of the body as a whole, threatening to take over the entire biomass of the body for its own purposes. To aid in obtaining that objective, it takes over the body's capacity to grow new blood vessels, and diverts the blood supply to its own needs instead of the needs of the rest of the body. As its reproduction is out of control, it overwhelms the body's ability to remove its wastes, and the toxins from its growth and death clog the systems of blood vessels, gall blad-der and liver. Unlike other cells in the body, if cancer cells can be carried from the place where they started to other locations in the body, they can attach themselves to that new location and begin to grow there—again, redirecting the local blood supply to serve them. Ultimately, unless some plague can be found to kill the cancer without killing the rest of the body, the body dies, totally absorbed by the cancer.

Humans are a bit like that. Many species of plant and animal will have popula-tion explosions ("bombs") now and again, but as they run through their natural food supply and attract their natural predators, the population crashes and gets back into balance—the immune system of the ecosystem, or of Gaia, has destroyed the danger. Generally, in a well-functioning ecosystem, the species are in balance. Now along comes the human species. Evolved as all other species, it is well adapted to the earth, and prospers. But when the population blooms, instead of dying back, it spreads, using its famous (or infamous) ingenuity to coopt new parts of the biota into food for itself, manufacture energy from beneath the earth, and destroy all competing species. (In a few isolated places, like Easter Island, human population follows the classic pattern of boom and bust—but leaves the natural environment infinitely more devastated than any other species could possibly have done.) As cancer kills the body, we will kill the earth, if we are not stopped. But who, or what, could stop us?

As intelligent cells of the organism, we alone of all the others have a choice. We can see, as above, what we are doing. We can, at least in theory, elect not to continue on our destructive path. We know what it would be to cure a cancer; we can use similar methods on our species. We can reduce our numbers, cut way back on our consumption of resources, reduce to nothing our toxic effects on the body in which we live. We can determine from a careful analysis of our ecosystem—a task we are very good at—how many people there should be, and how they should live, to protect the health of Gaia, the earth, the sustainer of all of us. It does not matter whether our duty to perform this reduction, this withdrawal of damaging intrusion, is to be derived from ultimate consequences (if we do not do it we are all dead, as per the Land Level 5 motivation, above), deontologically (we have a quasi-contractual duty of support for the earth that supports us, for instance), or ontologically (to live in health with the body of which we are a part is necessary for our nature). The duty of the cell, or organ, to serve and protect the body is a simple extension of its definition.

Again, this explanation works only if we accept several steps that may have few followers: first, we must accept the Gaia hypothesis, that the earth as a whole is best understood as a living organism, in which all living things are parts as to a whole; second, we must accept that from that perception, which may be very useful for many purposes, carries moral implications applicable to us as individual duties; and third, we must accept that such inchoate and diffuse duties can be acquired simply from an undifferentiated and unchosen status of human being—'found' duties, as it were. If these claims seem plausible, and many have found them to be, then our duty to protect the earth falls within the same class as the duty of the fetus not to harm its mother—biologically created and determined, but a duty nonetheless. If the claims seem implausible, and a greater number have found them so, then nothing of duty follows from our intimate participation in the web of life we know as the earth.

There is a further problem evident in this paradigm, a problem that has been called 'ecofascism'. My body works as a thoroughly authoritarian system, allowing no flexibility in roles or activities among the cells, all of which are required to serve the interests of the body at all times. (Cancer, as above, defies this authority.) It is possible for the state to work this way, as Plato pointed out approvingly in the *Republic,* modeling his state on the pattern of the human soul.[9] And indeed, I am very glad that my body works this way. But there is an ancient and correct tradition, which says that humans need freedom to function well, and that the organic model suits the human community on the one level, and the biotic community on another, very badly. (Aristotle criticized Plato on this score in his *Politics,* very effectively.)[10]

---

[9] Plato, *Republic,* many editions.

[10] Aristotle, *Politics,* Book II Chap. 4.

Justification Three: The Land as a Community

Probably the best candidate for a deontological earth ethic is from Aldo Leopold, the biologist and wildlife manager who became one of our best, in fact our primary, philosopher of the land.[11] Leopold's famous statement of the land ethic is from a section of that name in the final section of *A Sand County Almanac*, 'The Upshot'. His message, now become the centrepiece of all ecocentric ethics, is simple:

> … quit thinking about decent land-use as solely an economic problem. Examine each question in terms of what is ethically and aesthetically right, as well as what is economically expedient. A thing is right when it tends to preserve the integrity, stability, and beauty of the biotic community. It is wrong when it tends otherwise. (Leopold 1949)

The ethic was initially scorned by philosophers. John Passmore (1974), one of the first philosophers to ride the momentum of Earth Day 1970 to the publisher's with his 1974 volume *Man's Responsibility for Nature,* simply dismissed it; his countryman H. J. McCloskey called it "a retrogression to a morality of a kind held by various primitive peoples" (McCloskey 1983). J. Baird Callicott, Aldo Leopold's greatest exponent and interpreter, credits this misunderstanding to three very simple characteristics of the land ethic: it is "abbreviated, unfamiliar, and radical" (Callicott 1987). He proceeds to spell out its logic, tie it back into the philosophical tradition, and support its radical implications, in an argument we trace briefly.

The logic begins with two simple observations: First, moral obligation of some kind is universally acknowledged across the human race, for good evolutionary reasons. (Natural selection would predict that, had there been any human groups initially without such acknowledgement, they would have perished from the face of the earth.) Therefore we need not ask, why we *ought* to be moral, any more than we need to ask why we ought to have capillaries or external ears. Given the kind of creature we turn out to be, we could hardly be otherwise. (Callicott combines the accounts of human morality given by Charles Darwin, Edward O. Wilson, Adam Smith and David Hume to reach that conclusion; he might have added the more recent account given by Robert Wright in *The Moral Animal.*)[12] The second observation is that whatever the level of moral practice may be, here or elsewhere, the level of moral consciousness has risen slowly and inevitably from the dawn of human awareness, or at least from the time that Odysseus hanged the slave girls from a single rope (the incident that begins Aldo Leopold's account of the Land Ethic). The recognition of "moral considerability," of worthiness to have one's rights (however defined) and interests taken into account (Goodpaster 1978), spreads from the initial instinctive focus on the immediate family clan to the tribe, to the community, to the society as a whole, to non-humans, always proceeding by analogy with the last group deemed to be morally considerable. Worthy of note is the fact that many tribal groups recognize non-humans—animals, trees, even rocks

---

[11] The interpretation of Leopold's land ethic is taken from Callicott (1987).

[12] The editions cited by Callicott are: Darwin (1904), Wilson (1975), Smith (1759), Hume (1777), Wright (1994), Berreby (1996).

and mountains—as 'persons' long before they recognize as such the humans living in the next valley. Nothing in the human fabric, whatever the doctrinal strictures of theology and theologically oriented philosophers, prevents humans from conceiving of and honoring moral obligations to the rest of creation, obligations to the land. In that sense at least, the land ethic is neither unfamiliar nor radical.

We started our existence as a species in the heart of a biotic community, not as lord over it but as "plain member and citizen of it," in Leopold's words.[13] All the evidence suggests that for most of our existence—all except the last 6,000 years of it, in European reckoning, and considerably less than that for most of the human race—we acknowledged as part of ourselves the non-human neighbors and companions that made that life possible. In civilization—"cityfication," as Callicott translates it—we draw back from the nature with which we lived, we leave the animals with which we have evolved outside the city walls, and withdraw to an artificial environment inhabited primarily by other human beings. In company with the anthropomorphic gods and goddesses that emerge in the first myths of civilization, it becomes much easier to assume that all worth is contained in the human form. We now see ourselves as somehow 'transcendent', distinctly different from all other animals, and our myths, stories, and moral systems begin to change to contain this new assumption of superiority. Historically, the mythmakers, writers, storytellers, cosmologists and theologians have worked in the cities. In a self-reinforcing circle, our 'science' increasingly paints nature—non-human nature—as inferior, non-rational, a lesser order of being clearly fit to be dominated by us, and our 'theology', our account of gods and goddesses, increasingly paints us as created by them to rule nature for our own purposes.

Leopold homed in on the notion of 'community' to describe the natural world of which we form a part, specifically rejecting (after a period of trying it out) (Callicott 1987, p. 202) the notion of Nature as one huge all-encompassing (and dominating) organism. The community is essentially a passage of energy in which all participants cooperate:

> Land, then, is not merely soil; it is a fountain of energy flowing through a circuit of soils, plants and animals. Food chains are the living channels which conduct energy upward; death and decay return it to the soil. The circuit is not closed… but it is a sustained circuit, like a slowly augmented revolving fund of life. (Callicott 1987, p. 203)

This process augments itself in evolution, a trend over very long periods of time to increase the diversity of the biota. Since that process is the core of what is good in nature, it is our duty to maintain that diversity. Our position as 'plain member and citizen' of the community of the living world requires that we treat our fellow citizens with respect and appreciation, and conservation of biodiversity is only one of the obvious steps to take.

The integrity—and the beauty—of the process that is the soil, as described above, provides the needed 'intrinsic' or 'inherent' value of nature (as opposed to the merely instrumental value of commodifiable resources or recreational opportunities).

---

[13] Leopold, cited in Callicott (1987, p. 204).

From this vast process, from which we draw and in which we participate, we derive the duty of respect, fulfilled in the avoidance of damage and the effort to restore the process where its integrity has been lost—in short, all the activities of environmental conservation.

Coda: Why the Outrageous Young Men Were Right

Let us return to the current controversy, the infuriating suggestion that environmentalism ought to be abandoned in favor of more contemporary causes. Of course the young men are right, that environment is not, or is not any longer, the kind of buzz word that will attract liberal votes. Insofar as liberalism entails nothing but individual freedom—civil liberties in the public square, equal justice for all, but also the rights to play the market for all its worth, the right to consume anything you can buy, and the right to feel good about it as long as you are not hurting anyone else—anyone else visible and near—environmentalism is profoundly anti-liberal. That's not a fact that makes us feel very good, but it's a fact nonetheless.

On the other hand, maybe we should feel good about it. Liberalism has not been of lasting help to the land. Contemporary conservatism, of course, is even less help, having been monopolized by neo-liberals, sectarian theocrats and nativists. But it would seem that the ultimate initiative for the land is coming from the real conservatives, those who are recapturing the skills of organic farming on small and medium plots, selling fresh food to local markets, limiting reliance on long-distance (fuel-consuming) transportation, while rediscovering the pleasures of working together with neighbors on simple tasks that provide a sufficient life. The young men were right. Environmentalism cannot, and should not, recapture liberalism, let alone progressivism. If we can recapture conservatism—a revival of classical conservatism and the defense of the commons—that political philosophy will furnish the best home for environmentalism (although we may learn to call it something else). But the point of this paper, besides a vindication of the young men, is an expansion of the grounds on which we recognize acts as environmentally sound. We may seek support for environmental measures completely outside the political framework, in the economic world preferred by business. In the end, there is not only one set of teachings for the environmentalists—on the contrary, the defense of the land will appear in dozens of guises at many levels of public discourse.

References

Aquinas, T. (1270). *Summa Theologiae*, 1, 2; Q. 90 article 1.
Austin, J. (1998). *The province of jurisprudence determined*. New York: Hackett. (Reprinted from 1954 edition).
Barringer, F. (6 Feb 2005). Paper sets off a debate on environmentalism's future. *The New York Times* Sunday, 18.

Benyus, J. M. (1997). *Biomimicry: Innovation inspired by nature*. New York: William Morrow.

Berreby, D. (24 Sept 1996). Enthralling or exasperating: Select one: David Sloan Wilson, scientist at work. *The New York Times: Science Times*, Tuesday, C1.

Bix, B. (Spring 2005). John Austin. In *The Stanford Encyclopedia of Philosophy*. (http://plato. stanford.edu/archives/spr2005/entries/austin-john/).

Callicott, J. B. (1987). The conceptual foundations of the land ethic. In B. Callicott (Ed.), *Companion to a sand county Almanac: Interpretive and critical essays* (pp. 186–217, 187). Madison: University of Wisconsin Press.

Darwin, C. R. (1904). *The descent of man and selection in relation to sex* (p. 97). New York: J.A. Hill and Company.

Diamond, J. (2005). *Collapse: How societies choose to fail or succeed*. New York: Viking.

Elkington, J. (1998). *Cannibals with forks: The triple bottom line of 21st century business*. Gabriola Island: New Society.

Foderaro, L. W. (7 March 2005). In a debate over trash burning, it's rural tradition vs. health. *The New York Times*, B1.

Goodpaster, K. (1978). On being morally considerable. *Journal of Philosophy, 22,* 308–325.

Hardin, G. (1968). The tragedy of the commons. *Science, 162,* 1243–1248.

Hawken, P., Lovins, A., & Hunter Lovins, L. (1999). *Natural capitalism: Creating the next industrial revolution*. Snowmass: Rocky Mountain Institute.

Hobbes, T. (1962). Of the natural condition of mankind as concerning their felicity and misery. In M. Oakeshott (Ed.), Leviathan (p. 100). New York: Collier.

Holmes, O. W. Jr. (1897). The path of the law. *10 Harvard Law Review, 457,* 461.

Hume, D. (1777). *An enquiry concerning the principles of morals*. Oxford: Clarendon.

Kohlberg, L. (1981).*The philosophy of moral development: Essays on moral development*. San Francisco: Harper and Row

Kristof, N. D. (12 March 2005). I have a nightmare. *The New York Times* Op-Ed, Saturday.

Leopold, A. (1949). *A sand county Almanac and sketches here and there* (pp. 224–225). New York: Oxford University Press.

Lovelock, J. (1979). *Gaia: A new look at life on earth*. New York: Oxford University Press.

Lovelock, J. (1988). *The ages of Gaia: A biography of our living earth* (p. 5). New York: Bantam.

McCloskey, H. J. (1983). *Ecological ethics and politics* (p. 56). Totowa: Rowman and Littlefield.

Passmore, J. (1974). *Man's responsibility for nature: Ecological problems and Western traditions*. New York, Totowa: Charles Scribner's Sons, Rowman and Littlefield.

Ponting, C. (1993). *A green history of the world: The environment and the collapse of great civilizations*. New York: Penguin.

Sachs, J. (2005). *The end of poverty: Economic possibilities for our time*. New York: Penguin.

Smith, A. (1759). *Theory of the moral sentiments*. London: Millar, Kinkaid and Bell.

Speth, G. (2004). *Red sky at morning: America and the crisis of the global environment*. New Haven: Yale University Press.

The New York Times. (2003) Logging jobs benefit pygmies, but imperil their forest home. *The New York Times*, 6. (16 Feb 2003).

Wilson, E. O. (1975). *Sociobiology: The new synthesis*. Cambridge: Harvard University Press.

Wright, R. (1994). *The moral animal: Why we are the way we are: The new science of evolutionary psychology*. New York: Pantheon.

Part IV
Local Development, Global Sustainability: Case Studies in Development Contexts

Our last three chapters concern the need for sustainable development and distributive justice in developing countries.

Chapter ten asks us to consider why *all* development must be just and sustainable.

Chapter eleven reminds us that good intentions for development are not enough, if the cultural integrity of the communities we engage with is not maintained.

Chapter twelve asks us to listen to the voices of people in developing countries, and consider what development means to them.

Chapter 11
Sustainable Development Following Conflicts: The Critical Role of Security and Justice

Vandra Harris

The satisfaction of human needs and aspirations is the major objective of development. The essential needs of vast numbers of people in developing countries for food, clothing, shelter, jobs—are not being met, and beyond their basic needs these people have legitimate aspirations for an improved quality of life. A world in which poverty and inequity are endemic will always be prone to ecological and other crises. **Sustainable development requires meeting the basic needs of all and extending to all the opportunity to satisfy their aspirations for a better life** (WCED 1987, Ch2 Para4).

In this chapter I will argue that in post-conflict and transition societies, effective security sector reform (SSR) is key to sustainability of economic and social development. Indeed, without rule of law and functioning security systems such as police forces and prisons, progress made through social development projects is threatened by insecurity. Similarly, a functional security sector can help to expand people's capability set, and to support the expansions made by access to education and improvements in health. Police capacity building is therefore an example of a key strategy of sustainable development, and is appropriately funded from national development budgets, as is the case in Australia.

This chapter begins with a discussion of the term sustainable development, pointing to the sense in which it is a tautology, since genuine development *must* be sustainable. The second section examines SSR as a critical component of development in post-conflict and transition societies, which is expanded in the third section through a discussion of the Regional Assistance Mission to Solomon Islands (RAMSI) as an example of how security and justice can be prioritized in post-conflict environments. Nominating police rather than a department of foreign affairs or development as the lead agency on that mission demonstrates the importance of security and justice reform following conflict, but it also has important ramifications for the boundaries between domestic and international policy, and for some of the traditional conceptions of development. The chapter concludes with a consolidation of the argument that a functional justice system is a prerequisite for sustainability,

V. Harris (✉)
RMIT University Melbourne, Melbourne, Australia
e-mail: vandra.harris@rmit.edu.au

© Springer Science+Business Media Dordrecht 2014
S. Sandhu et al. (eds.), *Linking Local and Global Sustainability,* The International Society of Business, Economics, and Ethics Book Series 4, DOI 10.1007/978-94-017-9008-6_11

177

and that SSR must therefore be a primary development focus in transition and post-conflict societies.

[Sustainable] Development

The Brundtland Report (World Commission on the Environment and Development (WCED) 1987) brought sustainable development into the global spotlight. Only a year before, the UN General Assembly passed Resolution 14/28, clearly stating that every individual and all peoples have a right "to participate in, contribute to, and enjoy economic, social, cultural and political development, in which all human rights and fundamental freedoms can be fully realised" (United Nations 1986, Art 1). This resolution on the Right to Development marked a shift in which it was recognized that simply holding human rights does not ensure their fulfilment, and that wealthier countries have a responsibility to the world's poorest, through effective development support. *The Brundtland Report* extended this, highlighting that the form development takes is as important as development itself.

With an explicit focus on the interaction between the development and the physical environment, *The Brundtland Report* is most commonly quoted for its definition of sustainable development as meeting present needs without compromising future ones (WCED 1987, Ch 2, Para1). The report appears to recognize that physical resources cannot be separated from other development processes and goals, as shown in the quote at the beginning of this chapter, pointing to the importance of meeting not only people's needs but also their aspirations for improved lives for current and future generations. It does not support unfettered growth, pointing to unsustainable living standards in some parts of the world and calling for "equitable access" to limited resources (WCED 1987, Ch2, Para5, 10).

Sustainability has entered the vernacular, used lightly and often, with its definition somehow implicit. In most cases, the meaning has environmental connotations, referring to the importance of defending environmental priorities against rapacious economic progress. At a more nuanced level, it is widely accepted that there are three pillars or components of sustainability: the environment, the economy and society. These pillars are interdependent, with the best outcomes for each component arising from strength in each sector and balance between them (Victor 2006, p. 91).

Development (in the sense used by NGOs and government and international agencies in the context of attempts to improve lives and livelihoods in developing countries) always aims to meet basic needs, improve lives, create equitable access to resources and ensure that future generations are healthier, better educated, and better able to sustain themselves and their families. The authors of the first *Human Development Report* summarized this, explaining that "The basic objective of development is to create an enabling environment for people to enjoy long, healthy and creative lives" (UNDP 1990, p. 9). These aims are not always met, and there will always be disagreement on the best way to meet them, but as aims they remain central to the development exercise, whether or not it is labeled sustainable.

From a sustainability perspective, people have the opportunity to make choices that look beyond their own needs to account for their aspirations and the needs and aspirations of others when they have options, but these are notably limited in extreme poverty. Development requires a redistribution of resources (usually from countries with high development levels to those with lower measures) in the interests of meeting needs and aspirations—particularly of those people least able to achieve them without intervention. According to the United Nations, the fundamental purpose and function of development is to enlarge people's choices (UNDP 1990, p. 1, 2011, p. 1), so effective development gives people the option to make sustainable choices. Development therefore confers a particular perspective on the pillars of sustainability, aiming for a specific range of outcomes rather than general attention to the three areas of environmental protection, social justice and poverty alleviation.

With some force, it has been claimed that poverty elimination provides critical support to the other pillars of sustainability, since people will give priority to their unmet basic needs over other concerns (Victor 2006, p. 95). Indeed, the sustainability movement has been criticized for a misplaced rich world sensibility, projecting the concerns of wealthy and environmentally unsustainable societies onto the poorest countries in which many concerns stem from their failure to meet the basic needs of all citizens, "Because, when basic needs become an integral component of a developmental model, the question of unsustainability does not arise" (Nayar 1994, p. 1327).

Therefore while the *Brundtland Report* introduced the term 'sustainable development' into the mainstream, its definition is simply that of effective development: "meeting the basic needs of all and extending to all the opportunity to satisfy their aspirations for a better life"—in other words, enlarging people's choices. Development is "an investment exercise", intrinsically concerned with the diverse aspects of human lives in the medium- and long-term (Barakat and Chard 2010, p. 175). Even with a concern for durability and the needs of future generations, adding 'sustainable' does not expand the meaning of 'development', for it is not development if the gains are not enduring and shared. Indeed, the United Nations Development Program (UNDP) notes that *intra*-generational equity is as important as *inter*-generational equity, for it would be "distinctly odd if we were deeply concerned for the well-being of future—as yet unborn—generations while ignoring the plight of the poor today" (UNDP 1994, p. 13). In this sense, 'sustainable development' is a tautology—or, to put it another way, sustainable is a superfluous adjective.

It is therefore unsurprising to discover that key development approaches share fundamental tenets of the approach set out by the authors of the *Brundtland Report* and two decades of the *Human Development Report*, and refined for quarter of a century by theorists and practitioners alike. One of the clearest examples of this can be seen in the capabilities approach developed in the 1980s by renowned academic philosopher Martha Nussbaum and Nobel Prize-winning economist Amartya Sen. In this approach they recognize that there are many factors that enable or impede people in their striving to achieve the outcomes that they value (their 'valued ends'), and that as such it is not simply a person's *ability* to achieve something, but their *capability* to do so—how their environment interacts with those abilities. These capabilities are the diverse "combinations of things a person is able to do or be", and they influence an individual's (dis)advantage "in terms of his or her actual ability to achieve the various valuable functionings as part of living" (Sen 1993, p. 30).

The interaction of ability and capability results in a 'capability set'—the array of outcomes available to an individual in light of the context in which he or she lives. Armed with this knowledge, Sen and Nussbaum argue that development should focus on increasing each person's capability set—that is, removing barriers and enhancing supports to help people achieve the outcomes they value. Adopting the terms of sustainability, development must therefore focus on how to protect (and enhance) the environment, achieve social justice, and alleviate poverty in order to eliminate barriers to people's valued ends.

On this basis, it is fair to say that development is concerned with *enabling environments*, or ensuring that each person lives in a context that fosters their ability to meet their aspirations or valued ends. Stability and security are fundamental components of enabling environments, since the threat or reality of conflict and personal violence limit a person's mobility, education and earning opportunities and access to health care and other services. A focus on creating and maintaining a well-functioning security sector is therefore critical to development, which is measured by a range of indicators including education, health and income. In countries emerging from conflict, stability is particularly important for achieving the kinds of development outcomes that will support the transition to peace by encouraging investment (individual, national and international) and increasing access to education, health care, markets and services.

Security and Justice Are Critical to Development

One thing that is well known about conflict-affected countries is that they struggle to maintain peace in the medium-term. Following a complex statistical analysis of post-conflict societies, Collier et al. (2008, p. 467) conclude that for any country, "The entire post-conflict decade faces a high level of risk" for return to conflict. This is reflected in the focus of many national development agencies, including those of Australia and Great Britain, which prioritize post-conflict societies in their programs. It is also reflected in a slow learning curve on the part of UN peace interventions, which in the 1980s and 1990s were focused on the quick implementation of elections and a subsequent rapid withdrawal. In the last decade the UN has increasingly recognized that transformation takes a long-term, tailored commitment, and that elections do not of themselves signify the achievement of peace and democracy.

With a quarter of the world's population living in "fragile and conflict-affected states or in countries with very high levels of criminal violence" (World Bank 2011, p. 2), it is critical to understand the dynamics of the transition from conflict to acceptable stability and peace. Importantly, development and peace interact: development requires a level of peace and stability to make progress, while peace can be fostered by development gains (Commission on Human Security 2003, p. 7). Conversely, conflict severely limits development, with civil war in a developing country costing on average "more than 30 years of GDP growth" (World Bank 2011, p. 5), which of course has a significant impact on the country's human development. Of the 48 countries designated as "least developed countries" (LDCs) by the UN, almost half are conflict-affected—and just over one third of conflict-affected countries are LDCs (Cortez and Kim 2012, p. 2).

Development is therefore a critical concern following conflicts—contexts which have quite specific characteristics and demands, but which nonetheless require the usual focus of development on building the capacity of people and institutions. In addition to concerns associated with low human development, the specific conditions of post-conflict environments include "the unravelling of the fabric of society, the weakening or complete breakdown of those institutions and relationships that would normally enable the society to respond to its own needs or to negotiate assistance as sovereign peoples" (Barakat and Chard 2010, p. 173). These characteristics give focus to the areas that must be central to post-conflict development: rebuilding social relationships and trust and rehabilitating institutions, as a foundation for the broader capacities needed to expand people's choices.

Security concerns have an important (if not always acknowledged) resonance for those concerned with development because instability, inequity and dysfunction within the security sector impact the poor and marginalized more than other areas of society. This is played out in direct experiences of violence and crime, as well as failures to meet people's needs and ensure their access to services and to justice. This increased vulnerability in turn decreases people's access to resources required to improve their lives, such as a secure livelihood, education, health and other services (OECD 2007, p. 13). Thus, while poverty alleviation facilitates positive action in the diverse aspects of sustainability, failures of security and justice undermine economic development, and therefore social and environmental development as well.

SSR has therefore become increasingly important in international interventions to assist with transitions to peace and development. Much more than the input of foreign troops to maintain peace long enough for warring parties to start to coexist, it is a multi-sectoral approach that aims to build a long-term foundation for comprehensive, equitable nationally-managed stability and justice. Guidelines published by the Development Assistance Commission of the OECD note that there are three key aspects of this approach:

> The SSR policy agenda covers three inter-related challenges facing all states: i) developing a clear institutional framework for the provision of security that integrates security and development policy and includes all relevant actors, ii) strengthening the governance of the security institutions; and iii) building capable and professional security forces that are accountable to civil authorities. (OECD 2005, p. 16)

SSR therefore addresses capacity and resources of a wide range of sectors within the nation in question, requiring extensive and highly skilled engagement—including police, military, judiciary, courts, prisons, and functioning institutions such as schools, health services and government departments.

The notion of "mainstreaming" permeates the development sector, encompassing the notion that a particular concept (e.g., gender, disability) needs to be a key consideration in every sector for there to be effective impact. A key example of this is the notion that gender must be considered not only in the education sector, but also in areas such as governance and security, in order for there to be broader opportunities for girls and boys, and for there to be broad social change towards a more gender-equitable society. SSR requires a similarly overarching view, and has broad reach into key development sectors, but has not achieved mainstreaming into programming. According to the OECD, a lack of strategic coherence across programs and between donors is the critical challenge facing development donors, requiring greater consistency and integration between sectors, and particularly across government (OECD 2007, p. 13). This strategic coherence must become a key driver in national development priorities of both donors and host governments in order to ensure that development is achieved and maintained as countries negotiate the rocky path to stability and growth.

Sustainability Through Security and Justice

An effective security sector is a consolidation of the rule of law, according to which (at its most basic) the law applies equally to all. This fundamental concept is so familiar to those who experience it that it seems redundant to raise it, however citizens of less democratic societies often find that power and status have more impact on the application of the law than "the entitlement of all to equal protection and equal benefit of the law" (Arbour 2012 n.p.). Failures of rule of law perpetuate inequities and maintain the power of those who have money, political control, or the ability to use physical force against others. This raises alarm bells for those with concern for development, since it points once more to mechanisms that prevent the poor and marginalized from achieving their valued ends.

In many post-conflict societies, international intervention will include an SSR component, which as the name suggests focuses on reforming the various arms of the security sector—whether by strengthening existing institutions or replacing or rebuilding them. The aim of SSR is "to create a secure environment that is conducive to development, poverty reduction, good governance and, in particular, the growth of democratic states and institutions based on the rule of law" (GFN-SSR 2007). It achieves these aims in a variety of ways, but primarily through the peace dividend conferred by functioning institutions and personnel.

At its most obvious, a functioning security sector increases trust in security and justice institutions. This is most easily measured in terms of access to, or use of, those institutions, particularly in the reporting of crimes (see Goldsmith and Harris 2012). Low trust in police and the justice sector leads to low reporting, for communities do not have confidence that reporting will lead to satisfactory outcomes.

A key example of this is the response to 'women's issues'—that is, crimes against women, particularly of a sexual or gender-based nature. These are often viewed as belonging to the private sphere, to be dealt with in that realm alone. As a result, women face many barriers to bringing these concerns to public arenas, and those who do so "may face severe socio-cultural consequences" (Salahub and Nerland 2010, p. 265). A rise in reporting of gender-based violence can therefore be a strong indicator of confidence in the security sector, which in turn represents a significant step towards security and development for women, traditionally overrepresented amongst the poor.

An effective security sector also contributes to a positive investment climate, and private investment is a key "engine for growth and poverty reduction" (World Bank 2005, p. 19)—indeed, a much more sustainable driver of development than foreign aid. The cost of a civil war is incurred by both the country and its neighbours, and takes a range of forms, from obvious financial costs to the destruction of infrastructure, spread of disease and interruption of education; this cost has been calculated at US\$ 64 billion for a "typical civil war" (Collier 2007, p. 32). Post-conflict societies therefore require significant investment to help recoup those losses and to build new institutions and sources of economic growth.

It has been noted above that post-conflict countries face a high risk of relapse into conflict in the first four to five years—a risk calculated variously from one in four countries to almost one in two countries. This provides a strong disincentive for investment by large and small businesses, compounded by the disruption to markets, and the low capacity and risk-aversion common to new or transitional governments (IFC n.d., p. 21). These adverse conditions must be addressed quickly to ensure that as international peace and development interventions scale down, there is a local economy that is able to provide jobs and foster growth in a more enduring manner than is provided by aid. The strongest evidence of the impact of improving investment climates can be seen in the extraordinary poverty reduction achieved in both China and India (World Bank 2005, p. 31).

Effective security and justice contribute to a conducive investment climate through certain implicit assurances. The primary example is in the protection of resources, investment and markets by preventing and punishing crimes and acts of terrorism or insurgency that would threaten investments. This in turn reinforces stability and security capacity, as investors are less likely to create their own security mechanisms, which can drain capacity from national security sector institutions, and potentially promote competing interests. Benefits extend well beyond this more obvious area, however, for example ensuring that employees are able to travel to and from work safely.

A third important area that is improved is corruption. In its 2011 annual report, Transparency International (2012, p. 36) notes that "Corruption not only makes poor people poorer. It also diverts resources from schemes meant to meet society's most basic needs, such as sanitation and healthcare." This diversion occurs from the highest level of government and intergovernmental funding, right down to the individual level of ordinary people having to make choices between paying a bribe or protection money and meeting basic needs of food, shelter and clothing for their family. In many countries corruption permeates security and justice mechanisms, making rule of law impossible.

These factors are components in a broader process of development that facilitates the fragile shift away from conflict, which can be consolidated by prioritizing "citizen security, justice and jobs" (World Bank 2011, p. 11). These three elements promote sustainability in national development because they enable citizens to participate actively in the change and growth that are taking place in their society—making choices about their valued ends, and increasing their capability to achieve them. While development agencies may focus on expanding those choices by building schools for children's education, a secure environment is required so that boys and girls are safe at those schools and on the journey there and home. Where men and women are threatened by state and non-state violence they may not be able to leave their homes to work or to collect water and firewood. Basic functionings such as these are denied people in environments where justice and security sectors are fragile, corrupt or dysfunctional. This denial severely constricts choices and capabilities, diminishing people's ability to prioritize sustainability in their day-to-day lives.

Without rule of law and functioning security systems such as police forces and prisons, what progress is made through social development projects is threatened by insecurity. Citizens are inhibited in their participation in development processes and their access to positive outcomes by the threat of violence. Institutions, infrastructure, investment and people's heath are all threatened by physical violence that accompanies instability and failures in rule of law. Resources are redirected from social development to containing or participating in conflict. Reform and strengthening of security and justice sectors contributes to the stability that is critical to development as opposed to relief, which is primarily focused on saving lives (Barakat and Chard 2010, p. 174). A focus on security and justice must therefore be at the forefront of development interventions in post-conflict societies.

A Multi-sectoral Approach

RAMSI is a strong example of what it means in practice to place a priority on security and justice within a broader intervention. In 2002, the *Solomon Islands Human Development Report* produced by the Solomon Islands government and the United Nations identified the archipelago in the South Pacific as facing four key medium-term challenges: "restoring the country's productive and export potential; repairing and upgrading the country's public infrastructure; revitalising the country's social and human development; [and a] focus on increased financing of provincial programmes" (Government of Solomon Islands 2002, p. 74). The country was classified by Australia's Department of Foreign Affairs and Trade (DFAT) as a failed state as a result of the broad-ranging effects of an enduring and worsening political and security crisis that rendered the country "a kind of post-modern badlands, ruled by criminals and governed by violence" (DFAT 2004, p. 13). For several years the country had experienced ethnic conflict that had not only severely damaged the economy but also "led to the collapse of the police force" and an associated fragmentation of social order (Dinnen 2009, p. 70). In the face of escalating unrest, and after repeated requests from the Solomon Islands government, RAMSI was formed in 2003.

The mission has a number of features that distinguish it from other well known international interventions. Firstly, it involves only states in the region, drawing personnel from 13 Pacific Island Forum (PIF) states and was initiated by the Solomon Islands' own government. It does not operate under the auspices of the United Nations, but rather is led by Australia, which is a member of the PIF. Finally, it is police-led, giving a clear priority to the justice and security sectors. RAMSI has three pillars, representing the priority areas of the intervention: law and justice, economic governance and growth, and machinery of government. In an echo of contemporary UN interventions, RAMSI was designed as a three phase project, with a commencement phase in 2003, consolidation in 2004 and what was originally designated as a final phase focused on sustainability and self-reliance phase (Morgan and McLeod 2006, p. 419). A fourth phase (transition) has been announced more recently, recognizing that significant progress has been made and that a shift is necessary from a post-conflict framework to a more standard development approach.

Nominating police as the lead agency rather than a department of foreign affairs or development recognizes the importance of security and justice reform as foundational for sustainable development following conflict. It also has important ramifications for the boundaries between domestic and international policy, and for some of the traditional conceptions of development. These three issues will be addressed in turn, after a brief summary of RAMSI's key security and justice activities and achievements in the last decade.

Expectations of interventions are generally very high following conflict (Barakat 2010, p. 12) and when they are conducted on such a large scale, therefore RAMSI had a double dose of high expectations. Indeed it is appropriate to expect that a massive investment of financial and human capital in a very small nation should effect a significant and sustainable transformation. It was instability and a weak security sector that led to RAMSI's initiation, and a recognition of the interaction between security and development that shaped its structure. Responding to security and development simultaneously is the only way to meet these high expectations, however prioritizing security (at least initially) is key to the sustainability of the intervention.

As in any intervention, RAMSI has been credited with both successes and failures. A measured critique recognizes that the two coexist: in a relatively brief time of transformation, some "ugly" security and justice practices have emerged, yet there has been significant improvement in a range of areas, including improved security and success in targeting the worst levels of corruption in a state in which "Zero tolerance of corruption would mean no-one left standing to run the nation" (Braithwaite et al. 2010, p. 151). In spite of high investment it is unrealistic to expect to comprehensively restructure a nation's power base and introduce (and fully implement) widespread legal reform in just 10 years. Effective intervention can certainly set a nation upon such a trajectory, but such rapid change would not be sustainable, not least because it is unlikely to be matched by local ownership and capacity. Indeed, Della-Giacoma (2012) has noted that the self-determination evident in the East Timorese refusal to comply with directives of the intervening mission in their country should perhaps be regarded as one of its successes. Progress will therefore be uneven and will require an enduring commitment.

Consistent with its SSR focus, RAMSI has prioritized the restructuring and capacity building of the police force, now known as the Royal Solomon Islands Police Force (RSIPF). The mission's largest personnel component was 330 international police from the region (primarily Australia), clearly demonstrating the police focus from the outset, supplemented by a smaller military force and civilian personnel (Dinnen 2009, p. 70). The task of international police included both 'in-line policing' (the day-to-day functions of policing such as patrolling, responding to crime and so on) and capacity building (working collaboratively with local officers to expand their ability to perform policing effectively and manage their functions without external assistance). Placing policing in the lead also extended to ensuring that broader security and justice functions were improved as a matter of priority, including prisons, courts and justice mechanisms. While the results have not always been deemed to be most appropriate for the local environment, it can also be said that "Few developing countries have courts of law in their capital as professional and independent as the Solomons'" (Braithwaite et al. 2010, p. 155). Another measure of success can be seen in the relative stability and security that has led to a significant reduction of international police and return to performance of policing functions by the RSIPF, with the coming phase of RAMSI focused on "work[ing] with RSIPF to strengthen its capacity and further develop it as a modern and effective police force" (RAMSI n.d.)

As such, this mission has been founded on the belief that effective security and justice mechanisms contribute significantly to an environment conducive to economically, socially and environmentally durable development. The significant civilian component working to build capacity in a range of government sectors has helped to form a civil sector with greater capacity to fulfill these roles effectively in a more stable and peaceful environment as RAMSI scales down. This comprehensive and integrated approach is important in ensuring resources are available for these important governance mechanisms rather than being diminished by an enduring requirement to respond to conflict.

The important point here is that the environment is enabling, not determining. A more secure environment has allowed for improvements in the provision of health and education services in Solomon Islands, yet employment opportunities remain low, with 60 % of the surveyed population reporting subsistence as a key or sole occupation in 2007 (ANU Enterprise P/L 2007, p. 16). While government (often with support of international development partners) is primarily responsible for changes in service provision, job growth depends on factors such as domestic and international confidence that stability will endure, and that corruption and red tape will not interfere with business. This confidence takes time to build, but is enabled by a secure environment with an effective security and justice sector.

Local confidence in stability and personal safety is also important in determining the willingness of citizens to participate in development activities and commit to the changes necessary to transform the nation—indeed such participation is both expensive and risky, particularly for those most vulnerable in a society. Although there was a major conflict in the capital city in 2006, well over half (59 %) of responses to the first Solomon Islands People's Survey that year indicated that "the law and order situation had improved in the past year [while only] 9 % said it had deteriorated" (ANU Enterprise P/L & Australian National University 2006, p. 7). In the 2011 survey, the same proportion (59 %) reported always feeling safe in their communities, with only 5 % saying they rarely feel safe (ANU Enterprise P/L 2012, p. 5).

The development progress as measured by the UNDP has been uneven, as is commonly the case. No statistics were recorded for the years 2001–2004, however Solomon Islands' Human Development Index (HDI) rating improved from 0.479 in 2000 to 0.502 in 2005 (UNDP 2012). In the following 6 years it grew significantly (to a peak of 0.514) before subsiding to 0.510 in the most recent measurement, 2011. These figures indicate not only the way development indicators may lag behind major events and interventions, but also the fluctuations. Timor-Leste is a close neighbour of Solomon Islands and has experienced a similarly fluctuating record of human development through the period of massive external intervention (also with a key focus on SSR).

The difficult reality for interventions such as RAMSI is that it has been shown that when significant change is achieved in fragile states it originates from within that nation (Anderson 2005, p. 3). That is to say that externally imposed solutions are often thrown out after the external actors leave, while solutions generated either within or in close collaboration with the community, and supported by appropriate financial and capacity-building resources, are much more likely to be sustained and successful. In this sense, external interventions are bound to have only short-term success unless they work with the community to devise local solutions and build the capacity of local people to implement and maintain them (see for example Chambers 1997). Thus a focus on security and justice is necessary for sustained development in post-conflict environments, but it is not of itself sufficient.

Transcending Policy Silos

This mission has been played out in an era that has seen significant changes in practice reflecting the prominence gained by the interaction between security and development in international debates and policy. A key reason this has gained so much traction is the conviction that instability in a developing nation will quickly lead to instability in neighboring states, and that this will lead directly to security threats to richer, more stable nations. This leads to policy formulations in which, for example, AusAID (the Australian Agency for International Development) named the Australian Federal Police (AFP) as a key agency in the delivery of development

(AusAID 2006, p. 4), and in which one sixth of Australia's federal policing funding comes from its aid budget.

For Australia as a RAMSI contributing nation, this has had important policy ramification because a key facet in this engagement has been the blurring of domestic and international policy-making, in the sense that the AFP deployment in Solomon Islands relies on Australia's 'domestic' policing policies and budgets as well as its 'international' aid and foreign affairs policies and budgets. The challenge here is that governments tend to seal domestic policy off from international policy, with specified agencies and budgets for international concerns, clearly separated from domestic agencies and budgets. Now, however, those areas must interact more intimately, in a process Reus-Smit calls transnational policy-making (2002, p. 24).

In 2004, the AFP established the International Deployment Group (IDG) in a world-first program to respond to the increasing demand for able police available for rapid international deployment. With over 12,000 deployable personnel, the budget for international deployments in 2011–2012 was AU$ 346.623 million, of which AU$ 217.7 was drawn from the Australia's international development budget rather than the usual funding sources (the budget portfolio of the Attorney General's Department). Thus, while IDG personnel are drawn from domestic forces and deployed as members of the AFP, two thirds of their costs come from the nation's international budget area. Furthermore, there is exchange of liaison staff between the IDG and AusAID and planning for international deployments increasingly builds on development principles, signifying stronger interaction between policing and development concerns (see Harris 2010).

This transnational policy-making in turn sees national police—whose substantive training and experience are in the context of their home nation's security and justice mechanisms and historic development of policing—deployed in the name of international policy in vastly different contexts. Predictably, this raises questions of police suitability to their hybrid role of both policing and development, and their ability to integrate with other development actors (see Harris and Goldsmith 2012). Specific training, integrated policy development and a learning-focused approach have seen the IDG develop increasing skills in this area, giving personnel an effective foundation for the complex practice of security and justice reform in post-conflict environments.

Connecting Security and Development in Practice

In spite of this there remains a disconnect between traditional development actors and security and justice mechanisms (see Harris and Goldsmith 2012). This is in spite of the clearly shown negative impact of violence on development outcomes (see World Bank 2011). The reality is, however, that security and justice actors in many countries have a poor reputation for equity and justice—and in many cases, this reputation is well earned. Development workers therefore face the conundrum of how to engage with these sectors and support their transformation, without supporting corruption and perpetuating violence. Indeed, they face a complex set of calculations to ensure that they do not contribute to instability in the pursuit of development aims (Anderson 1999, p. 1), even before they start to engage with potentially compromised security and justice actors.

Such a reorientation is, however, critical in the current era of development practice. A key reason for this is that the coming decade will require a reorientation of development funding as middle-income countries continue their success in pulling their own citizens out of poverty. The greatest number of the world's poor will soon be found once again in the low-income countries—half of which are conflict-affected. Development agencies thus find their operations increasingly taking place in environments that require a particular focus on security and justice, and it is more efficient for them to collaborate with agencies already experienced in delivering such services (albeit in different circumstances) than to reinvent this particular wheel. Added to this is the stark reality that "Providing aid in complex settings entails danger", such that complete safety is "simply impossible" for local and international development staff (Anderson 1999, p. 65). As such, development agencies share local populations' need for stability, rule of law and effective justice institutions.

This interaction is taking place organically in some settings, as security and development personnel find themselves sharing the same operational space. Co-location does not necessarily lead to collaboration, as has been noted elsewhere (Harris and Goldsmith 2012, p. 1028). Much more is required to facilitate this interaction and overcome issues of mutual suspicion and distrust. Training of development and security personnel must take a lead in this process, giving individuals in each field useful knowledge about the history, values and priorities of their respective Other, as well as giving them opportunities to meet and engage with each other in the relatively safe and unhurried environment of education and training. This happens to a limited extent in the pre-deployment training of the IDG, which adopts a multidisciplinary approach to training and draws on experts from a range of fields. It also happens in a less formal manner in some tertiary development programs and through invitations to participate in each other's training courses (as for example is done by the Australian Defence Force in its major annual training exercise).

In each of these areas a more comprehensive approach is needed to ensure that coherence is achievable in the messy, complex space of post-conflict development and reconstruction. Development requires many inputs, and requires that they interact effectively in order that the achievements will endure in the medium- and long-term. Sustainability will not just happen by accident; rather it must be carefully planned and creatively executed. Prioritizing security and justice reform in these contexts is a critical enabler of sustainability, and it must be supplemented by coherent policy and practice that ensures that the various development sectors work in harmony rather than at odds.

Conclusion

Development processes are focused on achieving positive medium- and long-term impacts that will expand people's choices by building their capacity and that of the institutions that should serve them in a functioning society. If these positive impacts cannot be sustained and do not contribute to the equitable distribution of resources, the process cannot be accurately called development. It is therefore unnecessary to add the adjective 'sustainable' because it is already expressed in the term development.

When development processes are enacted in societies that are experiencing conflict or have recently interrupted such conflict, there must be special attention given to the breakdown of relationships, trust and institutions that characterize these contexts. In particular, the high risk of return to conflict must be considered, for it will be a powerful disruption to development, potentially derailing it altogether. As a result, a focus on security and justice mechanisms is critical, with a focus on ensuring that local institutions and personnel have the capacity to create and maintain stability. A stable environment in which rule of law functions enables effective development in other areas, which in turn expands people's choices in a manner that allows them to work towards social, economic and environmental sustainability.

RAMSI prioritized security and justice in this way, with some critical successes in its first decade, but still has some distance to go. The most significant achievement is a level of stability that allows the regional partners to plan a reduction of their engagement and focus on development rather than conflict factors. In the process, it has necessitated a significant policy shift in one of the key contributors, Australia; the resourcing, deployment and funding of Australian police to missions such as RAMSI has required the transnationalization of policy-making and budgeting. It has also seen the consolidation of the role of police in development arenas, opening new questions for development and police personnel alike.

This demonstrates that it is possible to prioritize security and development with the aim of creating an enabling environment for other development processes. The establishment of a safer and increasingly equitable society expands the capability set of ordinary Solomon Islanders—and within this spectrum of options is a much fuller participation in the nation's development and governance. As these options expand further, the durability of achievements is secured through the transition from external intervention to national governance, and Solomon Islanders are more able to exercise sustainable choices about economic, social and environmental development. There is a long way to go in the development of Solomon Islands, but the process so far is an effective model for post-conflict development that enables other (sustainable) development.

References

Anderson, M. B. (1999). *Do No Harm: How aid can support peace-or war*. Boulder: Lynne Rienner.

Anderson, I. (2005). *Fragile States: What is international experience telling us?* Canberra: Aus-AID.

ANU Enterprise P/L. (2007). *The people's survey 207*. Canberra: RAMSI.

ANU Enterprise P/L. (2012). *The people's survey 2011*. Canberra: RAMSI.

ANU Enterprise P/L, & Australian National University. (2006). *People's survey pilot 2006 Solomon Islands*. Canberra: RAMSI.

Arbour, L. (2012). The rule of law in a transitional democracy. International Crisis Group. http://www.crisisgroup.org/en/publication_type/speeches/2012/arbour-the-rule-of-law-in-a-transitional-democracy.aspx. Accessed 30 June 2012.

AusAID. (2006). *Australian aid: Promoting growth and stability*. Canberra: AusAID.

Barakat, S. (2010). Introduction: Post-war reconstruction and development-coming of age. In S. Barakat (Ed.), *After the conflict: Reconstruction and development in the aftermath of war* (pp. 7–31). London: I.B. Tauris.

Barakat, S., & Chard, M. (2010). Building post-war capacity: Where to start? In S. Barakat (Ed.), *After the conflict: Reconstruction and development in the aftermath of war* (pp. 173–190). London: I.B. Tauris.

Braithwaite, J., Dinnen, S., Allen, M., Braithwaite, V., & Charlesworth, H. (2010). *Pillars and shadows: Statebuilding as peacebuilding in Solomon Islands*. Canberra: ANU E-Press.

Chambers, R. (1997). *Whose reality counts? Putting the first last*. London: ITDG.

Collier, P. (2007). *The bottom billion: Why the poorest countries are failing and what can be done about it*. Oxford: Oxford University Press.

Collier, P., Hoeffler, A., & Söderbom, M. (2008). Post-conflict risks. *Journal of Peace Research, 45*(4), 461–478.

Commission on Human Security. (2003). *Human security now: Final report*. New York: Commission on Human Security.

Cortez, A. L., & Kim, N. (2012). *Conflict and the indentification of least developed countries: Theoretical and statistical considerations*. CDP Background Paper No. 13. ST/ESA/2012/CDP/13. Committee for Development Policy Secretariat, Department of Economic and Social Affairs, UN Headquarters, New York.

Della-Giacoma, J. (2012). *Self determination and peace operations in Timor-Leste*. Civil-Military Affairs Conference, Queanbeyan, Australia 28 May 2012. http://www.crisisgroup.org/en/publication-type/speeches/2012/della-giacoma-self-determination-and-peace-operations-in-timor-leste.aspx. Accessed 1 Aug 2012.

DFAT. (2004) *Solomon Islands: Rebuilding an island economy*. Canberra: Department of Foreign Affairs and Trade Economic Analytical Unit.

Dinnen, S. (2009). The crisis of state in Solomon Islands. *Peace Review: A Journal of Social Justice, 21*(1), 70–78.

GFN-SSR. (2007). *A beginner's guide to security sector reform (SSR)*. Birmingham: GRN-SSR International Development Department University of Birmingham.

Goldsmith, A., & Harris, V. (2012). Trust, trustworthiness and trust-building in international policing missions. *Australian & New Zealand Journal of Criminology, 45*(2), 231–254.

Government of Solomon Islands. (2002). *Human development report 2002: Building a Nation*. Windsor: Mark Otter.

Harris, V. (2010). Building on sand? Australian police involvement in international police capacity building. *Policing and Society, 20*(1):79–98.

Harris, V., & Goldsmith, A. (2012). Police in the development space: Australia's international police capacity builders. *Third World Quarterly, 33*(6), 1019–1036.

IFC. (n.d.). *A rough guide to investment climate reform in conflict-affected countries*. Washington, DC: International Finance Corporation.

Morgan, M. G., & McLeod, A. (2006). Have we failed our neighbour? *Australian Journal of International Affairs, 60*(3), 412–428.

Nayar, K. R. (1994, May 28). Politics of 'sustainable development'. *Economic and Political Weekly,* 1327–1329.

OECD. (2005). *Security system reform and Governance. DAC guidelines and reference series.* Brussels: Organisation for Economic Cooperation and Development.

OECD. (2007). *The OECD DAC handbook on SSR: Supporting security and justice.* Brussels: Organisation for Economic Cooperation and Development.

RAMSI. (n.d.). Transition. Regional Assistance Mission to Solomon Islands. http://www.ramsi. org/about/transition.html. Accessed 1 Aug 2012.

Reus-Smit, C. (2002). Lost at sea: Australia in the turbulence of world politics. Department of International Relations Working Papers 2002 (4). Canberra: Department of International Relations, RSPAS, Australian National University.

Salahub, J. E., & Nerland, K. (2010). Just Add Gender? Challenges to meaningful integration of gender in SSR policy and practice. In M. Sedra (Ed.), *The future of security sector reform* (pp. 233–280). Waterloo: The Centre for International Governance Innovation (CIGI).

Sen, A. (1993). Capability and well-being. In M. Nussbaum & A. Sen (Eds.), *The quality of life.* Oxford: Oxford University Press.

Transparency International. (2012). *Annual report 2011.* Berlin: Transparency International.

UNDP. (1990). *Human development report 1990: The concept and measurement of human development.* New York: United Nations Development Program.

UNDP. (1994). *Human development report 1990: New dimensions of human security.* New York: United Nations Development Program.

UNDP. (2011). *Sustainability and equity: A better future for all.* New York: United Nations Development Program.

UNDP. (2012). Solomon Islands country profile: Development indicators. United Nations Development Program. http://hdrstats.undp.org/en/countries/profiles/SLB.html. Accessed 7 Dec 2012.

United Nations. (1986). *Resolution 14/28.* New York: United Nations.

Victor, D. G. (2006). Recovering sustainable development. *Foreign Affairs, 85*(1), 91–103.

WCED. (1987). *Report of the world commission on environment and development: Our common future.* New York: United Nations.

World Bank. (2005). *World development report 2005: A better investment climate for everyone.* Washington, DC: World Bank.

World Bank. (2011). *World development report 2011: Conflict, security and development.* Washington, DC: World Bank.

Chapter 12
Sustainable Tourism and the Culture Economy: Does Certification Matter?

Azmiri Mian

Behind each painting, each dance, and each piece of music, there is a personal story. But we will not be able to continue to enjoy this precious knowledge and culture if we are not in a position to maintain and protect it. (Mick Gooda, Aboriginal and Torres Strait Islander Social Justice Commissioner 2011)

Introduction

Indigenous tourism provides Indigenous Australians an opportunity to tell their story in their way. It provides the chance to share their cultural insights and traditional practices and contemporary concerns with non-Indigenous Australians and international visitors. From a non-Indigenous perspective, Indigenous Australian imagery has long been recognized as an integral part of national branding (Pomering and White 2011). Increasing competition in the tourism market means that goods and services are no longer enough and that service providers differentiate their products by transforming them into "experiences" which engage the tourist (Richards and Wilson 2006, p. 74). Australia's National Long Term Tourism Strategy (2009) proposes that "the value of natural, cultural and heritage assets is likely to become increasingly important as consumers actively seek sustainable and authentic tourism experiences. The economic value of these assets is significant" (TRA 2011). In 2008, 23 million people visited Australia's cultural and heritage locations, of which 70 % were international visitors and 27 % of domestic visitors (TRA 2011).

Tourism Australia attracts international visitors through marketing Indigenous culture, distinguishing Australia in a competitive tourism marketplace. While such promotion makes sense in a marketing context, there are larger ethical issues that are underexplored in academic literatures and public discourse. Both tourists who seek Indigenous tourism experiences and the Indigenous communities and individuals who offer the tours operate in what we will refer to as the culture economy.

A. Mian (✉)
Business School, University of South Australia, Adelaide, Australia
e-mail: Azmiri.Mian@unisa.edu.au

© Springer Science+Business Media Dordrecht 2014
S. Sandhu et al. (eds.), *Linking Local and Global Sustainability,* The International Society of Business, Economics, and Ethics Book Series 4, DOI 10.1007/978-94-017-9008-6_12

Standards like certifications, codes and so on will subsequently create a reality of what is Indigenous about Indigenous tourism. It is not necessarily the case that standards can simply be said to 'improve' a situation. Rather, they bring about a reality of what Indigenous means and how it is related to the economics of the region. The standards create the cultural economy. This raises the issue of whether the reality is one that is ultimately acceptable to the Indigenous groups that are subject to tourism business.

Guides and codes have been developed to foster understanding such as the Respect Our Cultures (ROC) Program and certification within the ecotourism standards. In this chapter we discuss the needs for standards and certification, and how and if it translates to delivery of an ethical cultural experience and sustainability for the enterprise and/or community providing the experience. I ask whether standards and certification provide support to Indigenous tourism providers and argue that the standards fail to support Indigenous operators adequately.

Respect Our Cultures Framework

Accreditation and certification is a rigorous and challenging process for well-established tourism operators. For Indigenous tourism operators, various external factors can make it problematic in meeting the criteria, particularly as they are often operating in an informal economic setting. The ROC Program was originally developed in consultation with Indigenous communities, tourism operators and other stakeholders in the tourism industry to respect and protect Indigenous heritage, intellectual property and authenticity. The ROC Program is administered by Ecotourism Australia and is designed to meet tourist expectations in a professional and sustainable way, and is open to non-Indigenous operators to access accreditation (Ecotourism Australia n.d.). The ROC Progam states:

> In a competitive industry environment, tourism businesses that operate at national industry standards have the greatest potential to benefit from opportunities available. A business with ROC Program accreditation will be recognised in the industry as having sustainable business and environmental practices. The ROC Program is unique in that it also provides the recognition of cultural protocols and authenticity. (Ecotourism Australia n.d.)

Intellectual and cultural property rights are attributed to particular clan groups in Indigenous Australia. Therefore, it is ethically essential that Dreaming stories, spiritual beliefs, history, ceremony and art are not shared with tourists in exploitative ways. As culture is very significant, Indigenous people are cautious about the use of culture in tourism. Indigenous heritage, contemporary lifeways (Hutchins 2010; Turner and Clifton 2009), and intellectual property need to be respected and protected. To achieve this goal, the ROC Program has been identified as an essential tool (Ecotourism Australia n.d.).

The ROC is situated within the Australian Nature and Ecotourism Accreditation Program (NEAP), obtainable through EcoTourism Australia. Chester and Crabtree (2002, p. 171) state that "although the focus of ecotourism in Australia is primarily on natural values of an area, many of these sites are also have significant cultural value, particularly indigenous value, therefore minimal impact on the presentation of [Indigenous] culture, including involving indigenous communities in the delivery of the ecotourism product" (Chester and Crabtree 2002, p. 171). The ROC Program was launched in 2003 by Aboriginal Tourism Australia (ATA), and endorses both Aboriginal and non-Aboriginal tourism enterprises that follow specific cultural protocols, environmental management regimes and business practices in the context of tourism in Indigenous Australia (Ecotourism Australia n.d.).

One criterion concerns who began the standards setting process and how quickly representatives of Indigenous peoples were included. This has to do with the genuineness of the process. A second criterion concerns whether representatives of Indigenous groups were able to actually conceptualize the structure of the process. That is, we need to explore whether the protocols and norms behind the process incorporated ideas and values from the representatives of Indigenous peoples; this would have created a 'shared process'. A third criterion concerns how narrowly the standards were confined to supporting both consumer conceptions of Indigenous peoples and economic interests of operators. If the standards only serve as more ethical procedures for contracting with Indigenous peoples who ultimately must represent themselves in ways that conform to tourists' preconceived and uninformed expectations, then there is cause for worry.

Moreover, Indigenous communities possibly see tourism as more than a profit generator. It depends on the context in which the profits are generated. For example, are the profits generated in ways that will represent the culture well to the youth in the community? This is an important question as any business that will contribute to the intergenerational psychological problems of the community bound up with colonialism is problematic. A fourth criterion concerns the degree to which the standards address issues of reconciliation. Any standards for doing business between settler and Indigenous populations must have broader reconciliation as a somewhat pivotal part of it given the social disparities between these two populations. Economics is certainly not the sole driver of these disparities. A fifth criterion concerns the control to which Indigenous peoples actually have to veto or resist tourism business and to engage in alternative forms of tourism. There is an important issue as to whether ROC Program puts Indigenous people in situations where they have to compromise with very few options to do anything different.

In Australia, there are barriers to economic and enterprise development for Indigenous communities due to four major categories (Russell-Mundine 2007). These barriers are identified as:

- Economic—it is increasingly difficult for Indigenous communities to access the required capital. If in joint ventures they have a lack of control and there is lack of access to land ownership. Without legal deeds to a title it is almost impossible to get finance from a bank to commence a tourism enterprise.
- Resource—Indigenous communities have a lack of access to adequately trained managers, skills and training in tourism jobs, interest in interacting with tourists, or simply decide not to work.

- Cultural—the concern here is that in the process of customising Indigenous culture to attract and entertain tourists that culture may be distorted, exploited and undermined (commodified).
- Industry—high expectations and regulations of the mainstream industry in terms of professional delivery of the tourism product. Standards and certification, such as ROC Program sits within this framework (Russell-Mundine 2007).

The Theory of Standards

A critical issue in the establishment of environmental, economic and social sustainability in tourism is the delivery of assurance, usually through quality control systems. The term 'sustainable tourism' became popular after the release of the Brundland Report (World Commission on Environment and Development 1987). Sustainable tourism in this context is defined as tourism meeting the needs of the current generation without any compromise to meeting the needs of future generations (Bramwell and Lane 2011). At the most basic level it is applying sustainable development and practice idea to the tourism industry.

In tourism, codes of practice and ecolables are two of the main quality control mechanisms that attempt to provide the assurance that certain standards are met. Guides, codes and certificates fit into what is called, broadly, standards. A standard is a kind of criterion that is used to make judgments about an object, practice, process, human, group of humans, or other living thing or community. For example, in food systems, a fair trade standard indicates that a package of coffee, or other product, is produced under certain conditions, exchanged for a certain monetary value, and grown in a particular region. As in the case of fair trade, standards are not the same as law or regulations, even when laws or regulations employ something like standards. Standards, in the sense we are talking about, are voluntary insofar as it is organizations, individuals, companies, communities, and so on who promulgate them (Busch 2000, 2011; Hall 2010; Whyte and Thompson 2010).

The theory of standards is particularly important for the marketing of Indigenous tourism. Standards are used through certification and accreditation to vouch for certain kinds of tourism as being culturally sensitive, non-exploitative, and authentic. Standards of this kind would be particularly useful, from a business standpoint, for Indigenous tourism. They serve to create the reality of authentic cultural experiences—a reality that some tourists desire. Certification and accreditation legitimize certain practices as being authentic and silencing or marginalizing other practices. Moreover, tourism experiences that do not live up to these standards regimes are likely ascribed blameworthy labels such as 'inauthentic' and 'commercial'. In this case, standards create certain realities in order to make touristic practices more marketable in relation to the expectations of tourists.

Though voluntary, standards can quickly transform any network of human beings (Thompson 2011). Fair trade standards motivate producers to favour certain buyers; buyers play a larger role in evaluating what producers produce; consumers put pressure to be the favoured group in the supply chain. One way in which this occurs is through what are called tripartite standards regimes (Loconto and Busch 2010). These regimes involve a party that creates the standards, such as a fair trade organization, a party that certifies whatever the standard is supposed to constrain, and a party that accredits the certifiers. These parties may be different or one and the same, depending on the situation. Tripartite standards regimes, once their standards become more widely adopted, can completely transform the various connections in the network. For this reason, standards are a form of power.

Standards are not only a form of power in the traditional sense that they give some parties more leverage over others financially, politically, or socially. Standards have a more profound effect. Standards do not just distinguish good from bad products. Standards actually create the reality of whatever it is they have been deployed to constrain (Busch 2011). For example, in fair trade, standards do not just allow people to distinguish coffee produced one way as opposed to coffee produced another way. Rather, fair trade standards create the reality of what fair trade means. That is, the standards create the tastes associated with fair trade and the beliefs that consumerism can achieve justice for developing world producers. Lawrence Busch (2011) prefers to standards as recipes for reality.

As recipes for reality, standards always bear responsibility for doing violence to whatever has been excluded from reality (Busch and Whyte 2012). That is, standards can create realities that silence, marginalize and place blame on individuals, populations, non-human living and non-living things, and processes. For example, coffee producers and distributors who are not enrolled in fair trade standards can be perceived as immoral. Non-organic food production processes are perceived as repugnant. Animal health inspection standards may be impossible for Native American livestock producers to fulfil given barriers to access state veterinarians, forcing them out of a market that they depend on for their livelihoods. In each of these cases, standards are responsible for ascribing blame and for silencing and marginalizing various actors within the economic sectors to which they are applied.

Standards, Certification and the Culture Economy

The theory of the cultural economy states that in today's world there is a premium on selling the culture by way of cultural markers of a particular region in order to shore up competitive advantages (Ray 1998). The array of markers are "traditional foods, regional language, crafts, folklore, local visual arts and drama, literacy references, historical and prehistoric sites, landscape systems and their associated flora and fauna" (Ray 1998, p. 3). For communities, in this case Indigenous Australians, a culture economy can sometimes be seen as providing an opportunity to revalorize place and space through emphasizing certain features of a cultural identity that were previously suppressed through colonial practices. The ROC Program was implemented originally to provide protection over these aspects of cultural identity. Culture economy functions as an ethical economy by responding to the emergence of ethical consumerism reflected in this case as "support for marginalised societies in their struggle for sustainable development…" (Ray 1998, p. 15). Tourism is identified as one of the key strategies for economic development by the Australian Government for Indigenous Australians. We worry that the relevance of the ROC Program accreditation is problematic for Indigenous operators because as it is handed out to any tourism enterprise who claims to be 'green' and 'eco-friendly', and not owned or operated by Indigenous people.

Indigenous leaders may see the culture economy as a more benign possibility for advancing their communities' political self-determination and economic independence. There are several possibilities for why it might be seen as more benign. The culture economy may be a niche market that only that particular community can fill because of the uniqueness of its lifestyles. Indigenous peoples may see this market opportunity as a way for them to shape the perceptions of non-Indigenous peoples. Moreover, the demonstrable respect of tourists for Indigenous lifestyles can serve as a way of helping Indigenous youth to embrace their own cultural identities (Taliman 2011). The idea, then, is that if done right, the cultural economy can provide a means for Indigenous peoples to address the legacy of colonialism on their own terms while stimulating a better economy. But the culture economy can also be morally problematic. Many countries have had their own versions of festivals in the past where members of Indigenous groups acted in ways that appealed to non-Indigenous consumers. These situations are damaging to Indigenous persons' identities. They are also exploitative because they place consumer expectations in the hands of tourists who are unacquainted with Indigenous cultures. This is why standards are particularly important for promoting a culture economy that supports Indigenous self-determination and economic independence.

As travellers develop more interest in ecological and environmental issues, Indigenous tourism has become more influential in the Australian tourism industry, particularly the cultural issues. In 2007 a promotional tour to Europe was conducted by Indigenous Tourism Australia to attract international tourists to Australia by highlighting Aboriginal experiences to European travel agents and consumers (ITA 2007). In 2010, the Indigenous tourism sector represented 13 % of total international visitor numbers (TRA 2011) and a 2011 report to the Australian Indigenous Tourism Conference (Sherry 2011) identifies a growing market in Asia for Indigenous tourism.

Indigenous Tourism as a Contributor to Sustainability

Bunten and Graburn (2009) define Indigenous tourism as any service or product that is, (a) owned and operated at least in part by an Indigenous group, and (b) results from a means of exchange with visitors. Hall and Weiler (1992) describe Indigenous tourism as a form of 'special interest' tourism which depends on the primary motivation of the tourist, while Hinch and Butler (2007) describe it as a tourist activity in which Indigenous people are directly involved either through control and/or by having their culture serve as the essence of the attraction. Tourists look for a direct experience, involving a human element, with a more intimate and authentic contact than traditional cultural tourism where you visit a place, eat in a local restaurant and buy a few souvenirs (Hinch and Butler 2007).

Hinch and Butler (2007) have identified four different types of Indigenous tourism scenarios, based on two key aspects—the range of control and the Indigenous theme of the attraction:

- Non-Indigenous tourism: Low degree of Indigenous control, no Indigenous theme.
- Culture Dispossessed: Low degree of Indigenous control, Indigenous theme present.
- Diversified Indigenous: High degree of Indigenous control, with Indigenous theme absent.
- Culture Controlled: High degree of Indigenous control, Indigenous theme present.

Indigenous participation in tourism forces collective introspection: With the choice to make one's culture accessible comes a great responsibility as to how cultural, material and spiritual resources are dealt with. Tourism professionals often describe their work as sharing culture, whereas what they are actually doing is transforming the culture and ethnic identities into an alienable product commodified for tourist consumption (Bunten and Graburn 2009).

Indigenous tourism also links to environmental and nature-based tourism, arts and heritage, plus adventure tourism, in the sense that most of the time Indigenous peoples have a very special relationship to the land and their/the environment, and they have their own arts and architectural traditions. It can also be 'adventurous' as some communities live in very remote and hardly accessible areas, like the Indigenous peoples in central Australia.

As stated previously, in many parts of Australia, Indigenous Australians are the key stakeholders to economic development, and this is most often through tourism. Yet in places like Central Australia, they are the most disadvantaged of the population. Tourism is a major contributor to Australia's economy and provides opportunities for employment and cultural exchange. The Australian government continues to encourage the development of Indigenous cultural tourism in regional and remote areas of Australia. It can be argued that Indigenous culture is important to tourism development as it makes a significant contribution to tourism development. However, Indigenous people and communities have difficulty in securing more benefits because it is often difficult to compete in a market driven economy and the expectations of meeting institutional requirements (Zeng et al. 2010), in this case meeting tourism standards and certification.

With increasing need for certification and accreditation to operate in the global tourism industry today, one that continues to look for sustainable practices, Indigenous tourism operators are struggling to compete with non-Indigenous tourism operators for a fair share of the Indigenous tourism market (Vivanco 2007). Indigenous tourism certification, such as the ROC Program was originally intended to address this inequity and protect the authenticity of Indigenous cultural experience (Andrews and Buggey 2008). Indigenous tourism operators want to be better understood in how they do their business, and be recognized as the appropriate providers of an Indigenous experience of their land, stories, art and dance (Whyte 2010). However, what has inadvertently happened in practice is that the ROC Program has been designated a position within the ecotourism accreditation framework, on the assumption that this will allow for social and environmental sustainability of destination community.

Moreover, Indigenous peoples often suffer from greater social disparities, such as poverty and childhood obesity, and less political participation, given their population numbers, rural locations, and social invisibility within settler societies. In this context, tourism operators engaged in the cultural economy should do so appropriately; standards become a way of achieving this. One would expect that standards will bring together operators, communities, and customers around a reality of Indigenous tourism that will be conducive to economic growth and sustainability as Indigenous communities understand them.

The Indigenous tourism experiences have a common thread in its delivery of cultural knowledge, lifestyle and beliefs of Indigenous Australians. The National Aboriginal and Torres Strait Islander Tourism Industry Strategy (NATSITIS) define Indigenous tourism as inclusive of all forms of participation by Indigenous Australians in tourism by being:

- Employers
- Employees
- Investors
- Joint venture partners
- Providers of Indigenous cultural tourism products
- Providers of mainstream tourism products (ATSIC 1997).

For the purpose of marketing, Tourism Australia defines Indigenous tourism as "a tourism experience or service, which is majority owned or operated by Aboriginal people and/or operated in partnership with non-Indigenous people" (Tourism Australia n.d.). However, the accreditation and certification does not necessarily align with this.

In the current political climate, the Australian Government is investing \$ 5.2 billion to close the gap in Indigenous disadvantage, through funding for employment, education, health services, community development and community safety. The 2012–2013 Budget continues the Government's long-term efforts to overcome decades of underinvestment, and continues to improve the lives of Indigenous Australians (Macklin 2012). On one hand tourism is heavily promoted and funded for rural and remote Indigenous communities, on the other hand certification standards are required for Indigenous tourism enterprises to be competitive in the national and international tourism markets, such as the ROC and the Champions Programs.

Generally, Indigenous tourism is identified in having a competitive advantage in the tourism marketplace and economic advantages for the host communities.

Zeng et al. (2010) argue that in recent times, Indigenous tourism operators are experiencing difficulties in sustaining their businesses. Difficulties lay in the uncertainty of demand for the experience, not just from international visitors but also the domestic market. From the supply perspective, most Indigenous tourism businesses are small and often located in remote areas or travel to remote areas and often, due to disadvantage, do not have the finances or business capacity to keep up with institutional requirements to stay in the industry. Indigenous presence is of great benefit to the tourism industry. Indigenous peoples are present from the beginning of the supply chain, as artists for example, to being customer sales people in shops (Zeng et al. 2010).

Standards for Indigenous Tourism

The evaluation of standards should be consistent with what standards do. Standards make reality out of what was invisible. So the reality-making aspect of standards must be tested, not just, say, the aggregated economic outcomes of a tripartite standards regime. The key question, then, is whether the reality of indigeneity suggested by the ROC Program is one that serves primarily non-Indigenous business interests in the cultural economy, or whether it is one that reflects adequately a reality conducive to Indigenous peoples achieving what they would like to from the emerging cultural economy, which may go beyond just revenues or jobs as tour guides.

Bunten (2010) believes that Indigenous tourism enterprises prefer to have collective ownership to ensure the cultural integrity of the enterprise and the stewardship of the land and resources. This may come at an economic cost, but any sacrifice of cultural and social relationships must be carefully weighed when embarking upon new business ventures. Mentoring from Indigenous Business Australia (IBA) enables a fledgling business to develop goals and strategies while maintaining the core values of safeguarding country, culture and heritage. Governmental, financial and statutory requirements can often overwhelm new operators, especially if they have had little prior experience in private enterprise. IBA is an Australian government-sponsored organisation that "promotes and encourages self-management, self-sufficiency and economic independence" within a respectful cultural and social context that understands the needs of Indigenous people (IBA n.d.). This support allows enterprises to focus on maintaining cultural integrity with the necessary training to handle mundane but essential details such as documentation and approvals. Indigenous tourism offers local employment opportunities and, in many cases, allows young people to stay on country (Whitford and Ruhanen 2010).

Balancing the benefits and costs of Indigenous tourism demands that tourism operators develop models that allow them to participate on their own terms. By insisting that core values are not diluted in the process of gaining traction in a highly competitive industry, Indigenous tourism can contribute to the well-being of their communities. It is often considered necessary for Indigenous tourism enterprises to exceed the standards of their Western counterparts in order to negate the expectation that they may operate unprofessionally (Bunten 2010).

Hinch and Butler (2007) state that overall Indigenous tourism occurs within the context of a global tourism industry that is dominated by non-Indigenous actors. Even though the range of Indigenous ownership and control of tourism businesses has grown steadily in recent years, when trying to identify who owns these businesses, it turns out that most of them belong or are managed by non-Indigenous entrepreneurs (Butler and Hinch 2007).

The state of play currently in Australia is that of the 48 ROC Program certified tourism operators, 12 are 100% Aboriginal owned and operated and two are what would be called a hybrid model, meaning that the enterprise is jointly owned and operated by Aboriginal and non-Aboriginal people. Of the 75% of operators who are claiming to provide an Indigenous experience, almost half do not have any marketing information about Indigenous tours or experiences on their website, many of these are the larger organizations with a competitive edge (Ecotourism Australia n.d.). There are anecdotal observations of this situation impacting smaller Aboriginal owned enterprises who are forced to close their doors as they cannot compete in the market place. Nor can they claim the space rightfully in the ethical cultural tourism experience realm, as many who claim to offer it, in fact don't.

Authenticity, Culture and Branding Identity

Any systematic debate of cultural tourism needs to be positioned within wider transformations of culture and economy. Activities that tourists can engage in has erupted in the different types and range of 'niche experiences' (Mowforth and Munt 2003), fuelling what has been termed the 'experience economy' (Richards 2001), advancing the idea of cultural tourism (Stebbins 1996). Richards (1996, p. 24) describes cultural tourism as "the movement of persons to cultural attractions away from their normal place of residence, with the intention to gather new information and experiences to satisfy their cultural needs", while Raj (2004) defines it as travel experiencing the arts, heritage and special character of a place. While neither of these attempts offers much beyond traditional definitions of tourism (Urry 2002), Stebbins' (1996, p. 948) approach is more suggestive, when he argues: "Cultural tourism is a genre of special interest tourism based on the search for and participation in new and deep cultural experiences, whether aesthetic, intellectual, emotional, or psychological".

Authenticity is a concept well known in the tourism literature and has been an ongoing concern as cultures and their 'products' are sold in the global tourism marketplace (Zeng et al. 2010). Authenticity refers to the trueness a tourism experience, such as a festival, an art, a cuisine, or a ritual, and keeps to its traditional origins and manifestations. Because the processes of tourism commodifies such experiences, the concern is that this commercialization will undermine that experience's authenticity as the experience is modified to cater to the consumer's demands and desires (Zeppell 2001). Authenticity is a concern for most of the stakeholders in Indigenous tourism. Indigenous people are concerned with the authenticity of their cultures, landscapes and traditions and any threats to their integrity because it is often viewed as the foundation of a people (Andrews and Buggey 2008). To say that Indigenous people are concerned with authenticity does not mean that they do not allow for change and evolution in cultural practices; what it does mean is that what is the essence of the culture must keep its integrity for the people to continue the cultural practice because it remains meaningful for them. The tourists are concerned with authenticity because they do not wish to have a contrived or 'theme-parked' experience as Zeppel (2001) shows. They may not always be right about what is exactly authentic or not, but nonetheless they are concerned if they think they are being sold an inauthentic experience (Mac-Cannell 1999).

Returning to the Indigenous tourism context, the issue of authenticity has concerned both the tourism industry, Indigenous tourism organizations such as Aboriginal Tourism Australia (ATA) and Indigenous Australian communities. The concern with authenticity in this context includes the exploitation and mis-use of Indigenous Australian cultures by some non-Indigenous tour operators and tour guides, and a worry that some Indigenous Australians could harm the integrity of their cultures through the commercialization processes of creating Indigenous tourism experiences. MacCannell (1973) argues that cultural products are staged to look authentic, focusing on the preconceived stereotypes, and calls this illigitimacy *stage authenticity*. The tourism sector has bowed to the demands of the tourist seeking authentic experiences by providing commodified authenticity, therefore certification of the standards may be offered to others to ensure demand is met when required (Pomering and White 2011). As a result of these concerns, Tourism Australia launched its ROC Program as a tool to help ensure authenticity in Australia's Indigeneous tourism enterprises (Tourism Australia n.d.).

Conclusion

Guides and codes, such as the ROC Program and accreditation has been developed to bridge the divide between the mainstream tourism industry which uses Indigenous imagery, tourists who seek Indigenous tourism experiences, and Indigenous communities and individuals who offer Indigenous experiences. We challenge that although the original intent was to meet these outcomes in the implementation process, the authenticity of the experience has been lost. For Indigenous tourism operators to be better positioned in the global tourism industry they must be recognized as the appropriate providers of an Indigenous experience of their land, stories, art and dance.

Acknowledgement I acknowledge this land as the traditional lands of the Kaurna people and that I respect their spiritual relationship with their country. I also acknowledge the Kaurna people as the custodians of the greater Adelaide region and that their cultural and heritage beliefs are still as important to the Kaurna people today.

References

Aboriginal and Torres Strait Islander Commission [ATSIC], Australia, Office of National Tourism [ONT], & Pty. Ltd., F. (1997). *National aboriginal and Torres strait islander tourism industry strategy (NATSITIS)* (A. Ont (Ed.)). Canberra: ATSIC.

Andrews, T. D., & Buggey, S. (2008). Authenticity in Aboriginal cultural landscapes. *Journal of Preservation Technology, 39*(2–3), 63–71.

Australia's National Long Term Tourism Strategy. (2009). Commonwealth of Australia.

Bramwell, B., & Lane, B. (2011). Critical research on the governance of tourism and sustainability. *Journal of Sustainable Tourism, 19*(4–5), 411–421.

Bunten, A. C. (2010). More like ourselves: Indigenous capitalism through tourism. *The American Indian Quarterly, 34*(3), 285–311.

Bunten, A., & Graburn, N. (2009). Current themes in Indigenous tourism. *London Journal of Tourism, Sport and Creative Industries, 2*(1), 2–11.

Busch, L. (2000). The moral economy of grades and standards. *Journal of Rural Studies, 16*, 273–283.

Busch, L. (2011). *Standards: Recipes for reality*. Cambridge: MIT Press.

Busch, L., & Whyte, K. (2012). On the peculiarity of standards: A reply to Thompson. *Philosophy & Technology, 25*(2), 243–248.

Chester, G., & Crabtree, A. (2002). Australia: The nature and ecotourism accreditation program. In M. Honey (Ed.), *Ecotourism and certification: Setting standards in practice* (pp. 161–185). Washington,DC: Island Press.

Ecotourism Australia. (n.d.). Summary of respecting our culture program 2009. http://www. ecotourism.org.au/roc.asp. Retrieved 4 Aug 2012.

Gooda, M. (2011). Indigenous designs, stories and culture are valuable sources of knowledge. *Human Rights Commission media release*. http://www.humanrights.gov.au/about/media/media_releases/2011/66_11.html. Retrieved 4 Aug 2012.

Hall, D. (2010). Food with a visible face: Traceability and the public promotion of private governance in the Japanese food system. *Geoforum, 41*(5), 826–835.

Hall, C. M., & Weiler, B. (1992). *Special interest tourism*. London: Belhaven Press.

Hinch, T., & Butler, R. (2007). *Tourism and indigenous peoples: Issues and implications*. London: Butterworth-Heinemann.

Hutchins, F. (2010). Indigenous capitalisms: Ecotourism, cultural reproduction, and the logic of capital in Ecuador's Upper Amazon. In F. Hutchins & P. Wilson (Eds.), *Editing Eden: A reconsideration of identity, politics, and place in Amazonia* (pp. 3–37). Lincoln: University of Nebraska Press

Indigenous Business Australia. (n.d.). http://www.iba.gov.au/business-ownership/. Accessed 4 Aug 2012.

Indigenous Tourism Australia. (2007). Indigenous tourism operators confirmed for first roadshow. http://www.indigenoustourism.australia.com/news.asp?sub=0643. Retrieved 4 Aug 2012.

Loconto, A., & Busch, L. (2010). Standards, techno-economic networks, and playing fields: Performing the global market economy. *Review of International Political Economy, 17*(3), 507–536.

MacCannell, D. (1973). Staged authenticity: Arrangements of social space in tourist settings. *American Journal of Sociology, 79*, 589–603.

MacCannell, D. (1999). *The tourist: A new theory of the leisure class*. Berkeley: University of California Press.

Macklin, J. (2012). Budget 2012−13 Investing to close the gap on Indigenous disadvantage. Minister's Media Centre. http://ministers.deewr.gov.au/macklin/budget-2012-13-investing-close-gap-indigenous-disadvantage. Retrieved 4 Aug 2012.

Mowforth, M., & Munt, I. (2003). *Tourism and sustainability* (2nd ed.). London: Routledge.

Pomering, A., & White, L. (2011). The portrayal of Indigenous identity in Australian tourism brand advertising: Engendering an image of extraordinary reality or staged authenticity? *Place Branding and Public Diplomacy, 7*(3), 165–174.

Raj, R. (2004). The impact of cultural festivals on tourism. *Journal of the College of Tourism and Hotel Management, 4,* 66–77.

Ray, C. (1998). Culture, intellectual property and territorial rural development. *Sociologia Ruralis, 38*(1), 3–20.

Richards, G. (1996). *Cultural tourism in Europe*. Wallingford: CAB International.

Richards, G. (2001). The experience industry and the creation of attractions. In G. Richards (Ed.), *Cultural attractions and European tourism* (pp. 55–69). Wallingford: CAB International.

Richards, G., & Wilson, J. (2006). Developing creativity in tourist experiences: A solution to the serial reproduction of culture? *Tourism Management, 27*(6), 1209–1223.

Russell-Mendine, G. (2007). Key factors for the successful development of Australian indigenous entrepreneurship. *Tourism: An International Interdisciplinary Journal, 55*(4), 417–429.

Sherry, N. (2011). Need for Indigenous tourism to target emerging markets. http://minister. innovation.gov.au/sherry/mediareleases/pages/needforindigenoustourismtotargetemerging-markets.aspx. Retrieved 4 Aug 2012.

Stebbins, R. (1996). Cultural tourism as serious leisure. *Annals of Tourism, 23*(2), 948–950.

Taliman, V. (2011). Indian country taps international tourism market. Indian country today media network. http://indiancountrytodaymedianetwork.com/article/indian-country-taps-internation-al-tourism-market-23593. Accessed 4 Aug 2012

Thompson, P. (2011). There's an App for that: Technical standards and commodification by technological means. *Philosophy & Technology, 25*(1), 87–103.

Tourism Australia. (n.d.). Aboriginal Australia. http://www.aboriginaltourism.australia.com/. Retrieved 4 Aug 2012.

Tourism Research Australia. (2011). *Indigenous tourism visitors in Australia*. Canberra: Tourism Research Australia.

Turner, N. J., & Clifton, H. (2009). It's so different today: Climate change and indigenous lifeways in British Columbia, Canada. *Global Environmental Change, 19*(2), 180–190.

Urry, J. (2002). *The tourist gaze* (2nd ed.). London: Sage.

Vivanco, L. A. (2007). The prospects and dilemmas of Indigenous tourism standards and certifications. In R. Black & A. Crabtree (Eds.), *Quality assurance and certification in ecotourism* (pp. 218–240). Norfolk: Biddles.

Whitford, M. M., & Ruhanen, L. M. (2010) Australian indigenous tourism policy: practical and sustainable policies? *Journal of Sustainable Tourism, 18*(4), 475–496.

Whyte, K. P. (2010). An environmental justice framework for Indigenous tourism. *Environmental Philosophy, 7*(2), 75–92.

Whyte, K. P., & Thompson, P. B. (2010). A role for ethical analysis in social research on agrifood and environmental standards. *Journal of Rural Social Sciences, 25*(3), 79–98.

World Commission on Environment and Development (1987). *Our common future: The Brundtland report*. Oxford: Oxford University Press.

Zeng, B., Gerritsen, R., & Stoeckl, N. (2010). Contribution of Indigenous culture to tourism development. *International Journal of Culture and Tourism Research, 3*(1), 165–184.

Zeppel, H. (2001). Aboriginal cultures and Indigenous tourism. In N. Douglas & R. Derrett (Eds.), *Special interest tourism* (pp. 232–254). Brisbane: Wiley.

Chapter 13
Impact of Oyster Farming on Rural Community Sustainability in North Vietnam

Janine Pierce and Wayne O'Connor

Introduction

The challenge for all communities is to sustain their populations while ensuring the natural environment is sustained to meet their environmental, economic and social needs. An increasing human population demands more water, food and land resources to survive. These challenges are occurring at a time of deforestation, soil erosion, greenhouse gases, black carbon, beef production, salination, pollution, climate change, and threats to marine ecosystems, including fish stocks, that are often depleted or over exploited, while demand for fish continues to grow, particularly in South East Asia (FAO 2012).

Producing sufficient food for the world's population involves the competing challenges of producing a variety of better quality food for those with more income, to feeding those with insufficient natural resources of land and water to produce food, or those with insufficient income to procure food. This chapter explores the notion of sustainability within the community sustainability context, illustrating an initiative implemented by the Ministry of Agriculture and Rural Development's Research Institute for Aquaculture No1 (RIA 1) and the NSW Department of Primary Industries (NSW DPI) with funding support from the Australian Centre for International Agricultural Research (ACIAR) in introducing oyster farming into North Vietnamese rural communities. Janine Pierce from the University of South Australia was involved in a project to research the social impact of oyster farming.

ACIAR is a statutory authority that operates as part of the Australian government's international development cooperation program, working in collaborative research partnerships. ACIAR seeks to benefit partner developing countries, by enhancing livelihood through strategies to improve agriculture productivity and sustainability. ACIAR routinely monitors the adoption and impacts of its projects through commissioning independent assessments.

J. Pierce (✉)
Centre for Rural Health and Community Development,
University of South Australia, Adelaide, Australia
e-mail: Janine.Pierce@unisa.edu.au

W. O'Connor
Port Stephens Fisheries Institute, NSW Department of Primary Industries, Nelson Bay, Australia

© Springer Science+Business Media Dordrecht 2014
S. Sandhu et al. (eds.), *Linking Local and Global Sustainability,* The International Society of Business, Economics, and Ethics Book Series 4, DOI 10.1007/978-94-017-9008-6_13

The main research question underpinning this study sought to gain additional perspectives for RIA No1, NSW DPI and ACIAR on the effectiveness of their aid and assistance in relation to the oyster farming initiative, specifically:

What Impact has Oyster Farming had on the Lives of Oyster Farmers and in the Wider Perspective of those in their Commune?

This particular study was conducted at the Ban Sen Commune level using the Photovoice technique and interpreting oyster farmer photos and diary comments through a Five Capitals Framework lens of evaluation. Although there are approximately 200 farmers involved in oyster farming, this study focussed on 10 farmers, a number consistent with Photovoice methodology (Wang et al. 1996).

How has the Introduction of Oyster Farming to Ban Sen Commune Affected Community Sustainability?

What Changes to the Five Community Capitals do Oyster Farmers Identify as Most Significant?

Community sustainability requires consideration of environmental, social and economic aspects to ensure that the community and its members can survive for today and tomorrow. In developing countries, a starting point to accelerating development comes through agriculture, a stable economic situation and poverty alleviation, for which placing value on agriculture is required (Timmer 1996). Challenges occur when increased need for food and water to produce more economic return may negatively impact on the environment, and on the people who build their survival and community existence there. The Brundtland Commission report (WCED 1987) identified key areas to address and these are reflected in the strategy of establishing oyster farming in Vietnam:

Consideration for levels of poverty: Oyster farming in Vietnam provides the chance for poor farmers to have the opportunity to integrate oyster farming into their income producing activities as a means to increasing income.

Building of wealth in developing countries: Oyster farming in Vietnam addresses this strategy from the grassroots level in poor communities.

Sustainability—the economic challenge: Establishing oyster farming in a poor area of Vietnam provided the catalyst to achieve more income which can result in a more sustainable quality of life.

The link between the environment and economic aspects: Primary Industries NSW in providing knowledge, skills and guidance, ensured consideration of the importance and interdependence of ecological considerations in determining the success of oyster farming and economic return.

Background Context of the Oyster Farming Area and Stage of Development of Oyster Farming

The farmed oyster industry along the North East coast of Vietnam has continued expansion since its inception in 2007. Australian shellfish experts from NSW DPI's Port Stephens Fisheries Institute were commissioned by ACIAR to assist development at Vietnam's government-owned, newly constructed oyster hatchery on Cat Ba Island. Under DPI guidance, local Vietnamese staff were trained in the various facets of hatchery operation, including algal culture, broodstock maintenance, larval rearing and nursery techniques. Today, over 100 million spat (small oysters) are now sold annually from the hatchery to small family-owned farms, providing a means to alleviate poverty and improve quality of life. Currently there are over 1500 poor coastal villagers employed in managing some 2200 oysters rafts with more labor required to operate an additional 1000 oyster rafts due for construction in 2013. Estimates suggest there are some 10,000 coastal village families that ultimately could become involved in the oyster industry.

This study was conducted in the Ban Sen commune in Van Don district, Quang Ninh province in Vietnam, which is one of the largest provinces along the North East coastlines of Vietnam. Quang Ninh province is both extensively mountainous and coastal, and includes over 2000 islands which extend more than 250 km along the coast. The province has four seasons but monsoons occur in summer. The largest islands in this province are Cat Bau and Ban Sen. The province has mineral and forestry resources, some manufacturing industry including shipbuilding, and farming and fishing activities, with increasing income from aquaculture. Tourism is attracting many tourists to the Province, with its water locations and the UNESCO World Heritage site of Ha Long Bay. The areas in which oyster farming were introduced were in lower income areas.

Comprehensive scientific production reports were prepared for ACIAR on the oyster farming initiative, but researchers acknowledged the need for an assessment of social and economic impact on the lives of farmers and their community. White et al. (2004) emphasized that aquaculture operations need to be vigilant of the social impact of expansion, and the importance for sustainable aquaculture practices that consider both natural and social systems. There had been a study in the Eyre Peninsula region in South Australia using the Photovoice method, which indicated mainly positive impact from introduction of the oyster industry (Pierce et al. 2008; Pierce and McKay 2008). The findings indicated a predominantly positive story of impact of oyster farming. However, not all stories of introduction of aquaculture into existing communities have been positive. Reports from Maryland (USA) suggested problems of disease, unsustainable management practices, governance, and contested water rights (Leffler 2003), while Mexican communities were argued to have experienced displacement of fishers as the result of pro-aquaculture policies (Perez-Sanchez and Muir 2003). In Vietnam there have been some negative impacts on local-level social resilience of communities, through undermining common property institutions; for example mangrove areas were privatized for the aquaculture businesses (Adger 2000). Thailand has also experienced negative impact from shrimp farming related to algal blooms, fish deaths, mangrove loss, and release of diseases (Lebel et al. 2002). Overall the social impact of aquaculture is not well understood (Jolly 2010). To achieve sustainability in the longer term economic growth must be accompanied by a balance and compromise among the environmental and social priorities of the community.

Measuring Community Sustainability: Selection of Methodologies

Achieving a sustainable community is considered a long-term goal, therefore assessments at intervals has value in ensuring the community is moving in the right direction (Roseland 2005). There are various forms of community sustainability assessment which include tools such as indicators, surveys, focus groups, monitoring reports, geographic information systems, community mapping or rankings, and community sustainability assessment models. Examples of these that have been developed for use in the community context include the community indicators of Orange County California (2012), in the Australian context (MacGregor and Fenton 1999; Pepperdine 1998), in New Zealand (Pomeroy 1997), and through the work of Pintér et al. (2005).

Photovoice is a community assessment tool that was selected for use in this study. Photovoice was used in a South Australian oyster community by Pierce and McKay (2008), and was considered appropriate to apply to the Vietnam oyster farming context. Photovoice was first developed by Caroline Wang and Mary Anne Burris in 1994, when they developed a picture story approach in their research into rural women in Yunnan Province. Wang and Burris gave the women cameras so that they could tell their own stories via photos. The goal of this Chinese study was to influence policies and programs that impacted on the women. This approach reflected the philosophy of Paulo Freire (1993) who advocated the value of education for critical consciousness in which photos are a form of code that enable community participation and community member empowerment. Rose (2001) highlights the societal trend to an area of study termed 'visual culture', in which knowledge and perceptions of reality are increasingly conveyed through visual images. Photos reflect back to the individuals taking the photos, the community, and in turn to decision-makers, the narratives of the photos and collective stories, of realities and perceptions of community members. The value of Photovoice in this study was that oyster farmers were empowered to give their perceptions of impact on them and on their communities of initiatives to encourage oyster farming. Wang and Burris (1994) emphasize the value of the Photovoice method as community members have an insider understanding and insight into their community in a way that outsiders do not. Taking photos as a collaborative participatory methodology has value for participants to share their world and their perceptions of it, which in turn conveys insights to the audience and those in governance and decision-makers on participant issues. It transcends language barriers and the limitations of the written word. It provides the richness of visual data, and is mostly directed by the participants themselves with only initial theme prompts. Photovoice is a qualitative research method that can provide a supportive dimension to quantitative data.

The challenge in using the Photovoice method is how to assess the degree of community sustainability from these photos. Hall (1997) argues that a visual image may be interpreted differently by different viewers, and that an explicit methodology is required to justify the interpretation. Therefore a supportive lens of analysis

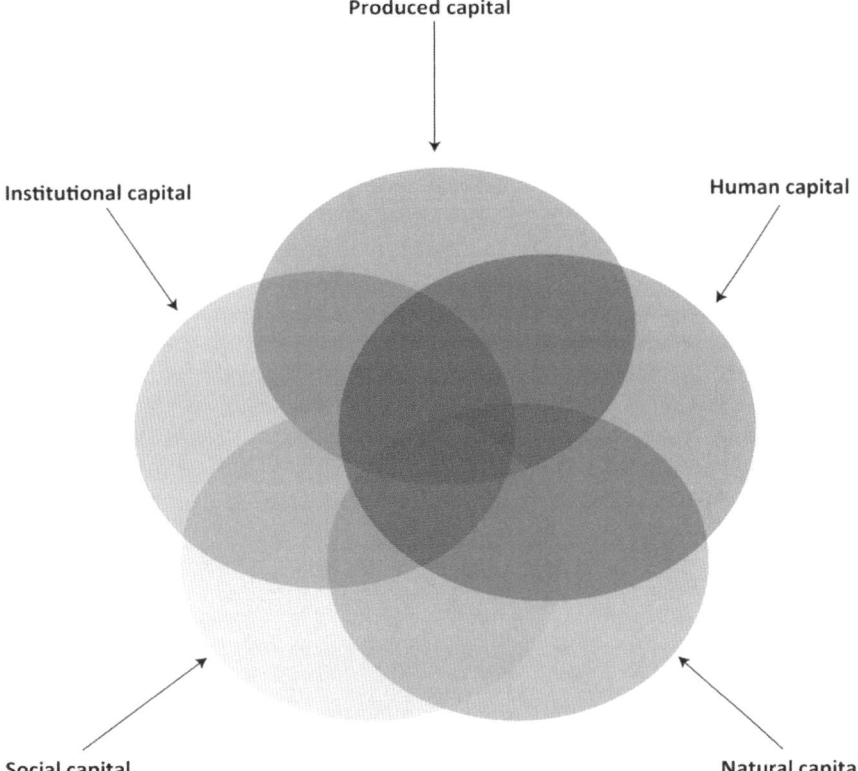

Fig. 13.1 Five capitals framework. (Source: interpreted from explanation of Cocklin and Alston (2003))

for Photovoice was considered necessary to assist decision-makers in assessing oyster farming's overall impact on community sustainability.

A community assessment method adopted to interpret photos in the rural Australian context is the Five Capitals Framework (Cocklin and Alston 2003). This community assessment tool provided the lens through which South Australian oyster community sustainability was assessed (Pierce and Mckay 2008). This framework was also considered relevant to the Vietnam oyster farming context, which was similarly rural, although different in cultural, income levels, and political aspects. It is argued that a sustainable community needs to be rich in five capitals: natural, human, social, institutional, and produced (Cocklin and Alston 2003). Social capital is considered to be the central ingredient identified by O'Meara (1999), which is inclusive of the qualities of a 'vibrant' sustainable community inclusive of commitment, shared vision, participation, coordination and partnerships. This capitals-based framework can also be used to assess whether stocks of capitals are increasing or diminishing (Cocklin and Alston 2003).

The framework (Fig. 13.1) divides community sustainability needed dimensions into five interrelated capitals:

- *natural* (natural resources, ecosystem services and aesthetic value)
- *human* (knowledge and skills of individuals, innovation, commitment to place, health)
- *social* (productive networks and shared values, relationships, goodwill)
- *institutional* (institutional structures in the private, public and third sectors)
- *produced* (the built environment, harvested or manufactured goods and monetary resources).

A capitals analysis enables assessing sustainability in relation to how the stocks of capitals are increasing, maintaining, or declining, and how goods and services generated by these capitals are flowing. Assessing impact of introduction of oyster farming aligns well with this form of analysis.

Combining Photovoice with a capitals assessment has value as it is considered important to involve potential users in the assessment (Lehtonen 2004), in this case the community members. The Photovoice method enabled a gateway to access a capitals story of the oyster farming impact.

The following stages of Photovoice methodology were used in this study (Wang et al. 1996):

Recruitment of participants: This was done by Vietnam ACIAR staff and key local oyster farming leaders. During this stage the nature of the study, the fact it would require photo-taking on themes included in the diary over a 6 day timeframe and to be accompanied by diary entries, completion of ethics approval for release of photos, and camera usage guidance was carried out. Time was spent on this aspect of the study as it was considered necessary to build rapport and trust for the process and with the research team (Neuman 2006). Wang et al. (1996) recommended a Photovoice study has 8–12 participants as an ideal and manageable size. Ten oyster farmers involved in this study were selected, all from the same commune, including three females and seven males. There was some representation from part-time and full-time oyster farmers.

Telling stories: This stage required oyster farmers to take photos to represent loosely framed themes mentioned in the diary, and support these photos with explanatory comments to provide a context to the photo. The timeframe was 6 days. The questions themes listed in the diary were:

1. How has oyster farming impacted on you?
2. Is your village/commune more or less likely to develop since oyster farming began?
3. What is good about oyster farming in your village/commune?
4. What is bad about oyster farming in your village/commune?

Codifying of issues and themes: After 6 days, when it was confirmed that all farmers had completed the task all the cameras and diaries were collected. The photos were loaded onto a laptop computer. This was done in conjunction with the farmers to ensure the diary comments matched the photos. Diary comments were then translated into English and photo data was then recorded under each farmer in a powerpoint file in both English and Vietnamese with the first photo recording the farmer and location under a photo.

Findings from the Study

Photos reflecting positive impact in produced capital dominated, with focus often being on new financial acquisitions enabled by oyster farming income, with attendant quality of life enhancement such as transport via motor bikes and boats. Photos were taken of better houses new community buildings built from oyster farming income, which were more able to withstand typhoons. In this area of Vietnam there is a poor household ranking, and in several instances comments were made of people being able to move off the poor household list since beginning oyster farming. The link was made in diary comments that oyster farming had enabled these acquisitions, which in turn had come through human capital enhancement of new knowledge and skills (human capital) and support to develop these skills (institutional capital).

Most photos presented a positive view of the impact of oyster farming, however there were some negative aspects presented. Oyster farmer comments are included beside each photo, accompanied by types of capitals represented in the photos as interpreted from diary comments. Although only some of the photos are presented here, the later discussion on how photos reflect the five capitals is reflective of all the 134 photos taken by participants.

Natural Capital

Positive Environmental Impact

The oyster industry as with all farming initiatives in this commune is connected to and dependent on the effectiveness of production of a natural resource commodity (Krannich and Luloff 1991). The environmental impact on oyster farming was reflected in relation to an increased awareness of need for purity of water for oyster farming, and the need to keep it this way. More health conscious practices resulting in improved quality of drinking water for commune members had been introduced, as well as more health aware practices in improved sanitation and human water management (Fig. 13.2), all of which benefit the whole commune. New infrastructure relating to water and sanitation had been assisted by oyster farming income. The ability to build oyster farming infrastructure from available natural resources (for example bamboo), in turn also funded further wood farming, which was also identified in a couple of photos.

Fig. 13.2 Introduction of
new water wells (capitals:
natural, human, produced)

Fig. 13.3 Negative environmental impact (capitals:
natural, produced)

With money from oysters, 100% of households in the village had clean water
wells. They don't have to use water from open stream for cooking as in the past.

However, there were some natural capital photos taken with perceived negative
impact due to oyster farming, mainly relating to parasites that were impacting on
another aquaculture species: Tu Hai clams, which are co-located on aquaculture
farms near oysters (even though these are not oyster parasites). Also identified was
impact on the natural environment from oyster farming residue (Fig. 13.3).

Harvesting oysters is not scientifically proper. (Residue from) on-farm harvesting makes changes to ecological environment, affecting a lot to culturing
of other species

Human Capital

Human capital is often argued as being the key factor needed to achieve regional
adaptation and growth (Stayner 2003). Keeping people in rural communities,

Fig. 13.4 Human capital
positive impact (capitals:
human, social, Produced)

particularly the young, is needed to sustain the community into the future which presents a community sustainability challenge. Lawrence (2005) makes the link between out-migration from rural communities, mainly younger people, due to insufficient employment. With the introduction of oyster farming to this area of Vietnam has come more jobs, which also encourages more younger people to stay in their commune. A number of photos of children implied a more positive future for them since the introduction of oyster farming (although there was no specific mention about this being due to jobs). There was mention that income from oyster farming would enable covering costs of increasing education for children. This increase in human capital would assist the whole community. As farming in this area of Vietnam is often diversified, more seasonal jobs in oyster farming not only provides extra income, but also keeps people busy and active, provides income at times when there is no work in other areas of farming, and can improve mental well-being, which is another facet of human capital. Some participants also referred to commitment to place in keeping young people in the commune due to jobs in oyster farming (Fig. 13.4), with others indicating commitment to place by mentioning they had plans to expand their oyster farms and to create more jobs for those in their commune.

> Attracting workers, creating jobs for farmers and young people, so that they do not have to go to work in other locations.

A shortage of meaningful jobs was the main cause identified by young people leaving their Australian rural communities (Alston and Kent 2004). A couple of photos from this study did indicate that working in oysters was often repetitive, boring and tiring as it was very labor intensive (Fig. 13.5). This negative human capital aspect associated with oyster farming was also mentioned as an issue for oyster workers in the Eyre Peninsula in a South Australian oyster study (Pierce et al. 2008).

Health is another aspect of human capital. The value of oysters in introducing a protein-rich food to commune members was highlighted in several photos.

Fig. 13.5 Human capital
negative impact (capitals:
human)

Social Capital

Social capital is viewed as an essential element needed in determining the strength of
a rural community's key attributes that indicate propensity for sustainability (Smailes
and Hugo 2003). Social capital is reflected in the community context to the degree to
which a community has cohesion, shares with others and has a common vision. Social
capital can also be reflected in how people feel about and demonstrate their commitment to their community or 'place', whether it is considered in the physical sense of
geographic location, or what is perceived in the feeling people have of their place.

Place becomes imbued with a symbolic meaning when it is connected to the
cultural values and social interactions that occur within that space (Soja 1996). This
integration of geographic place associated with a meaningful sense of place then
becomes a space in which can exist a culture of communal efforts in connecting
people for shared community building of places to work, to pray, to create buildings and spaces of community utilities. Collectively these ways of acting indicate
the community members experience a sense of a common fate. There were photos
of a new community house which oyster farmers had contributed to and which all
community members would benefit from; there were photos of a new rice husking
machine bought by an oyster farmer which could be used by others in the commune.

Pride had increased in community members as some had moved from the poor
housing list, some had better houses, and some had more items to increase their
quality of life which also reflected an improved level of job success. There were
many photos that emphasized positive aspects of social capital in this study. Aspects
of trust, enhanced community spirit, commune members working together to help
each other on the oyster farms, or in improving their village in using money received from oysters featured in photos and associated diary comments. There were
a number of photos which indicated that oyster farmers as individuals were feeling
happier with their involvement in oyster farming and the enhanced sense of happiness and renewed community spirit they were feeling. Oyster farmers also took
photos of other community members who reflected this increased sense of happiness since oysters. Harvesting oysters is often done in a group which helps to build
social cohesion. One example of this was a women only oyster farm (Fig. 13.6),
which may be a comfortable working environment for widows or single women.

Fig. 13.6 Social capital
positive impact (capitals:
social, human, institutional,
produced)

Fig. 13.7 Social capital
positive impact (capitals:
social, human, produced,
institutional)

The ladies are together happily harvesting oysters to raise funds. The community becomes stronger, thrives together on economy.

There were a number of photos that indicated a wider social impact on the community and how oyster farming had provided the chance to enrich and sustain the community. One example was of a shuttle boat purchase which, although possibly considered to be produced capital through providing a shuttle boat to ferry commune members, is also a means of connecting commune members to each other. The shuttle boat enables more ease in lifestyle, but also more human capital links through more chance to network, travel to a job or school, and demonstrates an entrepreneurial nature and a community focus (Fig. 13.7).

With money from oysters, a villager also bought a shuttle boat to transfer passengers around and about the village.

A study by Kawakami and Aton (1998) linked geographic place to how people interact in stating that people define their environment in relation to both physical and social environments, and that social contexts and interactions demonstrate and confirm community values. A clear example of this was provided in photos relating to the significant

Fig. 13.8 Institutional capital
negative impact (capitals:
institutional, produced)

destruction by the typhoon of oyster farming infrastructure for some farmers. Photos
showed farmers assisting other oyster farmers who had experienced significant losses
to rebuild. These photos demonstrated a strong social capital component and trust to
work together and to help others. Working together is an indicator of community spirit
and caring relationships in a shared place (Warburton 1998). The link between social
capital and produced capital as identified in oyster farming in this study has also been
indirectly alluded to by Knack and Keefer (1997), who have identified a correlation
between increasing levels of trust and an increase in economic prosperity.

There was a strong focus on positive social capital-related photos, however no
negative photos relating to social capital impact since oyster farming was taken up
by farmers.

Institutional Capital

Institutional capital in communities comes through three areas: the public sector, the
private sector (including private business and non-government), and not-for-profit
organizations (Cocklin and Alston 2003). There were some photos relating to raising
funds through collective oyster farming business activity (Fig. 13.6), and a number
of other photos that indicated oyster farmers were focused on building and expanding
their business. Figure 13.7 showed the photo of the ferry bought as a business to assist
community members in travelling around the commune, which connects institutional
capital to social capital for the good of the community, and links to human capital in
being entrepreneurial. There were photos that oyster farmers took to express a need
for more financial support from government to expand their oyster business, and one
photo that expressed gratitude for government and other given to establish their oyster farm. There were some photos reflective of institutional capital issues reflective
of difficulties for oyster farming with lack of regulation of oyster pricing which was
impacting negatively on their economic return from oyster farming (Fig. 13.8).

There should be more wholesale agencies, so that the trade between farmers
and consumers is more convenient

Produced Capital

As this commune is in a lower income level, it is not surprising that the most often mentioned capital in the photos was produced capital, with emphasis placed on more money to improve material possessions, quality of life or to fund other types of farming.

Produced capital encompasses financial resources and physical products that have been harvested or manufactured, including the built environment of housing, roads, boat ramps, water management systems, other buildings and financial assets (Cocklin and Alston 2003). Out-migration from rural communities presents the challenge of maintaining produced capital, as any financial contraction will result in job reductions, reduced spending and more out-migration (Tonts 2005). New industries such as the oyster industry can assist in redressing this trend. Sustaining and building produced capital in a community is required to not only provide jobs and income that helps to fund community projects, but also to encourage young people to build their future in the community. The value of oyster farming was highlighted in several photos which emphasized that oyster farming was an efficient way of farming as the time from seed to harvesting was relatively short, which results in a faster turnaround for the farmer. Also, the input costs were relatively low compared to the economic return.

Vietnam rural oyster communities operate from a diverse rural base in which oyster farming is only one income stream. This type of farming mix has the desirable propensity to be sustainable as argued by Herbert-Cheshire and Lawrence (2003), so that a decline in one area may be offset by a growth in another. While these farmers remain relatively poor, it could be argued that the introduction of oyster farming into the economic base of the commune has reduced their resource dependency risk. Photos were often of the economic improvement in their lives and the lives of those in their commune since the introduction of oyster farming. Produced capital was positively represented in photos and diary comments. Recurring photo themes highlighted improvements of the economic base both for oyster farmers and their workers. Photos were also of improvements to infrastructure across a range of areas including transport, better and stronger houses, and personal belongings such as karaoke machines, community houses and enhanced community infrastructure, in particular housing. There were a number of photos taken of motor bikes which enables more efficient use of time, as well as more social status and enhanced mobility. Purchase of a motor bike not only relates to produced capital, but to the social issue of pride and enhanced shared community spirit identified by Everitt and Annis (2002). A defining comment associated with a couple of photos which indicates the link between produced capital and social capital, was in moving from the poor household list which indicates improved income and improved social status. Other farming requirements to make labor easier and more productive had been assisted by oyster farming income with purchase of rice pluckers and fertilizers.

Some photos indicated the downside of produced capital in relation to challenges in oyster farming. A particular recurring theme related to erratic and sometimes lower oyster income than had been hoped for due to low prices being paid for oysters. Other photos captured the impact of the most recent typhoon (2011) on oyster

Fig. 13.9 Produced capital
negative impact (capitals:
produced)

farming infrastructure, and oyster farms which had required rebuilding and lost income. This damage had been extensive as oyster infrastructure is mostly located in one area, so impact of the typhoon was on oyster rafts, oyster houses, boats used in transporting oysters and workers, and on oyster worker accommodation (Fig. 13.9).

> Although there were losses and damages after the natural disaster, farmers are still overcoming the difficulties, repairing rafts and continuing to invest in oyster farming.

Conclusions

Social capital improvement in oyster farming is dependent on and intrinsically linked with other capitals. It has been shown in this study that measuring the overall impact of a new environmentally sensitive industry on community sustainability needs to be assessed holistically through a range of interconnected aspects. Photo data was often explained by oyster farmers in diary comments as relating to several capitals. This is indicative of the assertions of Smailes and Hugo (2003) and Dibden and Cocklin (2003), who argue that the Five Capitals Framework is limited if capitals are considered separately, as there is an interconnectedness between them.

This study has generated an integrative perspective of impact of ACIAR's funding and NSW DPI's technical guidance, in implementing oyster farming into the Ban Sen Province in Vietnam. The method used in this study of using a Photovoice methodology in conjunction with a Five Capitals Framework interpretation highlighted a number of areas of impact for oyster farmers across the five capitals: natural, human, social, institutional and produced. The Five Capitals Framework as a lens through which to view Photovoice data from this study in the developing country of Vietnam was a useful methodology, and produced similar types of social and other capital impacts as in the study in South Australian oyster farms (Pierce and McKay 2008).

Overall impact from the ACIAR initiative of introducing oyster farming into Ban Sen Province has been portrayed as mostly positive across the five capital aspects. Produced and social capital were conveyed most often in photos of impact of oyster farming. In a poorer community an increase in assets and income would be expected to be a priority, as income is needed to sustain life. However, in the process of enhancing produced capital, farmers told photo stories of how social capital has also been enhanced within their commune. There have been benefits to the commune from oyster farming, with increased protein foods, more oyster farm jobs, better transport and a community house.

Oyster farmers through the Photovoice medium were enabled and empowered to articulate their perceptions of the good and bad impact of this new industry. Negative impact was conveyed across all five capital areas, with particular impact in the environmental and produced capital areas. In produced capital negative photos related to lack of power to control oyster pricing, as this was currently, and also likely to produce in the future, a less predictable income, as were lower prices from sometimes small-sized oysters resulting from imported seed. Some other mentions of negative impact were in relation to natural capital (parasites and natural elements of the typhoon), human (some oyster processing jobs were boring), no negative social capital mentions, institutional capital (issues relating to problems in oyster prices that might need government intervention). Positive impacts from oyster farming are addressed under each of the three research questions.

Research Question 1: What Impact has Oyster Farming Had on the Lives of Oyster Farmers and in the Wider Perspective of those in their Commune?

This study found that oyster farmers had increased their income and thereby their quality of life through jobs for their families, the chance for family members to work and stay together for the future, and in providing seasonal jobs for commune members. Shifting from the poor household list was a point of pride, as was a lift in community spirit, new and better houses, and motorbikes to make transport more efficient.

Research Question Sub Question: How has the Introduction of Oyster Farming to Ban Sen Commune Affected Community Sustainability?

There has been a wider impact on the commune in more jobs to keep the young in the commune, a new industry to help achieve more income and raise workers to a better and healthier standard of living, improve sanitation, increased protein source from oysters, more community cohesion through workers and families working together, and a community house. These aspects were some of the community sustainability indicators from the data.

Research Question Sub Question: What Changes to the Five Community Capitals do Oyster Farmers Identify as Most Significant?

Photos relating to produced, social and human capital were most represented. This industry is helping poorer farmers to improve their financial standing and acquire more assets and build their oyster business and other farming interests. Human capital is reflected in more skills, more jobs particularly for their children, and more money to fund education for the children, which will ensure more sustainability for the commune. Sell and Zube (1986) found that concerted working together to sustain what is valued can work towards strengthening sense of place and commitment to the place. In this study social sustainability appears strengthened through more commitment to place in building a future in the commune and the commune members strengthening their social fibre in working together on oyster farms.

It is recommended that a holistic assessment such as the Five Capitals Framework be used in assessing social impact of a new industry such as oyster farming, or in general assessment of sustainability of a rural community. Using a Photovoice method in conjunction with the Five Capitals approach has value due to its simplicity in engaging and empowering community members, and in ensuring authenticity in capturing participant data. The Photovoice method in conjunction with the Five Capitals Framework has relevance to be applied to other developing communities, in assessing impact of aid assistance and new programs, not just on social impact, but on all community sustainability dimensions. The implications of the approach in this study was that the methodology was relevant to programs in a developing country that start at the farming level, as the potential strengths or vulnerabilities of the environment are included.

Acknowledgments Gratitude is expressed to the many people and organizations who made this study possible. Particular thanks is accorded to the ten oyster farmers who so willingly committed their time to this project and produced both photos and written explanations to tell their story of the impact of oyster farming. The efforts of Nguyen Thi Thanh An, Geoff Morris and Kieu Xuan Hung from ACIAR are warmly acknowledged, as is the assistance of Cao Truong Giang, Cao Van Hanh and Pham Van Nhiem, and Dr Le Xan, from RIA1. Thanks also to Mr Pham Ngoc Chanh (boat driver). The firsthand background information provided from local authorities at the commune and district levels was of great assistance in the conduct of this study.

References

Adger, W. N. (2000). Social and ecological resilience: Are they related? *Progress in Human Geography, 24*(3), 347–364.

Alston, M., & Kent, J. (2004). Coping with a crisis: Human services in times of drought. *Rural Society, 14,* 214–227.

Cocklin, C., & Alston, M. (Eds.). (2003). *Community sustainability in rural Australia: A question of capital?* Wagga Wagga: Centre for Rural Social Research, Charles Sturt University.

Dibden, J., & Cocklin, C. (2003). 'Tarra' Victoria. In C. Cocklin & M. Alston (Eds.), *Community sustainability in rural Australia: A Question of capital?* (pp. 177–201). Wagga Wagga: Centre for Rural Social Research, Charles Sturt University.

Everitt J., & Annis, R. (2002). The sustainability of prairie rural communities. In C. Bowler, N. Bryant, & N. Nellies (Eds.), *Contemporary rural systems in transition: (2), Economy and society* (pp. 213–222). Walingford: CAN International.

Food and Agricultural Organization (FAO). (2012). *FAO yearbook: Fish and aquaculture statistics.* http://www.fao.org/economic/ess/ess-publications/ess-yearbook/yearbook2012/en/. Accessed 20 Feb 2013.

Freire, P. (1993). *Pedagogy of the oppressed: New revisited 20th anniversary edition.* New York: Continuum.

Hall, S. (1997). Introduction. In S. Hall (Ed.), *Representation: Cultural representations and signifying practices* (pp. 1–12). Berkshire: The Open University Press

Herbert-Cheshire, L., & Lawrence, G. (2003). Monto, Queensland. In C. Cocklin & M. Alston (Eds.), *Community sustainability in rural Australia: A question of capital* (pp. 10–37). Wagga Wagga: Centre for Rural Social Research, Charles Sturt University.

Jolly, C. (2010). Aquaculture and socio-economic growth and development: Enabling policies and partnership for improved benefits. Global conference on aquaculture 2010, Thailand. http://www.fao.org/docrep/015/i2734e/i2734e00.htm. Accessed 22 Feb 2013.

Kawakami, A., & Aton, K. (1998). *Native Hawaiian curriculum development: A study identifying critical elements for success.* Paper presented at the meeting of the national Education Association, Nashville, TN. http://www.eric.ed.gov/ERICWebPortal/search/detailmini.jsp?_nfpb=true&_&ERICExtSearch_SearchValue_0=ED447972&ERICExtSearch_SearchType_0=no&accno=ED447972. Accessed 4 Feb 2013.

Knack, S., & Keefer, P. (1997). Does social capital have an economic payoff? A cross-country investigation. *Quarterly Journal of Economics, 112,* 1251–1288.

Krannich, R., & Luloff, A. (1991). Problems of resource dependency in US rural communities. In A. Gileg, D. Briggs, R. Dilley, O. Furuseth, & G. McDonald (Eds.), *Progress in rural policy and planning* (pp. 5–18). London: Belhaven.

Lawrence, G., (2005). *Futures for rural Australia: From agricultural productivism to community stability.* Rockhampton: Central Queensland University.

Lebel, L., Nguyen, H. T., Amnuay, S., Suparb P. U., & Buatama, L. T. H. (2002). Industrial transformation and shrimp aquaculture in Thailand and Vietnam: Pathways to ecological, social, and economic sustainability? *Journal of the Human Environment, 31*(2), 311–323.

Leffler, M. (2003). Oyster farming vs Oyster hunting. http://www.mdsg.umd.edu/issues/chesapeake/oysters/history/conflict/. Accessed 20 Feb 2013.

Lehtonen, M. (2004). The environmental-social interface of sustainable development: Capabilities, social capital, institutions, *Ecological Economics, 49,* 199–214.

MacGregor, C., & Fenton, M. (1999). *Community values provide a mechanism for measuring sustainability in small rural communities in Northern Australia.* In Country Matters Conference Proceedings, 20–21 May. Canberra: Bureau of Rural Science.

Neuman, W. (2006). *Social research methods: Qualitative and quantitative approaches.* Sydney: Pearson Education.

O'Meara, M. (1999). *Creating and maintaining a vibrant community.* In Country Matters Conference Proceedings, 20–21 May 1999. Canberra: National Convention Centre.

Orange County Community Indicators Report. (2012). http://ocgov.com/civicax/filebank/blobdload.aspx?BlobID=4126. Accessed 14 Feb 2013.

Pepperdine, S. (19–24 April 1998). *Making peoples' values count: Measuring rural community sustainability.* Paper presented at 18th Annual Meeting of the International Association for Impact Assessment, Christchurch, New Zealand.

Perez-Sanchez, E., & Muir, J. (2003). Fishermen perception on resources management and aquaculture development in the Mecoacan estuary, Tabasco, Mexico. *Ocean Coastal Management, 46,* 681–700.

Pierce J., & McKay, J. (2008). Our community capitals as we see them through photovoice: Cowell oyster industry in South Australia. *Australian Journal of Environmental Management, 15,* 159–168.

Pierce, J., Thompson, K., Sharp, R., & Mckay, J. (2008). *Their world is an oyster: Final report to the Eyre Regional Development Board*. Adelaide: Hawke Institute for Sustainable Societies. The University of South Australia in conjunction with the School of Commerce, Division of Business, University of South Australia.

Pintér, L., Hardi, P., & Bartelmus, P. (2005). *Sustainable development indicators: Proposal for a way forward*. Prepared for the United Nations Division for Sustainable Development (UN-DSD) IISD Publications Centre, United Nations.

Pomeroy, A. (1997). *Social indicators of sustainable agriculture*. Wellington: Ministry of Agriculture.

Rose, G. (2001). *Visual methodologies*. London: Sage.

Roseland, M. (2005). *Toward sustainable communities*. Canada: New Society.

Sell, J., & Zube, E. (1986). Perception and response to environmental change. *Journal of Architectural Planning and Research, 3,* 33–54.

Smailes, P., & Hugo, G. (2003). "The Gilbert Valley" South Australia. In: C. Cocklin & M. Alston (Eds.), *Community sustainability in Rural Australia: a question of capital?* (pp. 65–106). Wagga Wagga: Centre for Rural Social Research, Charles Sturt University.

Soja, E., (1996). *Thirdspace: Journeys to Los Angeles and other real-and-imagined places*, Cambridge: Blackwell.

Stayner, R. (2003). Guyra, New South Wales. In C. Cocklin & M. Alston (Eds.), *Community sustainability in rural Australia: A question of capital* (pp. 38–64). Wagga Wagga: Centre for Rural Social Research, Charles Sturt University.

Timmer, C. P. (1996). Agriculture and economic growth in Vietnam. *Research in Domestic and International Agribusiness Management, 12,* 161–203.

Tonts, M. (2005). Competitive sport and social capital in rural Australia. *Journal of Rural Studies, 21,* 137–149.

Wang, C., & Burris, M. (1994). Empowerment through Photo Novella: Portraits of participation. *Health Education & Behavior, 21*(2), 171–186.

Wang, C., Burris M., & Xiang Y. P. (1996). Chinese village women as visual anthropologists: A participatory approach to reaching policymakers. *Social Science & Medicine, 42*(10), 1391–1400.

Warburton, D. (1998). A passionate dialogue: Community and sustainable development. In D. Warburton (Ed.), *Community and sustainable development: Participation in the future*. London: Earthscan.

White, K., O'Neill. B., & Tzankova, Z. (2004). *At a crossroads: Will aquaculture fulfil the promise of the blue revolution?* Sea-Web Aquaculture Clearinghouse Report, Providence, Rhode Island, USA.

World Commission on Environment and Development [WCED]. (1987). *Our common future*. Report of the World Commission on environment and Development (chaired by Gro Harlem Brundtland, and referred to as the Brundtland report). Oxford: Oxford University Press.

Chapter 14
Conclusion

Stephen McKenzie, Sukhbir Sandhu and Howard Harris

Sustainability: End States, Goals and Processes

At the beginning of this volume, we argued that that it is almost impossible to make a full and properly scientific assessment of the activities of an individual organisation in relation to global sustainability, and even where it may be possible, it would be well beyond the capability of many small- to medium-sized enterprises. For this reason, we have not tried to define global sustainability as an end-state. Instead, we focus on developing goals for human activity at the local and organisational level, and on systematically improving our relationships with communities and the wider environment. That focus has given rise to a definition of *a local to global sustainability initiative* as:

> A collective, progressive and self-reflective activity, undertaken within communities, designed to develop more sustainable relationships with the natural environment, including its own members and members of other communities.

The preceding statement may place us in argument with theorists like Phillip Sutton, for whom the move to define sustainability as a *process* can be symptomatic of denial:

> As the scale of the task of achieving a sustainable environment and society has become apparent many people have tried to insulate themselves from the enormity of the challenge by retreating into small incremental changes. So some people have started to say that sustainability is a process of change and not an end state, and that it's the journey that counts, not the destination. (Sutton 2004, p. 2)

S. McKenzie (✉) · S. Sandhu · H. Harris
School of Management, University of South Australia Business School,
Adelaide, Australia
e-mail: Stephen.McKenzie@unisa.edu.au

S. Sandhu
e-mail: Sukhbir.Sandhu@unisa.edu.au

H. Harris
e-mail: Howard.Harris@unisa.edu.au

© Springer Science+Business Media Dordrecht 2014   225
S. Sandhu et al. (eds.), *Linking Local and Global Sustainability,* The International Society
of Business, Economics, and Ethics Book Series 4, DOI 10.1007/978-94-017-9008-6_14

Yet Sutton's subsequent definition of the 'destination' of sustainability is not so very different from our own position:

> The 'destination' of sustainability is not a fixed place in the normal sense that we understand destination. Instead it is a **set of characteristics of a future system**…But getting to the destination…doesn't mean that our lives become static. Achieving the 'destination' is the purpose of the journey but when we get there society and the environment will not be static. (Sutton 2004, p. 5, emphasis added)

We do not see that our definition of sustainability as a process is an act of denial. The lack of any static end-state for global sustainability is precisely why we view it as a 'work', an ongoing process of change. Our model for a local to global sustainability initiative presupposes that in most cases, we cannot fully comprehend the ideal global end-state that we are trying to achieve. This is why the development of appropriate local goals becomes so important. The sustainability goals for an organisation must be tangible enough so that we know when we are achieving them, yet also, fluid enough to ensure that we do not try to 'set and forget' our sustainability targets, and become unresponsive to inevitable changes in social and environmental conditions.

Returning to Sutton's 'set of characteristics of a future system'—what might these be? We argue that they must include the ability of organisations and communities to undertake sustainability initiatives, and also, a community that creates an enabling environment for businesses to undertake such initiatives.

On the first point, it is clear that flexible and agile organisations are inherently more likely to be sustainable than ones that are wedded to particular types of technology or patterns of consumption and cannot survive when circumstances change. As society and the environment shift, the businesses they host must adapt. And further, just as the ongoing work of any business is continuous, sustainability work must be continuous if it to be imbedded in the core of the organisation.

On the second point, we restate our position from the introduction: we cannot continue our way of life unchanged, and expect our business organizations to bear sole responsibility for the overall sustainability of our system. The ongoing work of sustainability will requires a two-fold conception of responsibility, in which businesses are responsible for their behaviour as guests, and society also bears some responsibility to create enabling conditions, so that businesses can be flexible and adaptable to change.

Various early chapters in the volume highlight the importance of individual judgement in organisational flexibility and agility. Chapter 2, in particular, challenges us to accept our ongoing responsibility to act on new and potentially unpalatable information about changes in technology, or the market. If this responsibility seems onerous, Chap. 4 brings some relief—seeing sustainability as an ongoing work, rather than as a condition in which all needs are met, may be more difficult, but it also engages with a broader and more generous view of human nature. As Sen wrote in 2004:

> Certainly, people have 'needs', but they also have values, and, in particular, they cherish their ability to reason, appraise, act and participate. Seeing people in terms only of their needs may give us a rather meagre view of humanity. (Sen 2004, quoted in Chap. 4 of this volume)

Subsequent chapters point to places where sustainability may be effectively embedded in the core business of any operation: in supply chain management (Chap. 6) and in product life-cycle analysis (Chap. 7). Neither of these are suggested 'end-states' for sustainability—they are holistic examinations of production and consumption that allow the managers of the case study companies to make informed decisions about improving their social and environmental relationships in a cost-effective way. Chapter 6 notes the ongoing nature of such work, and concludes with a call for:

> more flexible interaction between all firms involved, long-term and culturally grown partnerships and cross-organizational cooperation strategies between companies. These could then serve as a catalyst for change toward sustainable development, eco-efficiency, innovation and responsible business practices in order to benefit the supply chain as a whole. (Chap. 6, this volume)

Case Studies with Uncertain End-States

The book we have presented is an equal mix of theoretical papers and case studies. Two sections have dealt with ethical theory, and with the need for all of us to locate sustainability as a central part of our responsibilities as human beings. The remaining half of the volume is case studies from developed nations, developing countries, and development contexts. In these case studies, our contributors have pointed to organisations that are voluntarily guiding themselves through processes that have little to do with conventional CSR or Triple Bottom Line reporting. We have put these examples of local to global sustainability initiatives, in which organisations systematically seek ways to improve their relationships with the environment and with the human communities in which they are hosted.

We will conclude the volume by arguing for the case study approach, informed by theory, as a means to further develop the link between local and global sustainability.

The case study approach is very common in sustainability research. Successful examples of sustainable business practice are inspirational, and tales of unsustainable activities can be cautionary. Business ethics and sustainability courses at undergraduate level are generally full of both. Similarly, businesses and other organisations will naturally wish to promote their own successes in sustainability, and learn from the successes and failures of their counterparts.

Despite their ubiquity—or perhaps because of it—there have been a variety of criticisms of case studies in sustainability over recent years. In a meta-analysis of sustainability case studies, Corcoran et al. (2004) have criticized much current use of the technique, finding that many of the 54 case-study articles they studied lacked theoretical depth and transferability of findings. The review by Scholz et al. (2006) of Transdisciplinary Case Studies in sustainability found a deeper issue: many case studies suffered from having an 'ill-defined problem'. That is, while the initial state of unsustainability was clear enough, the 'goal' state of sustainability was not, and therefore it was not possible to adequately describe the transition from one state to the other. In regards to a particular regional sawmill industry, they noted:

> In this case it was not possible to precisely define the desirable target state…because it was, among other things, unclear how many and what types of sawing companies were beneficial for a sustainable regional development, or if sawing in [the region] contributed to sustainable development at all. (Scholz et al. 2004, p. 233)[1]

The problems faced by Scholz's team are shared by many organisations focusing on sustainability as an end-state. How do we know when we have achieved our objective? Can we determine exactly how we achieved it? Further, how do we know if what we are doing can ever be truly sustainable? Such questions loom particularly large when we attempt to contribute locally to global sustainability. Even in the case of trying to assess the effect on sustainability of an industry within a single region, the desired end-state can be unclear. Trying to determine such things on a global level is all but impossible.

In terms of academic and practitioner studies, the lack of certain end-states raises a different but related issue: what is the purpose of case studies in a situation in which the global end-state is not known? How can the case study approach demonstrate the effectiveness of a particular initiative, if it is has no set end-state to be achieved?

In our response to this issue, we are influenced in part by Oliver O'Donovan's view that the value of case studies in ethics education lies in the opportunity they provide to examine the processes which were employed by those involved in the case (O'Donovan 2002). Another influence is the work of Doug McKenzie-Mohr on Community Based Social Marketing (McKenzie-Mohr 2011). CBSM proposes that behavioural change for sustainability is most often—and most effectively—achieved at the community level, through projects that simultaneously remove barriers to an activity while also enhancing the benefits of that activity.

McKenzie-Mohr uses the term 'end-state' in a very specific sense, to indicate that the outcome of a sustainability initiative should be actual behavioural change, rather than the identification of a strategy that might (or might not) result in those behaviours. For example, if we wish for people in our organisation to use our paper recycling system, our target 'end-state' is not the creation of the recycling system—it is a situation in which people actually use it. We cannot ever suppose that our sustainability strategy will result in the behavioural change we actually want.

In a more general sense, thinking too much about 'end-states' may be undesirable, even at the local level. In 2006, a meta-analysis was conducted of 159 papers that measured the financial effect on companies that adopted sustainability measures. In most cases, single end-state metrics were employed to measure the effect—typically, the company's share price (Peloza and Yachnin 2008). The general pattern of most studies (80 %) was to describe the sustainability measure and then report on the effect on a single end-state metric: "if we behave well environmentally, our share price goes up, or maybe down, and we don't know why." The study

---

[1] Original text says 'sewing' instead of sawing. We have altered this.

concluded that such metrics were inadequate for managers wishing to know how to implement such measures, why they are financially successful, and particularly, how to manage and measure the cultural change around their adoption. The study's authors suggest a greater focus on intermediate measures—for example, employee satisfaction and retention, improved organisational processes, consumer awareness, and so on.

Based on these observations, our first suggestion is that case studies of local to global sustainability initiatives should not be primarily focused on whether they have achieved end-state goals or metrics, but rather, on the ongoing organisational processes that support the change. For example, the case study presented in Chap. 11 looks at sustainable development outcomes in the Solomon Islands. In such a situation, some end state-metrics (for example, household income) may be employed to measure the country's development progress, but ultimately, the real 'ends' are the things the people of the Solomon Islands value in their daily lives, and so development must focus on removing barriers and enhancing supports to help people achieve the outcomes they value. Consequently, the chapter's primary focus is not on end states, but on the importance of the security sector as an intermediate measure in fostering conditions that enable people to meet these ends.

Our second suggestion regarding case studies is that where end-states are conceived, they should focus on behavioural change rather than on the implementation of strategy, or on simple economic metrics. To take an example from our own volume (Chap. 12), the creation of a framework for accrediting sustainable cultural tourism operations is not, of itself, a fitting end-state; instead, we must ask if that strategy is actually working, and look for the existence of culturally valid and sustainable tourist operations as evidence. To take another example (from Chap. 13), the primary purpose of the case study is to demonstrate the processes by which people's capability to achieve their own value goals was enhanced. In many ways, the increase in produced capital was a means to the greater end of increased social capital, something so greatly valued by the villagers in the case study.

We hope that this volume has refocused your views on sustainability—from a set of formulae describing ideal static conditions, in which our needs are met in perpetuity, within the bounds of our eco-systems—towards a series of interwoven and dynamic relationships, backed by just ethical decision-making, which begin locally, and reach out to achieve impact the global level.

References

Corcoran, P. B., Walker, K. E., & Wals, A. E. J. (2004). Case studies, make-your-case studies, and case stories: A critique of case-study methodology in sustainability in higher education. *Environmental Education Research, 10*(1), 7–21.

McKenzie-Mohr, D. (2011). *Fostering sustainable behavior: An introduction to community-based social marketing*. British Columbia: New Society Publishers.

O'Donovan, O. (2002). *Common objects of love*. Eerdmans: Grand Rapids MI.

Peloza, J., & Yachnin, R. (2008). *Valuing business sustainability: A systematic review*. London: Research Network for Business Sustainability.

Scholz, R. W., et al. (2006). Transdisciplinary case studies as a means of sustainability learning: Historical framework and theory. *International Journal of Sustainability in Higher Education, 7*(3), 226–251.

Sen, A. (2004). Why we should preserve the Spotted Owl. *London Review of Books, 26*(3), 10–11.

Sutton, P. (2004). What is sustainability. *Eingana: The Journal of the Victorian Association for Environmental Education, 2004,* 1–7.

Printed by Printforce, the Netherlands